The RESCUER

June 6/13

To Lesa :

With best regards

Very sincerely

Judy Feld Carr

The RESCUER

The Amazing, True Story of How One Woman Helped Save the Jews of Syria

(Originally published as *The Ransomed of God*)

HAROLD TROPER

LMB
EDITIONS

To the Jews of Syria and all those
who helped rescue them

Library and Archives Canada Cataloguing in Publication

Troper, Harold Martin, 1942–
    The rescuer : the amazing true story of how one woman helped save the Jews of Syria / Harold Troper.

Originally published under title: The ransomed of God; Toronto : M. Lester Books, 1999. Includes bibliographical references and index.
ISBN 978-0-9781765-3-2

    1. Carr, Judy Feld. 2. Refugees, Jewish—History—20th century. 3. Jews—Persecution—Syria. I. Troper, Harold Martin, 1942– Ransomed of God. II. Title.

DS135.S95T76 2007   956.91'004924   C2007-904348-8

First published in paperback in 2007 by Lester, Mason & Begg Limited, 491 Davenport Road, Toronto, Ontario M4V 1B7. Originally published in hardcover in 1999 by Malcolm Lester Books as *The Ransomed of God: The Remarkable Story of One Woman's Role in the Rescue of Syrian Jews*.

Editors: Andrea Knight and Alison Reid
Book Design: Jack Steiner Graphic Design

Printed and bound in Canada.

07 08 09   5 4 3 2 1

CONTENTS

Photographs appear after page 150.

Isaiah 35:10

And the ransomed of God shall return,
And come with shouting to Zion,
Crowned with joy everlasting.
They shall attain joy and gladness,
While sorrow and sighing flee.

Adapted from *Tanakh: A New Translation of the Holy Scriptures According to the Traditional Hebrew Text* (Philadelphia: Jewish Publication Society, 1985).

PREFACE TO THE PAPERBACK EDITION

When this book was first published in 1999 as *The Ransomed of God*, a suburban Toronto synagogue invited me to give a talk about Judy Feld Carr's critical role in the rescue of Syrian Jews. Following my talk a number of people stayed on to ask questions or chat. After most had left, an older man took my arm and drew me aside. Apologizing for keeping me, he explained that he knew Judy Feld Carr slightly and had already read my book. The reason that he had come to my talk was that there was something about the book that bothered him and hoped that I wouldn't mind if he raised it with me. I told him I'd be pleased to answer any questions he had. Reassured, he looked me straight in the eye and asked what parts of the book were true and what parts were my invention. Taken aback, I told him it was all true; none of it was fiction. He stood there for a moment, shook his head in disbelief and, without saying a word, walked away.

The more I think about it, the more sympathy I have for readers who have trouble accepting that everything in this book is true. When I first heard the story of Judy Feld Carr's sub rosa activities on behalf of beleaguered Syrian Jews, I too was more than a little sceptical. To this day, I wonder at the improbability of anyone being able to do what Judy did. It is a truly amazing story that loses none of its wonder in the telling—of how a Canadian Jewish woman, raised in northern Ontario and now living in Toronto as a musicologist, wife, and mother to a blended family of six children, ran, for almost thirty years, a covert rescue operation that successfully secreted thousands of oppressed Jews out of Syria. Since the book was first published, my admiration for Judy's accomplishments has not lessened—just the opposite, especially in view of recent events.

Over the past few years we have all witnessed a dramatic change in the degree to which the West, including Canada, has been drawn into the eye of the Middle East storm. Who would have imagined in 1999 that talk of a "peace dividend" flowing from the collapse of Communism in Eastern Europe would, in the wake of the 9/11 attack on the twin towers in New York, be replaced by fears of a "clash of civilizations" between the West and the Islamic world?

Who would have foreseen that the United States and Britain would be bogged down in a protracted conflict in Iraq, Canadian and other NATO troops battling Taliban insurgents in Afghanistan, the Iranian regime developing nuclear weapons capacity, Lebanon again torn by sectarian violence and stumbling toward full-scale civil war, Hamas the democratically elected choice of the Palestinian people, the Israeli military mired in efforts to contain ongoing Hamas and Hizbullah terrorist attacks, and Western European states pondering the social and political implications of the dramatic growth in their Islamic populations?

And what of Syria? As it is now, so it was then—a closed and repressive police state, its governing elite tolerating no challenge to its authority and privilege. As Syrian authorities impose order with an iron fist, however, that same fist threatens what remains of the region's fragile stability. While people speculate about possible Syrian-Israeli talks, Syria remains a frontline state in the Arab world's ongoing conflict with Israel, the home address of Hizbullah and Hamas terrorist organizations, the backbone of efforts to subvert the elected government in Lebanon, and the closest regional ally of Iran. Recent headlines warn that Syria continues to violate even the most basic precepts of human rights with seeming impunity. Nor have Canadians been immune. In a tangled story of intrigue that involves Syrian, American, Jordanian, and Canadian security police and agencies, several Canadians of Syrian origin have been imprisoned in Syria and reportedly tortured while in custody. When the federal government announced an inquiry into possible Canadian missteps or, even worse, complicity in wrongful jailings, a letter to the editor of the *Globe and Mail* asked why the inquiry was not going to extend its investigation to include "the country in which they were tortured—namely Syria. It is almost as if we expect such behaviour from the Syrians."[1] Sadly, the letter writer may be right. That Syria routinely inflicts physical torture on those its prisoners was not news to Judy. When she rescued more than three thousand Jews from Syria, among them were several severely tortured Jews she bought out of Syrian prisons.

In light of what we now know of the Middle East and what has been revealed of Syria's role there, one cannot help but marvel at all that Judy, armed with clarity of purpose, steadiness of nerve, and passion for her cause, was able to achieve. Another quality that helped her in her task was an uncanny ability to work alone and in secret. There were few people in whom she dared confide, and those who knew anything about what she was doing also protected the cone of secrecy within which she operated. Any violation of that secrecy would not only have jeopardized Judy and her network, but would have also inflicted horrific punishment on the Jews of Syria who entrusted her with their lives and the lives of their children. She dared not allow that to happen.

In the late-1990s, even as she rescued some of the last Jews of Syria, Judy knew that her rescue work was drawing to a close and that the history of a Jewish community in Syria—a community that can trace its roots back through the biblical era—would also to be a thing of the past. That community's story and the story of their secret rescue deserved to be told and Judy very much wanted it be told. To her, the story is not so much about her secret rescue efforts as it is the story of the unyielding determination of beleaguered Syrian Jews to survive as Jews, to put their lives on the line to escape Syria so that they might live in dignity as Jews.

Of course, it was one thing for Judy to want their story told; it was another for me to do the telling. Writing this book was not something I intended to do. In fact, until I was approached to write a book about the rescue effort that delivered so many Syrian Jews to freedom, I knew nothing about it. What Judy was doing was a well-guarded secret—even many of those who contributed money to make the rescues possible were kept in the dark about how their money was being spent. So, how did I come to write the book? It began when I received a phone call asking me to meet with Judy to talk about a book she had in mind. This was not the first time someone had called me with a book publishing idea. As the author of several books, it was not unusual for individuals to ask if they could run ideas by me about writing a book or to ask advice on how to find a publisher for a manuscript. I thought that it was one or other of these topics that Judy Feld Carr wanted to talk about. I was wrong.

I agreed to meet Judy at her house one afternoon later that week. When I arrived, we chatted briefly as Judy ushered me into the family den where she served me tea. After some polite small talk, out of the blue, Judy explained that, just before I rang the door-bell, she had been on the phone making the final arrangements to bring a Jew secretly out of Syria. I didn't know what to say. I had no idea what she was talking about. Jews. Syria. Rescue. Bribes. I sat there in silence. I would later learn that Judy abhors a silence almost as much as nature abhors a vacuum. As I sat speechless, Judy just talked on, skipping from one story of organizing a rescue from Syria to another as if she was talking about organizing a luncheon in her synagogue. It all seemed crazy. I remember asking myself, what kind of a fantasy world is this woman living in?

I became more and more uncomfortable until Judy finally came to the reason for our meeting. Since the history of Jews in Syria was fast drawing to a close, she explained, it was time for a book to be written about that history and I was the logical person to write it. Still reeling from her disjointed stories of secret rescues and covert negotiations, I begged off. Important as such a book might be, I said, I was a historian of the Canadian Jewish experience. I knew noth-ing of the history of Syrian Jews and did not read or write Arabic. Thinking I had disqualified myself from the project, I offered to look into which historians were working on Jews in Arab lands. Perhaps one of them might be interested.

Judy didn't give up so easily. She explained she wasn't suggest-ing that I write a book covering the entire history of Syrian Jews. Rather, what she thought might interest me was writing a book on what she regarded as a largely Canadian Jewish topic: the organized rescue of Syrian Jews that took shape in Canada, in her own home. My mind was filled with images of Judy in her kitchen stirring soup with one hand and holding a phone in the other as she negotiated the liberation of Syrian Jews. It simply didn't compute. Thinking only of making a quick exit, I agreed that this was indeed an impor-tant Canadian Jewish story. Since Judy obviously knew more about this secret rescue project than anybody else could ever know, she was undoubtedly the best person to tell the story. Again, convinced I had found a polite way to remove my name from discussion, I sug-gested several Canadian publishers who might be interested and strongly advised that Judy approach them about supporting her book idea, perhaps even arranging for her to work with a ghost writer—as long as it was not me. Judy took a little more convincing, but she reluctantly agreed to talk with one or two publishers. I asked her to let me know how it all turned out and finally made it out the front door feeling more than a little relieved.

It wasn't long before I heard back from Judy. She wanted to meet again. Against my better judgement I agreed. Back in her den, I listened as she explained that her meetings with publishers had not gone well. She was now convinced that a self-authored memoir, even one written with the help of a ghost writer, was not the way to go. She insisted that the Jews who had escaped Syria deserved a book written by a respected historian, a book grounded in research that nobody would question.

I wasn't sure what she meant by research. Was she talking about just recording her stories and somehow weaving them together into a book? What reputable historian would blindly accept her stories about rescuing Syrian Jews? I didn't believe them. Why would anyone else? But how could I tell her to her face that her stories were just too fantastic to be credible? Taking the coward's way out, I told her that much though I appreciated the value in a book that would tell the story of a Canadian-engineered rescue of Syrian Jews, as a historian, I still did not feel it was something I could do. Any historian writing about the subject would naturally be grateful for her input, but her testimony was not in and of itself sufficient. A historian would require solid documentation, evidence-based research. As chance would have it, Judy had one of my books in her den. I pulled it off the shelf and turned to the endnotes, showing her page after page of the detailed notations on my use of oral testimony and original documents from the period I was writing about.

Judy listened calmly and then said, "Oh, is that all you want? Come with me." I followed her into her office where she pointed to a wall of filing cabinets. Pulling one drawer open after another, she explained that this one contained this; that one contained that. The files were disorganized, but it only took a few minutes to see that I was being offered a historical treasure trove of documentation. There were individual files on each and every rescue she had conducted; material on her fundraising; mountains of correspondence with Jewish organizations, governments, and international agencies; clipping files; and dated slips of paper with handwritten notes on the hundreds of her telephone calls. There were organizational records; minutes of meetings; protest fliers and photographs; receipts for airline tickets out of Syria and coded letters from operatives with whom Judy worked. There were Amnesty International Reports on human rights abuses in Syria and even Syrian translations of Syrian government legislation, decrees, and judicial hearings involving Jews. And there were letters of gratitude, many simply addressed to Mrs. Judy, from many of those whom she had rescued. It was all there, an almost thirty-year paper trail of Judy's work on behalf of Syrian Jews. I could hardly believe it. Judy's files would also act as a guide in locating other sources of historical documentation in government, or in organizational or private hands. But most of all, these files were proof positive that Judy was not making up anything. It was all true; I was hooked.

Completing my research took several years. During that time Judy allowed me unfettered access to her files and she generously made herself available to be interviewed and answer my questions. She also paved the way for me to talk with some of the people she had worked with and, at my request, interceded on my behalf to arrange several interviews with people who were, at first, hesitant about talking with me. But that was the limit of her involvement. In no way did Judy interfere in the direction of my research. Nor did I ask for or she volunteer assistance in defraying my research costs. In fact, she had no notion where my research was leading or what conclusions I was drawing. Only in the final stages of preparing the manuscript for publication did I allow her to read what I had written.

To Judy's surprise, much that she read was new to her. This was because my research took me well outside Judy's sphere of activity. I was given permission to examine the records of various government agencies and private organizations with whom Judy had dealings or that in some way intersected with the rescue of Jews from Syria. I also interviewed more than sixty individuals who, to one degree or another, knew about the Syrian Jewish issue or were otherwise involved with Judy and her sub rosa activities. Among those I interviewed were leaders of the organized Jewish community, Canadian and foreign diplomats who were aware of and at times abetted Judy's operations, experts on Syria and the Middle East, individuals whom Judy could count on for financial assistance or for Syria-specific information, contacts, and connections. Most importantly, I interviewed a number of Jews whom Judy had rescued from Syria—including several people who had endured horrific torture in Syrian prisons. Some twenty individuals agreed to talk to me only on the condition that our conversations would remain off the record. I have honoured their wishes.

It is also important to acknowledge that there are those who are part of Judy's story whose names I do not know, do not want to know, and I was never foolhardy enough to even think about contacting. These include the Syrians with whom Judy negotiated for the release of Jews. There were also the cross-border smugglers who would bundle Jews across Syria's borders along with whatever other contraband they were carrying. At one point, when I was well into my research, I was approached by two men who quietly explained that the Israeli authorities were aware of my research. They just wanted to inform me that my topic was a very "sensitive" one for the Israeli government. In no way did they threaten me, at least not overtly, nor did they ask that I forgo the project. Rather they suggested that it would be "helpful" to me and to them if, before publication, I were to allow them to read my manuscript to ensure its "accuracy." I told them no. What they were asking would compromise my scholarly integrity and that was not going to happen. No more was said and that was the end of it. I never heard from them again.

Whether the two men really thought I would actually let them read my manuscript or just hoped to cast a cautionary chill over my research agenda I do not know. I do know that Judy, even as she guarded her independence of action, was more than a person of interest to Israeli security and intelligence agencies. To this day, I doubt that they have come to terms with the fact that this Toronto woman, an intelligence outsider, an amateur, successfully ran her own do-it-yourself operations in Syria. Eight years after the book was first published, the Israeli intelligence establishment still talks about Judy's exploits. The Israel Intelligence, Heritage and Commemoration Center located north of Tel Aviv is home to a highly regarded Israeli research and information project devoted to exploring intelligence and terrorism issues of the day, including questions related to incitement to violence and international support and sponsorship of terrorism, particularly as they apply to Israel. The Center also publishes a Hebrew-language journal aimed largely at the Israeli intelligence community. The cover story of the October 2006 issue discussed the fiftieth anniversary of the 1956 Sinai War. The back page, however, was not about the Sinai War. It was a short essay honouring Judy Feld Carr, neither an Israeli citizen nor a member of the Israeli intelligence community. Judy is simply described as "married, a mother to six children and a grandmother to thirteen grandchildren; musicologist by training and vocation, a graduate of the University of Toronto"—not exactly the profile of an intelligence operative. But in something of a sneak-peak-behind-the-Israeli-security-curtain, the article notes that "Judy worked tirelessly for three decades in a very clandestine and secretive manner. Perhaps 'the most guarded secret' in the Jewish world was Judy's far-reaching and extremely secretive smuggling out and bringing to safe refuge more than 3000 Syrian Jews, a majority choosing to settle in the State or Israel." No doubt even the most seasoned of Israeli intelligence operatives would be left scratching their heads in wonder at how a self-taught non-professional could build "an elaborate and secure intelligence network, and through it, established key contacts in Syria and abroad, paying bribes to key influential officials [to secure the freedom of Syrian Jews]." The article ended with a simple "*Kol Ha Kavod!*" (All honour to Judy!)[2]

For all the praise that Judy has earned, there are still several key questions about her work that, even as author of this book, I have not been able to answer or answer completely. Prime among these questions is, what made Judy think that she could do what she did? What drove her? What gave her the chutzpah to think she would be able to pull off what any reasonable person would conclude was impossible? What enabled her to convert a passion for the plight of Syrian Jews into a secret and effective rescue network that in the end delivered more than 3,000 Syrian Jews to freedom? I'm not sure, but one thing is certain: there is no point in asking Judy. I've tried. Rather than taking time to reflect on who she is or why she does what she does, Judy just did, and, even if the gentleman who took me aside following my synagogue talk in Toronto refused to believe it was true, thousands of Syrian Jews know it is true and are forever grateful. It may well have been those few like Judy to whom Rabbi Hillel was referring when he said, "If I am not for myself, who will be for me? If I am only for myself, what am I?" And, particularly in Judy's case, "If not now, then when?"[3]

Thirty years after Ruben and Judy Feld first decided that they had to do something to ease the plight of Syrian Jews, Judy Feld Carr was once again in Ottawa. She had been there many times over those thirty years, sometimes to butt heads with politicians on the issue of Syrian Jews, sometimes to huddle with Canadian officials on how they might covertly assist in her work. But this time was different. Judy was not in Ottawa to meet with politicians or officials about Syrian Jews; her Syrian rescue activities were finally finished. On the afternoon of May 31, 2001, she was in Ottawa to accept the Order of Canada, the nation's highest lifetime achievement award. At a state ceremony at Rideau Hall, official residence of the governor general of Canada, Judy was called forward by Governor General Adrienne Clarkson and invested into the Order. After labouring in secret for so many years, on that day Judy stood and listened as a citation in recognition of her deeds was read aloud to assembled dignitaries and guests:

> [Judy Feld Carr's] story is one of international drama and suspense. Driven by a selfless concern for others, in 1973 she and her husband established a network to assist members of the Jewish community in Syria to obtain the right to travel outside their country. After his death a year later, she remained at the forefront of this movement and was known to those who sought her aid as simply "Mrs. Judy." Years of persistence and compassion resulted in more than [three] thousand people being able to leave the country. Today, she continues to work with human rights groups concerned with the plight of refugees.

---

[1] *Globe and Mail*, December 15, 2006, 22.

[2] Yochi Erlich, "Judy Feld Carr," *Mabat Malam*, October, 2006, 48.

[3] Quoted in *Pirkei Avot* (Ethics of the Fathers), 1:14

ACKNOWLEDGMENTS

My name is on the cover of this book but there would be no book were it not for the care and support of many people. My first debt is to Judy Feld Carr, who not only pressed this topic on me but also gave me privileged access to her home, her memories and her voluminous collection of files. I am also grateful to all those who shared their life experiences with me. All the people in this story are real. In cases where it is necessary to protect anonymity, names have been changed in the text.

I am grateful to the Ontario Institute for Studies in Education for giving me a seed grant to begin the research that evolved into this book, and I am also indebted to the Social Science and Humanities Research Council of Canada. Some of the formative research for this book was conducted in conjunction with an SSHRC-funded project I coordinated with Morton Weinfeld of McGill University. The result of this collaboration is a jointly edited book, *Ethnicity, Politics and Public Policy: Case Studies in Canadian Diversity* published by the University of Toronto Press.

A number of public and privately held manuscript collections were consulted for this book. I am much obliged to those custodians of the historical record who welcomed my inquiries and opened their papers to my research—George Gruen, Malka Hillel Shulewitz, Janice Rosen, and Alan Bowker. Many others also contributed to the successful completion of this project. I am particularly indebted to Arnold Ages, Frank Bialystok, Dwight Boyd, Michael Brown, Donald Carr, Vivian Darroch-Lozowski, Adina Dayan, Paula Draper, Rabbi Baruch Frydman-Kohl, Mohammad Javam, David Levine, Cyril Levitt, Marty Lockshin, Michael Marrus, Richard Menkis, Bernard Shapiro, Baruch Sienna, Jerry Silver, Linda Silver, Jan Silverman, Joan Somalchik, Janice Stein, Carla Troper, Ralph Troper, and Morton Weinfeld for their assistance, advice, and encouragement. The OISE/UT computer team, particularly Ron Arbuthnot, Dick Combeer, Tony Gallina, Avi Hyman, Bill Lewchow, Margaret Richards, and Jeanie Stewart, were always there when I tripped over my techno-ignorance.

I am grateful to Morton and Phyllis Weinfeld, Philip Silverman,

Ralph and Miriam Troper, and Adina and Yaacov Dayan for graciously opening their homes and refrigerators to me while I was on the road.

I am also indebted to Bev Slopen for her faith in this project, to Malcolm Lester and his partners, David Mason and Wesley Begg, for their commitment to republishing this book, to Alison Reid and Andrea Knight for their careful editing which makes this book read better than would otherwise be the case, to the much-missed Janet Hamilton who showed such generous good will toward this project, and to Rabbi Arthur Bielfeld and the Temple Emanu-El adult education program for allowing me a unique opportunity to dry-run this narrative. Words alone cannot express my gratitude to Cathy Lace and Ron Silvers for holding my hand through very rough times, and to my Tuesday gang for always providing a warm haven from the storm. Much love goes to my daughters, Carla and Sarah. They patiently accepted my long absences, surrendered the phone to me when I had to have it "for just a second," and politely kept their eyes from glazing over whenever I went on and on about my research. Most of all I am grateful to Eydie, my wife, for knowing what this research meant to me, for her keen eye, and for walking with me every step of the way.

The Determination to Survive

MURAD GUINDI REMEMBERS the aftermath of the 1947 United Nations vote to partition Palestine into two states, one Arab and the other Jewish. Even though he was only six years old, Murad's memories of the days following the vote are vivid. While Jews in Palestine and the West celebrated the United Nations vote, in Aleppo, Syria, where Murad lived with his parents, the vote sent fear through their Jewish community. Syria was a stalwart in Arab League efforts to thwart the creation of a Zionist state in Palestine, and the UN vote was a blow to the Arab cause. In Aleppo, public rage poured into the streets. Denied police protection, individual Jews were attacked and murdered. Jewish homes and businesses were looted and torched. Jewish holy books were set on fire.

Murad Guindi and his family, more fortunate than some, were hidden by Christian friends. Their sporting goods store was broken into, but they survived. In the uneasy calm following the riot, Murad's family decided to rebuild. Others didn't. Most of Syria's estimated forty thousand Jews fled. Many traced their roots to returnees from the Babylonian captivity or to those who sought refuge in Syria from the Inquisition and the expulsion of Jews from the Iberian Peninsula. Some took only what they could carry or easily convert to cash.

The Aleppo pogrom was not the first time that Syrian Jews had been singled out for attack. In the 1930s, during the French colonial administration, Syria emerged as a centre of Arab anti-Zionist sentiment. Throughout the Second World War, anti-Jewish and anti-Zionist demonstrations were common. Fearing that Syrian nationalist leaders might throw their support behind the Nazis and foment an insurrection, French authorities turned a blind eye to attacks on Jews. In 1944, the Jewish quarter of Damascus was twice sacked by mobs.

Any hope that the departure of the French from Syria and the creation of a sovereign Syrian state in 1946 might defuse anti-Jewish hostility was soon dashed. Independent Syria became an uncompromising opponent of Israel. When the mob attacked Aleppo's small Jewish quarter in furious reaction to the 1947 UN partition vote, authorities legitimized the violence with edicts that denied Jews the civil protections granted to other Syrian citizens.[1]

With Israel's Declaration of Independence in 1948, the failure of Arab military forces to crush the fledgling Israeli state translated into another round of attacks on local Jewish populations that were condoned, if not actually organized, by Syrian authorities. Once again, Jews were beaten and murdered, Jewish homes were looted, institutions were closed, and holy books were destroyed. An economic boycott of Jewish businesses and professionals was capped by seizures of Jewish property. Many Jews were left destitute.[2]

Faced with repeated threats to Jewish life and property, Jews who could escape fled to Israel or the West. This was not always easy. After 1948, legal emigration of Jews from Syria was officially prohibited to prevent them from resettling in Israel, thereby strengthening the Jewish state. But in the confusion of an unstable Syrian regime, many Jews found ways to leave illegally, crossing Syrian borders into Turkey or Lebanon and moving on to Israel or the West. In 1954 and again in 1958, the Syrian government temporarily lifted its ban on Jewish emigration for those willing to abandon their property. Then Syria's doors closed to the legal departure of Jews, trapping most of them in the country. An estimated five thousand Jews remained in Syria—approximately three thousand in Damascus, fifteen hundred in Aleppo, and another five hundred or so in the town of Qamishli, near the northern Syrian border with Turkey.

Syria is a tightly controlled police state, where Western notions of democratic freedom do not apply. The Muhabarat, the feared security police, are everywhere. But the iron heel of control fell particularly hard on the Jewish community, and a special section of the Muhabarat dealt only with Jewish affairs. Jewish identity cards were stamped in red with the Arabic word *Mussawi* (follower of Moses). State regulation tightly constrained Jewish business, social, and institutional worlds. Jews endured debilitating restrictions on commercial licences, rules against conducting business with government agencies, limits on the right to buy or sell property, barriers to operating a car or obtaining a telephone. Just to stay in business, many Jewish businessmen found it necessary to seek out a non-Jewish partner who, in return for allowing his name to be used in the business, walked away with much of the company's profits. Contacts with non-Syrians and non-Jews were restricted, mail was censored, and telephone calls, for Jews who were allowed telephones, were monitored. Even synagogue services often had Muhabarat agents in attendance. Jews knew that any infraction of the rules, no matter how minor, could be punished, and that Jews could not count on the courts for justice. There was usually no penalty for those who robbed, beat, or otherwise attacked Jews.[3] As late as 1992, a United States State Department report on human rights practices in Syria noted that "Jews, like all other citizens of Syria, are subject to close purview of the intelligence services, but are under more thorough surveillance than is the general population."[4]

The only escape was escape and many, especially young men, tried it. In 1958, at the age of seventeen, Murad Guindi made an illegal dash for freedom. He snuck across Syria's border into Lebanon, where he was apprehended by Lebanese authorities who handed him back to the Syrian border police. He paid the price for failure. Murad was interrogated, imprisoned, and tortured. He still lives with memories of the electric shocks and whippings he received from jailers intent on making him confess that he was attempting to get to Israel, Syria's enemy.

Four decades later Murad Guindi and his family are out of Syria.[5] So are virtually all Syrian Jews. In 1994, almost fifty years after he and his family survived the Aleppo pogrom of 1947, after almost fifty years of oppression and state-endorsed marginalization, the government of Syria finally permitted the departure of the remaining Jews of Syria. The Jewish presence in Syria is no more.

Memories of the struggle to maintain Jewish lives and dignity in Syria are still fresh. For many, there is also a deeply felt gratitude for a saving hand that came from abroad. Among the rows of shops that line the flea market in Yaffa, south of Tel Aviv, is one festooned with small plastic Canadian flags. In 1997, a Canadian tourist visiting Israel for the first time was making her way through the busy market when she saw the flag-bedecked shop. Curious, she stopped to talk with its proprietors. When they discovered that the tourist was not only from Canada but from Toronto, they became very excited. Did she know Mrs. Judy? She also lives in Toronto. Without waiting for an answer, the proprietors, two brothers, explained that they were originally from Syria, where they had been merchants. In Syria their lot had been bitter. They had surrendered hope of ever getting out, when Mrs. Judy delivered them into Israel. They would never forget her. And the Canadian flags? But a small token to honour the woman who brought them to freedom.[6]

Who is Mrs. Judy? Mrs. Judy, as she became known to the many who turned to her for help, is Judy Feld Carr, a twenty-five-year Canadian crusader on behalf of the Jews of Syria. Working out of her home in Toronto, Mrs. Judy struggled to bring the plight of Syrian Jewry to the attention of the world and campaigned for their right to emigrate. Less well known is that she was personally involved in ransoming thousands of Syrian Jews, covertly helping individual Jews and families find freedom, sometimes by buying them out of Syria one by one, sometimes by assisting their escape across Syria's borders into Lebanon or Turkey.

During the more than two decades covered in this narrative, others—individuals and organizations, Jewish and non-Jewish, the State of Israel and sympathetic governments, particularly the United States, France, Australia, and Canada—contributed their efforts to ease the plight of Syrian Jews. They all added their voices and their weight to the cause, lobbied on behalf of Syrian Jews, and can take partial credit for making possible the final Jewish departure from Syria in the early 1990s.

But Judy Feld Carr's contribution was significant and singular. Through the 1970s and 1980s, as she embraced the cause of Syrian Jews, she gradually learned that Syria was porous. She discovered that with money and connections, it was possible to reach from Canada into Syria and secretly ransom Jews out. With money and connections, it was possible to alleviate the plight of those in Syrian prisons. With money and connections, it was possible to support the families left behind.

Until recently, the story of Judy Feld Carr's efforts on behalf of Syrian Jews could not be told. As long as Jews remained in Syria, the work of Mrs. Judy and others had to be kept out of the public eye. But during the early 1990s, as part of the diplomatic jockeying that characterized the on-again-off-again Middle East peace process, Syrian authorities granted the remaining Jews of Syria permission to leave. Fewer than one hundred Jews now remain in Syria. It is now possible to publicly acknowledge the contributions of those who worked to ease the lot of Syrian Jews and, in the case of one woman, to rescue them. For Judy Feld Carr, Mrs. Judy, this acknowledgement has begun. On the wall of her home there is a framed 1995 letter from Yizhak Rabin, then prime minister of Israel.

Dear Judy,

Now that for all practical purposes, the entire Syrian Jewish community has left Syria, the time for thanks is here—first and foremost for you.

Words cannot express my gratitude to you for 23 years of hard and dangerous work, during which you devoted your time and your life to the Jewish community in Syria. To list all your varied activities for the rescue of this oppressed and tormented community would require a book. Very few people, if any, have contributed as greatly as you have.

The Jews of Syria who were rescued and the State of Israel owe you so much, and will never be able to reward you as you deserve.

This letter is not a summary of 23 years of extraordinary work for the Jewish people and the Syrian Jewish community. This is just say that our gratitude knows no bounds. And the rest will be told in history books.

Judy, the State of Israel salutes you.

Sincerely yours,
Yizhak Rabin[7]

This book begins to tell that history.

CHAPTER ONE

Half a World Away

JUDY FELD CARR—born Judy Leve—grew up half a world away from Syria, in Sudbury, a northern Ontario mining community. With a Jewish population of about forty families after the Second World War, it was hardly a major centre of Canadian Jewish life. The Jewish community, mostly small businessmen and their families, kept a low profile, and Jewish life was confined to family and synagogue. The community's small Orthodox synagogue housed most organized Jewish activities, including a small religious school. Outside of synagogue, many Jewish children participated in Young Judea, a Zionist youth organization that brought Israel-oriented youth activities into smaller Jewish communities across Canada. The organization also sponsored regional gatherings for isolated Jewish youth from across Ontario's north. Under Young Judea sponsorship, Jewish children in Sudbury journeyed long hours by train to participate in weekend retreats with Jewish children from other small towns. Summer meant two months of summer camp and an intense Jewish communal experience.[1]

Being openly Jewish in post–Second World War Sudbury was an isolating experience for Judy. The only Jewish child in her public school classroom, she felt exposed and different, and never more so than when she stayed away from school on Jewish holidays. She still remembers her pain as a little girl, singled out by her classmates, and subjected to anti-Jewish name-calling.

Judy Leve hated being the outsider at school, but her parents were uncompromising in their efforts to shelter her from what they saw as the seductive lure of the non-Jewish world. Even as a high school student, she was forbidden to go to school dances or date non-Jewish boys. There was no use arguing. Her father would not tolerate it—his word was law, and his influence extended beyond his gate. He imposed his definition of Jewishness on his community, and he was not above forcing the local rabbi to bend to his will. Hearing that a bat mitzvah had taken place in a Conservative synagogue in Toronto, he determined that his daughter would also have a bat mitzvah. A rare event even in the Conservative synagogues of larger Jewish communities, bat mitzvahs were unknown in the Orthodox world. The local rabbi, Orthodox and a Holocaust survivor, had to set aside his reservations and permit Judy to have her bat mitzvah in the synagogue. The event, a matter of some controversy among Sudbury Jews, again singled Judy Leve out.

Judy's father traded in furs with Native trappers in the Ontario north, which often required him to be on the road or in the bush for long periods. During his absences, Judy and her younger brother were under the care of their mother and maternal grandmother. Their mother's marriage had brought the two women to Sudbury from New York, and they never fully adjusted to the narrow constraints that small-town Ontario life and a small Jewish community imposed on them.

Judy Leve was six when the Second World War ended. When she was eight or nine, she remembers playing on the floor in her parents' bedroom while her father rearranged his dresser drawers. As he sorted personal items, he placed a collection of newspaper clippings on the floor near his daughter. Curious, she began leafing through them. They were cut from Sudbury and Toronto newspapers and contained articles about the Holocaust and the liberation of the concentration camps. She recalls her horror at seeing pictures of emaciated bodies and mass graves. Asking her father for an explanation, she was shooed away. The subject was taboo. The pictures disappeared.

This introduction to the Holocaust took on a human face when a Polish couple—displaced persons—became their neighbours.[2]

Shortly after Sophie and her husband moved into the boarding house next door, Sophie knocked on the Leves' door. She pointed to the *mezuzah* on the door frame of the house and asked, in hesitant Yiddish, if she had found a Jewish home. When she was reassured that this was a Jewish home and she was invited in, Sophie began to cry.

She became a regular in the Leve household. But Judy knew little about this warm, childless woman, who had become almost a second mother to her. She knew Sophie was a seamstress, married to a non-Jewish man, and that she had somehow survived a distant war. Whatever curiosity Judy or her parents might have had about Sophie's war experience, they never pressed her for information about her past, nor did she volunteer any. But one night in the Leve family living room, Sophie told her story. Calmly at first, she revealed that she had been married before and had two children by her first husband. One of her children would have been Judy's age, but neither they nor her husband had survived the war. She described her concentration camp experience and the horror of Nazi medical experiments that she had been subjected to. As words gradually gave way to tears, Judy and her brother were hustled out of the room and off to bed on the floor above. The French doors to the living room closed.

Refusing to be locked out, the two children crept back downstairs. In the shadowy darkness of the hallway outside the room, they huddled on the floor, listening to Sophie. She was screaming now, pouring out her pain at the atrocities she had endured, atrocities she had locked away inside herself. When Judy's mother left the room to get Sophie a glass of water, she discovered her children, her daughter's ear pressed against the door. The two were again banished to bed, but not before the sound of Sophie's tortured memories had become imprinted in Judy's mind.

Judy often visited Sophie after school, hoping that she would share something of her previous life, of her children, but she did not. Nevertheless, a special bond between Judy and Sophie grew stronger. It was Sophie who made Judy's bat mitzvah dress, a white gown with a "sort of a *tallith*," a prayer shawl, and a hat. Judy Feld Carr still has that dress.[3]

Judy Leve's identification as a Jew and commitment to issues of Jewish concern were strong by the time she graduated from high school in 1957. A Zionist, she had hoped to go to Israel as part of the Machon, a year-long leadership-training program for Jewish youth from the Diaspora. Although her father was an outspoken Zionist, a community stalwart on behalf of Israel, he forbade his daughter to go. Perhaps he was worried for her safety. The 1956 Sinai War had just ended, the ceasefire seemed fragile, and the first United Nations peacekeeping force was deployed in the desert to keep distance between Israeli and Egyptian troops. Resentful at her father's apparent hypocrisy, the usually assertive young woman nevertheless bent to her father's will. Instead of the Machon, Judy Leve moved to Toronto and enrolled in the Faculty of Music at the University of Toronto. She left Sudbury behind her.

At university, she became active in Hillel, the main campus Jewish student organization, but showed few signs of the kind of activism that later marked her life. During her third year at university, she became the head of music at Hillel—hardly a springboard to activism. That same year, she met Ronald Feld—Rubin, as he was known to his friends. He came to Hillel one evening and heard Judy Leve lecture on Jewish music of the fifteenth and sixteenth centuries. Rubin Feld was six years older than Judy. Born in Toronto, he grew up in of the heart of a bustling downtown working-class immigrant Jewish neighbourhood. Even after the war, his family remained in the inner city while many of their Jewish neighbours moved into the suburbs that stretched northward along Bathurst Street.

Rubin Feld showed little interest in Jewish community life or organized Jewish youth activities. According to Judy, as a twelve-year-old, Rubin wanted to forgo a bar mitzvah rather than devote the time and effort necessary to prepare. In the end, however, he did have a bar mitzvah. His father was a free thinker who nonetheless believed in the importance of Jewish community identity and the bonding power of celebrating Jewish life events. But throughout Rubin's youth, the lure of the synagogue was far less powerful than the lure of downtown pool halls.

Rubin's father, a tailor, died just as his son was completing high school. The family had never been rich but now money became a problem. If Rubin was going to make something of himself, he would have to pay his own way. He financed himself through university and medical school while supporting his mother and younger sister by working for the city, in the sewers. Judy argues that the job sharpened Rubin's Jewish identity. Years later, he confided that he tried to keep his Jewishness under wraps for fear that it might get him fired or bring him into conflict with his co-workers. He hated the deception and swore he would never again hide his Jewishness. After graduating from medical school and completing his medical training, he opened a general practice in a non-Jewish working-class neighbourhood in east Toronto.

As soon as Rubin Feld heard Judy Leve lecture at Hillel, he asked her for a date. She accepted. Ten days later, on their second date, Rubin proposed. The two were married in 1960. Their honeymoon was spent in Israel, the first visit to the Jewish state for either of them. It was a turning point in their lives. They fell in love with Israel. On their return, Rubin, who had had little previous involvement in Jewish communal affairs or activities in support of Israel, organized a Canadian support network for the Israeli medical profession. A second visit in 1965 strengthened the Felds' commitment to Israel.[4]

Like Jews around the world, the Felds only grasped how precious Israel had become to them during the spring of 1967, when the Jewish state came under serious threat. In *The Fixer*, Bernard Malamud declares that Jews have "stepped into history more deeply than others—it has worked out so."[5] Never was this more true than in May and June of 1967, a pivotal moment in modern Jewish history. On May 15, the Egyptian president, Gamal Abdul Nasser, mobilized his military forces and, two days later, ordered the United Nations to withdraw its peacekeeping forces from the Sinai Peninsula. Within a week, Egyptian troops, equipped by the Soviet Union, were massing along the Israeli border. Egyptian artillery batteries blockaded the narrow Straits of Tiran, the gateway to Israel's southern port of Eilat, effectively closing the waterway. Israel, declaring that free passage through the straits was guaranteed by international agreement, branded the Egyptian blockade an act of aggression. Meanwhile, other Arab states rallied behind Egypt and put their military forces on alert. Syria and Jordan, bordering Israel on the east, announced that their forces were committed to an all-out struggle with Israel, and several Arab states with no land border with Israel—Iraq, Kuwait, and Algeria—sent military units to stand with Egyptian and Jordanian forces.

Egypt was buoyed by popular backing in the Arab world and the Soviet bloc. The Egyptian military was well supplied. Nasser could afford to wait. Israeli government and military insiders were convinced that talk of a compromise solution was only diplomatic code for forcing Israel into making concessions. The Israeli economy was wearing down as large numbers of its military reserves were called up for duty. With no talks on the horizon and no hope of an Egyptian rollback, the military option grew more and more credible.[6]

Israeli military planners might have been satisfied that they could handle any Arab threat, but Jews in Canada, like many around the world, feared the worst. Israel was being forced into battle—one that might be its last. As their desperation grew, Diaspora Jews rallied in support of Israel. In no other period of modern Jewish history was the consciousness of Jews worldwide so at one with Israel. Many who had taken pride in their emancipation from the narrow strictures of Jewish parochialism were suddenly drawn back to a dormant sense of Jewishness. Those with no previous attachment to Israel, even former anti-Zionists, were inexplicably pulled to Israel's side. They held their breath, wondering why, for the second time in a generation, the existence of a major Jewish community could hang by a thread and nobody but Jews seem to care. And if a liberal, democratic Israel could be destroyed, what reason was there to believe that Jews anywhere would be safe? It had happened once in living memory. Now it was happening to the very state that had taken in so many Holocaust survivors.

In Montreal, Winnipeg, Vancouver, Ottawa, and Toronto, young Jewish men and women lined up to go to Israel, intending to volunteer on farms or take up the slack in the public service created as many were called up for military duty. Rubin Feld joined a group of doctors who volunteered to go. Other Canadian Jews dug deep and millions of dollars were collected.[7]

Anxiety suddenly turned to exhilaration. Israel delivered a hammer-blow assault on Egypt, Jordan, and Syria on June 5, 1967. A massive pre-emptive Israeli air attack demolished the Egyptian air force. Most Egyptian aircraft didn't even get off the ground. While Arab radio broadcast martial music and reported fictitious Arab victories on the battlefield, Israel ruled the sky. It took Israeli ground forces only three days to overrun the Sinai Peninsula. After Jordan and Syria halfheartedly entered the battle, Israel took another three days to occupy the West Bank of the Jordan River and East Jerusalem, formerly under Jordanian control, and wrest control of the Golan Heights from Syria. Israel stood victorious. For Canadian Jews, like Jews in other Western countries, the mixture of relief and joy at Israel's victory acted as a shot of communal adrenaline, revitalizing Canadian Jewish institutional life and cementing Canadian Jewish commitment to Israel's well-being and to the well-being of all oppressed Jews.

It is an irony of Canadian Jewish history that in the very moment of their euphoria at Israel's 1967 victory in the Six-Day War, Canada's approximately 200,000 Jews, like the Felds, had also never felt more Canadian: the year of Israel's victory marked Canada's centennial. The national mood was upbeat and the optimism was infectious. As the world beat a path to Expo 67 in Montreal, Canadian Jews were swept along in the exuberant expectations of Canada's boundless tomorrow. They truly believed the second half of the twentieth century belonged to Canada and, as Canadians, that future belonged to them too. The walls of exclusion were crumbling. In business, law, medicine, the arts, the academy, and local and regional government, Canadian Jews were accepted as never before.[8] By the late 1960s, Jews in Canada were confidently moving from the margins to the centre of civic life, comfortable as Canadians and as Jews.[9] From this emerged a new sense of empowerment. No longer in Canada by sufferance but by right, Jewish community activists began organizing and lobbying on issues close to the Jewish heart.

Judy and Rubin Felds' commitment to Israel and their Jewishness, heightened by the 1967 war, found expression in the Jewish Defence

League. The JDL, with its anti-establishment message of muscular Judaism, came out of the American Jewish scene of the late 1960s. The organization had no presence in Canada. Canadian Jewry considered themselves well served by a single overarching organization, the Canadian Jewish Congress, headquartered in Montreal with a number of semi-autonomous regional divisions across the country. Every shade of Jewish life—religious and secular, Zionist and non-Zionist, right and left—was represented under the Congress umbrella. Both inside and outside the Jewish community, the organization was regarded as the authoritative and representative political voice of Canadian Jewry. While splinter groups were not unknown, new populist voices in Canadian Jewish life were typically absorbed into Congress.[10]

The controversial, right-wing firebrand Rabbi Meir Kahane and several supporters established the Jewish Defence League in New York in 1968. The JDL found fertile ground in the growing turmoil of urban America. Black America was in revolt, and inner-city riots spread across the nation. Resistance to the Vietnam War was being organized on university campuses. Hope for political solutions from within the system was shaken by the murders of Robert Kennedy and Martin Luther King.

Many well-educated, young, and affluent American Jews opposed the war in Vietnam and joined in solidarity with black community protest. But many less affluent inner-city Jews had been left behind by the economic success that had swept so many of their confreres into the primarily white suburbs. They were apprehensive about being overrun by blacks as their neighbourhoods became more and more racially polarized and dispossessed in the name of school and workplace integration. The JDL built on their fears of a growing racial divide and on the heightened Jewish pride and new "tough Jew" image produced by Israel's victory in the 1967 war. The JDL promised militant intervention in defence of American Jews who were too poor or too weak to protect themselves. Kahane translated this self-styled guardianship of inner-city Jews into stewardship of other Jewish causes. On behalf of Soviet Jewry, he declared war on Soviet interests and institutions in the United States.

Many in the Jewish mainstream rejected Kahane's bare-knuckled style, undisciplined rhetoric, and go-it-alone tactics, but he was a magnet for publicity. Even though the coverage was not always flattering, the charismatic Kahane knew what the media said was less important than the fact that they said something. He dismissed negative attacks as orchestrated by a Jewish establishment who, he claimed, had abdicated its responsibility to protect inner-city Jews while currying favour with black leaders. He attacked Jewish leaders for turning their backs on Soviet Jews who cried out for help. Kahane's shrill voice and politics of the street made good press and brought in money and followers, but many who rallied to his call did not stay long. They were disillusioned by his leadership style or lack of coherent plan of action beyond fist-shaking confrontation. In the end, a Kahane biographer later noted:

> Kahane is always left with those on the fringes of society: teenagers from broken homes; drug addicts; *ba'alei tshuvah*—Jews who have recently returned to Orthodox Judaism and have abandoned their former lifestyles; residents of deteriorating neighborhoods in the United States and of development towns in Israel; unemployed; Arab haters; the unbalanced, looking for action.[11]

The twin catalytic agents of the Vietnam War and the urban black revolution were absent in Canada. So why did Kahane strike a responsive note with some in the Canadian Jewish community? In part, Kahane's swashbuckler image attracted a small group of Canadian Jews who admired his anti-establishment message. There might have been be no threat to inner-city Canadian Jews, but some people were always ready to believe that antisemitism was a constant danger that the Canadian Jewish establishment refused to address. They were excited by Israel's resounding defeat of its Arab enemies in 1967 and demanded that Canadian Jewish leaders confront homegrown enemies, real or imagined, with the same decisiveness.

In 1968, Rabbi Meir Kahane was invited to speak at Beth Tikvah synagogue, a growing, youthful, and Conservative congregation in upper-middle-class suburban Toronto. Judy Feld, now a mother of two boys, attended the Kahane lecture as much out of curiosity as anything else. She pressed into the standing-room-only

15

gathering just as the JDL founder was about to speak. She was immediately swept up by the enthusiasm of the crowd and the charismatic message of aggressive Jewish particularism and militant activism that Kahane delivered. He challenged his audience to get personally involved. Evoking memories of the Holocaust, he declared his determination to never let it happen again. He exhorted those in the hall to rise up as Israel had in 1967 and join him in the fight for Jews and Jewish pride. Judy Feld was electrified. Headstrong and impressionable, the woman who had been that isolated Jewish girl from Sudbury suddenly felt empowered. Flushed with excitement, she slowly circled the group around Kahane after his speech until she found an opening. What, she asked Kahane, could any one person do to help save the Jewish people? "Join the JDL," he replied.

She did. Shortly after Kahane's speech, Judy Feld read an ad in the *Canadian Jewish News* inviting all those who were interested in joining a Canadian wing of the JDL to attend an organizational meeting. To her surprise, she found herself the only woman amid the twenty or so men who showed up. The assembled group was very different from the image of street-hardened Jewish toughs projected by the JDL in the United States. The men who attended the Toronto meeting were young white-collar professionals and small businessmen who, like Judy, had been inspired by Kahane's lecture at Beth Tikvah. They shared his belief that Jewish leaders only wanted to maintain their positions of privilege and were wilfully blind to the real issues facing the Jewish rank and file at home and abroad. Echoing Kahane, they asserted that it was up to ordinary Jews like themselves to take back control of the communal agenda and redefine Jewish destiny.[12]

Then and there Judy Feld joined the JDL and soon brought her husband into the organization. She became a member of the local executive, and between 1969 and 1971 she served as the JDL co-chair for Ontario. She also got to know Kahane personally. He came back to Toronto to help his newly organized JDL branch-plant attract a wider community following and build up a financial war chest. A major fundraising event was announced for the Murray House, a large Jewish banquet hall more given to weddings and bar mitzvahs than political rhetoric. More than three hundred people filled the hall to hear the leader speak. Some who sympathized with the JDL message but dared not be seen at a JDL-sponsored event quietly contributed money.

Judy still remembers this time as one of the greatest experiences of her life. Kahane stayed with the Felds during his visit. An RCMP car conspicuously parked across the street from their house. There was a constant stream of supporters coming and going; talk was endless and exciting. Kahane, who impressed Judy Feld as a fiery speaker in front of a crowd, proved surprisingly subdued and relaxed in private conversation. But what she remembers best was that Kahane "always had this passion. It was the passion that got to me. He had this pride for Jews."[13]

CHAPTER TWO

The Jews of Despair

KAHANE FOCUSED his passion and that of his followers on the cause of Soviet Jewry. But he did not, as he claimed, single-handedly make it an issue. Mainstream Jewish leaders who were concerned that the radical right would run off with what was an increasingly emotional issue for American Jewry, had already brought to the cause the tactics of the American civil rights movement and the anti–Vietnam War protest in place of their usual quiet diplomacy. Kahane's critics have alleged that he was neither the originator nor the brains behind the JDL's anti-Soviet campaign. Rather, he was a plucky, self-styled demigod who knew a marketable product when he saw one. Some even asserted that the scrappy street fighter was only the JDL's figurehead while others with a broader vision, perhaps Israeli intelligence agents, masterminded his campaign.

If Kahane was only a figurehead, he was an articulate one. The JDL's clenched-fist logo and slogan Never Again, welding the cause of Soviet Jewry with raw memories of the Holocaust, was nothing short of brilliant. Quiet diplomacy, he warned, had not saved Jews during the Holocaust and it would not save them now. He called for high-profile and dramatic action to highlight the plight of Soviet Jews and give them hope. To do anything less was to be complicit in their oppression. In the United States, the JDL moved from words to sometimes violent confrontation.

In Canada, the JDL moved from words to publicity stunts. During 1968 and 1969, the Toronto JDL, Judy Feld Carr remembers, "decided to go public on the Soviet thing" and organized several events to dramatize the Soviet Jewish cause. The Toronto JDL was more flamboyant and attracted more media attention than the slowly mobilizing campaign of the Canadian Jewish Congress.

When a Soviet ballet troupe visited Toronto, the JDL picketed the event and handed out flyers denouncing Soviet abuses of human rights. In front of the media, the JDL and other activists attempted to shame ticket holders, some of them prominent members of the Jewish community, into tossing away their tickets and joining the picket line. When a large Soviet freighter docked in Toronto harbour, the JDL set up a film projector and screened a movie about the oppression of Soviet Jews on the white-painted hull of the ship. It was great theatre.

The signature event in the JDL's effort to highlight the cause of Soviet Jewry came in October 1971, during a nine-day visit of the Soviet prime minister, Alexei Kosygin, to Canada. After years of mistrust and hostility, the Cold War was showing the first signs of a thaw. For both Canada and the Soviet Union, a thaw promised rewards in increased trade, travel, and scientific co-operation. The Kosygin visit, which followed an earlier trip to the Soviet Union by Canadian Prime Minister Pierre Elliott Trudeau, was hailed as the opening of a new era of detente.

Kosygin's itinerary included a mixture of formal meetings with Canadian government leaders in Ottawa and a series of less formal visits to other Canadian cities for special events and meetings with leaders in business, industry, and finance. As planned, Kosygin and his party first arrived in Ottawa and then proceeded to Montreal, Vancouver, and Edmonton. The last stop on the Kosygin itinerary was Toronto, where the highlight of his Toronto visit was to be a black-tie banquet given by the Canadian Manufacturers' Association in the Great Hall of the futuristic-looking Ontario Science Centre.

Security for the Kosygin trip to Toronto was tighter than for any previous distinguished visitor in Canadian history, including members of the Royal Family. A security team made up of the RCMP, the Ontario Provincial Police, and the Toronto police, working in co-operation with Soviet security officials, wrapped a protective blanket around Kosygin and his party. Security officials knew the visit would generate peaceful protest, and where possible, they worked with protest groups to ensure that demonstrations did not breach security or threaten public safety. Security officials were concerned that anti-Communist groups from dispossessed minorities who had immigrated to Canada from the Soviet Union and its satellites since the Second World War were a threat to the Soviet leader.

They had reason to worry. In Ottawa, as Trudeau and Kosygin walked from the main entrance of the Parliament Buildings to a waiting car, an anti-Communist Hungarian refugee broke through police lines. Before police could grab him, the protester tackled Kosygin. The Soviet leader was shaken but unharmed. The assault, an embarrassment to Canadian officials, was seen on television around the world and underscored the threat posed by demonstrators.

Eastern European anti-Communist groups received approval for a mass demonstration on the street in front of the Ontario Science Centre on the night of the Kosygin banquet. The Canadian Jewish Congress also seized on the Kosygin visit to publicize the plight of Soviet Jewry. The issue for the Jewish community was the human rights of Jews in the Soviet Union, not the particular ideology of the state, and they rejected overtures to join in one mass event in front of the Science Centre. Instead, Congress organized its own separate demonstration. Twelve thousand members of the Jewish community gathered in a suburban park. In a light drizzle, carrying signs reading Let My People Go, the crowd began a half-mile protest march to a large park across the street from Kosygin's hotel. There, amid a sea of signs and glowing candles, Elie Wiesel addressed the crowd. Wiesel, a Holocaust survivor and author of The Jews of Silence, a 1966 book about the awakening of Jewish identity in the Soviet Union, appealed for Jews in the North American Diaspora to support this modern-day miracle.[1] After Wiesel finished speaking, several thousand people, largely young adults, organized an all-night vigil. The rest of the crowd quietly dispersed.

Judy and Rubin Feld and other JDL stalwarts had their own strategy to publicize the plight of Soviet Jews: they intended to disrupt the Kosygin banquet itself. A wealthy Jewish businessman and JDL supporter who was invited to the banquet passed on his two well-positioned banquet tickets to a member of the JDL executive. As part of the plan, Judy ordered a red suit from a dressmaker and had a matching banner-size length of cloth silk-screened with the Russian word for freedom, *SVOBODA*, Freedom for Soviet Jews, and the hammer and sickle. The secret banner became the kerchief of the red outfit she would wear into the banquet.

Judy had originally planned to attend the banquet with her JDL co-chair, a hospital pharmacist. Just days before the event, the executive of the Toronto JDL decided that Judy should not go. Rubin was negotiating a licence to operate a nursing home. The primarily white-collar professionals on the executive understood that Judy's arrest might put the licence approval at risk, and there were other JDL members only too ready to step in. Reluctantly, she passed the red suit on to her replacement.

On the night of the banquet, the Felds, their young son Alan, and a band of other JDL supporters carrying Soviet Jewish protest signs joined the crowd of anti-Communist demonstrators in the street facing the Science Centre. Meanwhile, the two JDL activists with banquet tickets made their way into the building with the other invited guests. They passed through the tight security checks and took their seats for the dinner. At the appointed moment, with the world press and television cameras recording the event, the two stood up and unfurled the kerchief. Police and security agents were on them in an instant, and they were quickly hustled out—but not before they had made their point to an audience of millions. "It made Russian television, world television, all of the newspapers from page three of the *New York Times* to *Maclean's* to page one of the *Star* and the *Globe* and everything else....We [the JDL] were made."[2]

Later that evening at the Feld house, the mood was festive. Media coverage spotlighted the Soviet Jewry issue, but even more important to the small group who gathered at the Feld home, it spotlighted the audacity of the JDL. Canadian Jewish Congress leaders were furious. The stunt had been effective, but costly. It had eclipsed the larger community demonstration, and even worse, Congress leaders claimed that it had pulled the attention of the media away from the plight of Soviet Jewry. Congress insiders were not about to forgive the headline-grabbing JDL upstarts for stealing the show.

The Science Centre episode was a last hurrah for the original group who had first formed the JDL branch in Toronto. By the time of the Kosygin visit, the Soviet Jewry campaign had become a centrepiece of Jewish community concern, and the JDL lost their special reason to champion the cause. Interest in the JDL, Judy Feld Carr recalls, "sort of dried up." Founding members drifted away and the leadership of the JDL was left to others.[3]

Members of the original inner circle of the Toronto JDL turned to other things. Many redirected their energy inward, to families and careers. Rubin and Judy Feld now had three children, two boys, nine and six, and a one-year-old daughter. By 1971, Rubin not only had an active medical practice but he and a partner were also involved in building their licensed nursing home. Judy, who had finished her master's degree in music education at the University of Toronto in 1968, was busy juggling motherhood and a career.

But for some of the JDL firebrands, including the Felds, the pull to Jewish activism and the excitement of protest were not so easily set aside, and they were gradually drawn to related causes. For Rubin Feld it was Syrian Jewry. Why Syrian Jewry? Looking back, Judy believes it was a natural extension of his JDL experience and the influence of Meir Kahane. In 1970, during a second stay in the Feld home, Kahane had told them about the problems of Syrian Jews and condemned mainstream Jewish leaders for their neglect of another oppressed community. Syrian Jews endured in isolation as the most oppressed outpost of Diaspora Jewry, and world Jewish leaders did not care about their suffering. The JDL had a track record of stirring up Jewish protest. They had succeeded with Soviet Jews. Why not Jews in Arab lands?

Kahane was long on bravado but short on fact. Jewish leaders were far from ignorant of the situation of Jews in Arab lands. In 1969, the same year that Judy and Rubin Feld joined the JDL, a crisis of Iraqi Jews was high on the Canadian Jewish agenda. The situation of the small Iraqi Jewish population had deteriorated rapidly after Israel's victory in the 1967 Six-Day War and the Ba'ath Party's accession to power in Iraq under Hassan al-Bakr in July 1968. To consolidate its control by eliminating its foes and warning others of its iron-fisted response to any opposition, the Iraqi regime announced that it had smashed a Zionist spy ring. A "revolutionary tribunal" held secret trials, found fourteen men, mostly Jews, guilty of treason, and sentenced them to death by public hanging. International appeals for clemency and for a review of the trial proceedings and evidence fell on deaf ears.

> At dawn on January 27 [1969], the men were hanged, one by one, from tall wooden gallows in a macabre celebration in Liberation Square. They were dressed in red prison garb.... Baghdad Radio summoned the mob to "come and enjoy the feast." Some 500,000 men, women and children paraded and danced past the scaffolds and through the city to rhythmic chants of "Death to Israel" and "Death to All Traitors."[4]

The public hangings did not end the reign of terror. Further arrests, sham trials, and executions of alleged Israeli spies left the few thousand Jews of Iraq terrified. The Canadian government joined in the condemnation of the Iraqi executions. But Israeli and Western Jewish leaders knew that the sounds of condemnation would not remove one Iraqi Jew from danger. In Iraq it was open season on Jews. Individuals were kidnapped and never heard from again. Jewish property was confiscated or looted. Jews were removed from jobs, barred from educational institutions, and denied the protection of the law and the police.[5]

Without an immediate reversal in Iraqi policy, the only solution was to get the few thousand Jews out of harm's way—out of Iraq. Since the Iraqi government was not about to permit its Jews to emigrate to Israel, the answer was to arrange the wholesale emigration of Iraqi Jews to the West.

A few days after the public hangings in Baghdad, Mitchell Sharp, Canadian minister of External Affairs, and Saul Hayes, executive director of the Canadian Jewish Congress, met in Ottawa to discuss the possibility of Canada offering itself as a safe haven for Iraqi Jews. There was a timely precedent. Canada had just resettled twelve thousand Czechoslovak refugees displaced in 1967 and 1968 after Soviet forces trampled Alexander Dubcek's reformist regime, crushing any hopes of democratization that had flowered during the short-lived Prague spring. During question period in the House of Commons, the Conservative foreign affairs critic had asked the External Affairs minister why Jews of Iraq and other Arab lands should not get the same kind of welcome Canada had given Czechs and Slovaks. The minister had replied that the government was giving the matter "serious consideration."[6]

The minister was saying as much as he dared in public about a Canadian plan to intercede in support of the emigration of Iraqi Jews. Sharp had given the green light to officials in External Affairs and the Department of Immigration to hammer out a scheme that might convince the Iraqi government to allow Iraqi Jews to emigrate to Canada.

The obstacles to any successful resettlement plan were formidable. No plan would work if Iraq was not prepared to let the Jews leave. Would representations on behalf of Iraqi Jews be regarded as meddling in Iraq's internal affairs or as a sign that the West was bowing to Jewish interests? In the charged political climate of the day, either of these conclusions by Iraqi authorities might jeopardize the very Jews Canada intended to help. And could a Canadian approach to Iraq be kept quiet? Iraq would not co-operate in any mass departure of its Jews if it meant international discussion of its human rights record.

If an approach to Iraq was to work, should the first approach be made though an intermediary—perhaps the Red Cross or the United Nations high commissioner for refugees? Would other Western countries join in a Canadian initiative? Holland and New Zealand were flagged as possible partners. Would the government of Iraq allow the Jews to leave without guarantees that they would not end up in Israel? Under Canadian law, it was impossible to refuse individuals the right to leave Canada for another country that welcomed them. What role would the Canadian Jewish community play in a Canadian resettlement program?[7]

At a meeting with Canadian Jewish Congress leaders on February 14, 1969, the minister of External Affairs pledged his department's co-operation. But the Jewish community had to choose between "publicity and 'practical results.'" The Canadian initiative could not be turned into a propaganda bonanza for themselves or for Israel. Congress leadership agreed. A week later, the issue of the movement of Iraqi Jews to Canada was presented to Cabinet. Cabinet was supportive but cautious, suggesting that Canada's approach to Iraq be not only for Jews from Iraq but for Muslims as well. This would allow the Jews to leave without Iraq having to acknowledge that Jews were being granted any special privileges.[8]

An interdepartmental committee started working on a detailed plan of action. But the likelihood of a Canadian initiative co-ordinated with one or more like-minded states was disappearing. The Dutch concluded that any direct approach to the Iraqis would be counterproductive.[9] The Canadian officials were increasingly concerned that the Dutch might be right, but they continued trying to iron out problems in the plan.

External Affairs officials favoured waiving routine immigration procedures to get the movement of Jews out of Iraq started, but Immigration officials were reluctant to set aside their rules and regulations. They all agreed, however, to propose that the UN high commissioner for refugees be asked to make the first approach to Iraq on Canada's behalf. The high commissioner might be able to sell the Iraqis on the benefits of letting a group of people who might be causing their government concern emigrate to Canada.

Officials recommended that no publicity be given to the scheme until it had either been rejected by the Iraqi government or accepted and implemented.[10] However, even if the proposal was accepted, the Iraqi government could not be expected to let the Jews know about the emigration program, and the Canadian government would not be welcome to do so. Here was a role for the Jewish community through its international connections.[11]

The proposal that eventually went to Cabinet for approval called on Canada to approach the problem of Jews in Iraq as a normal immigration movement, but also underscored the need for diplomatic talks with the Iraqi government to ensure both its co-operation and a guarantee of safety for Jews applying to go to Canada. The Jewish Immigrant Aid Society (JIAS) would provide appropriate assistance to Iraqi Jews who arrived in Canada and ensure that these immigrants would be cared for without major public cost.

The proposal was confirmed by Cabinet on June 26, 1969, but in the end, the Canadian initiative was superseded by events.[12] The international outcry that began with the hangings in Baghdad may have convinced the Iraqi regime that its assault on the small Jewish community was doing it more harm than good. The reign of terror had succeeded in consolidating the regime's hold on power by eliminating or silencing opponents. By late 1969, a more confident Iraqi regime felt free to turn its attention to other problems, such as exploiting Iraq's potential oil wealth, dealing with a separatist threat from Iraqi Kurds, and improving Iraq's profile internationally.

Iraqi officials granted Jews permission to leave. Some Iraqi Jews, too terrified to wait for an exit visa or not believing that official permission to leave Iraq would ever be granted, secretly headed north into Kurdish areas. Sympathetic Kurds with connections to Israel, which reportedly supplied arms to Kurdish rebels, helped smuggle Jews out of Iraq. The Iraqi regime may even have turned a blind eye to the illegal passage. Whatever Jews could not carry with them, they left behind. Once out of Iraq, most Iraqi Jews made their way to Israel with the assistance of Israeli authorities. Others immigrated elsewhere, some to the United States, some to Holland, and some to Canada.

The horrific situation of Syrian Jewry was also an issue of concern for both Diaspora leaders and Israel. The 1967 Israeli victory which had brought recriminations against the Jews of Iraq also turned Syria against its small Jewish population. Syria had suffered humiliating defeat at the hands of Israeli forces, and Syrian Jews dared take no public pleasure in Israel's victory. Whatever relief and joy they savoured at the victory, the five thousand Jews of Syria knew that the price of their attachment to Israel would be high. And this is exactly what happened. Many Syrians made the small Jewish community a scapegoat for their nation's humiliation. Syrian Jews suffered wholesale attacks and state-sanctioned terror. There was a rush of arbitrary arrests and torture, public assaults, and looting and

confiscation of Jewish property. The entire community was subjected to restrictions on their freedom of movement, forcible quar-
antine, barriers on economic activities, discrimination in education,
and denial of access to medical facilities. There was no point in
turning to the police or courts for protection: to be a Jew in Syria
was to be judged an enemy of the state.

Syria had its own warped logic in punishing Jews for the
nation's military defeat at the hands of Israel. Israel proclaimed itself
the Jewish state and therefore Israel's victories were hailed as Jewish
victories. As the Syrian military licked its wounds, as Syrian parents
buried their sons, as Jews stood as conquerors on occupied Syrian
soil, as Jews around the world proclaimed Jewish unity, why should
Syrians distinguish Syrian Jews from Jews elsewhere, from Israeli
Jews, from the Zionist enemy? Syrians were unable to crush Jews on
the battlefield, but at least they could crush them at home.

Syria and its allies in the 1967 war were not only enraged by
their defeat on the battlefield but by the fact that it was Jews who
had caused Arab armies to suffer a humiliating loss of face.
According to Raphael Patai, an Arabist and student of Middle
Eastern cultures, Arab states know that in war there are winners and
losers. The attack on Jewish minorities after the 1967 military
defeat, he believes, came from a conviction that defeat by Jews left
no room for honour.

> Losing to a greater opponent is an honourable defeat; to lose to Jews
> is something else again. "The Arabs have looked down on the Jews for
> many centuries. As long as they were subservient and behaved as the
> Arabs wanted, they were tolerated," says Patai. "But to face the fact
> that these subservient people suddenly have changed and are strong
> enough to defeat us, this is a bitter pill to swallow."[13]

Just three months after the Arab defeat, the World Islamic
Congress met in the capital of Syria's neighbour and ally, Jordan.
The gathering passed a resolution sanctioning attacks on Jewish
minorities in Arab lands.

> Jews in Arab Countries: The Congress is certain that the Jewish com-
> munities living in Islamic countries do not appreciate the Muslims'
> good treatment and protection over the centuries.... The Congress

declares that the Jews residing in Arab countries who contact the Zionist circles or the State of Israel do not deserve the protection and care which Islam provides for the free non-Muslim subjects living in Islamic counties. Muslim Islamic Governments should treat them as aggressive combatants. Similarly, the Islamic peoples, individually and collectively, should boycott them and treat them as deadly enemies.[14]

As a survival strategy, Syrian Jews learned to keep their heads down. But this was not without cost. Extortion of Jews was so common in Syria that Syrian Jews just accepted it as part of the cost of doing business, of getting by, of keeping the authorities at bay for another day. This was something that Jews shared with other Syrians who were easy prey to administrative greed and corruption. However, because Jews had no patrons or family connections in high places, they were particularly vulnerable. There was no shortage of Syrian officials ready to pocket that extra payment, that little gift for even the simplest service. As one Syrian Jew recalled bitterly, "We were paying for the air we breathed."[15]

With Syrian Jewish life so uncertain, so dangerous, and so bitter, most Jews wanted to leave, but a ban on Jewish emigration was rigidly enforced. Even temporary travel abroad on business, to visit family or for life-saving medical treatment unavailable in Syria, was impossible for Jews. Eventually, Syrian authorities would lift their absolute ban on temporary Jewish travel abroad, but to get authorities to even consider a humanitarian or business application for temporary travel abroad required lots of money—for extensive financial bonds that had to be put up against the traveller's return and for bribery, gifts given to officials in hope of their assistance. Approval of an application to travel abroad temporarily for humanitarian reasons was another market commodity to be bought and sold, and if Jews wanted to buy, they had to pay premium prices. For all but the wealthiest Jewish merchants and their families, permission for temporary travel abroad was as rare as it was expensive.

When Jews could go abroad on a temporary visa, they were never allowed to travel in complete family units. A key family member—perhaps a mother or even a young child—was always held back as a hostage against the return of those who were allowed out. And what if someone did not return as promised? The remaining family forfeited not only the cash bond deposited with the authorities but often their freedom as well. Family members of those who did not return, sometimes even children, could be arrested and imprisoned as a punishment for those who were beyond the reach of Syrian authorities. There was no mistaking the warning to Jews who might not return: others would pay dearly. In spite of all this, and often with the blessing of parents who were willing to face prison if it bought freedom for children, some did not come back.

Illegal escape appealed to those with meagre financial resources or to unmarried Jewish men. Often they made the risky journey in the company of a smuggler, likely more adept at trafficking in contraband than in transporting people. For those who successfully escaped, it was worth the price they had to pay the smuggler. Once safely out of Syria, escapees usually made contact with the local Jewish community or clandestine Israeli operatives who helped them get to Israel. Those who were caught could expect prison and torture.

Whatever Israel might do for them had to be done carefully; any contact between Syrian Jews and Israel was considered treasonous by the Syrian regime. With agents working in both Lebanon and Turkey and, no doubt, inside Syria, Israel monitored the situation of Syrian Jews and lobbied international organizations and friendly states to intervene on their behalf. Syrian Jews who managed to reach Israel were assisted in establishing new homes.[16]

The crisis of Jews in Arab lands was also a pawn in the Middle East political game. The Israeli occupation of the West Bank, Gaza, and the Golan Heights following the 1967 war left hundreds of thousands of Palestinian Arabs under Israeli jurisdiction. Arab states, eager to delegitimize the Israeli occupation and turn Western support away from Israel, pounced on charges of Israeli human rights violations in the occupied territories. In the battle of comparative and competitive human rights violations, the treatment of the Jews of Syria was a counterpoint to Arab accusations of human rights violations by Israel.

Even in its propaganda battle with Syria, the Israeli government had to be circumspect so as not to compromise the safety of Syrian Jews. But individual Israelis and groups organized and spoke out on behalf of Jews in Syria and other Arab lands, sustaining Israel's propaganda effort. The main Israeli advocate for Jews in Arab lands was the World Organization of Jews from Arab Countries (WOJAC), headquartered in Tel Aviv. WOJAC was dismissed by some as the handmaiden of Israeli government propaganda, and by others as a noisy, single-interest lobby group, a squeaky wheel pushing Israel and Jewish organizations for more activism on behalf of Arab Jews. Guilty on both counts, WOJAC was still a significant publicist for these issues. The organization gathered and distributed information on the situation of Jews in Arab lands, lobbied the Israeli government to be more responsive to the Israeli settlement problems of these Jews, and pressed for compensation from Arab countries for property left behind or taken from Jews who had left. In publications and conferences in Israel and abroad, WOJAC profiled the plight of Jews, like those in Syria, who were still in Arab lands.[17]

Despite Kahane's JDL rhetoric, Jewish organizations outside Israel did take up the cause of Syrian Jews. In 1971, the World Jewish Congress, headquartered in Paris, acknowledged that "apart from the Jewish problem in Soviet Russia, the Syrian plight has become our problem No. 2."[18] In the wake of the 1969 Baghdad hangings, a Committee of Concern for Jews in Arab Lands was organized in the United States under the wing of the American Jewish Committee. The AJC prided itself on being non-Zionist and remained determined to make clear that it was not acting as an agent of Israel. Originally founded in 1906 to prevent the infraction of the civil rights of Jews in any part of the world, over the years, the AJC continued to organize on behalf of Jews facing oppression. It was only natural that it should also organize on behalf of the Jews of Syria.

The Committee of Concern was set up as an independent, nondenominational committee with no formal ties to the Jewish community.[19] A non-Jew, the retired U.S. Army General Lucius D. Clay, was installed as chair. This was not the first time that the much-respected and decorated General Clay reached out to Jews in distress. He had been a ranking American field officer directly involved in the liberation of Nazi concentration camps. As the American military commander in post-war occupied Europe, he was also reportedly in sympathy with the survivors—a fact that set him apart from many others in the highest ranks of the military.[20] Once back in civilian life, Clay became a partner in Lehman Brothers, a major New York investment firm. Among the senior partners in Lehman Brothers was Oran Lehman, who was active in the AJC. After Clay had agreed to head the Committee of Concern, his involvement was hands-on, unlike that of many of the other prominent non-Jews who lent their names to the committee's letterhead and board. Under Clay, the committee received a budget from the AJC and an AJC staff member, George Gruen, was seconded part-time to support their work.

The Clay Committee of Concern became the model for similar ones elsewhere, especially in France. Of all Western states, France had the longest and most intricate relationship with Syria, going back through the pre-war years when Syria and neighbouring Lebanon fell under French colonial administration. After Syrian independence in 1946, France retained a proprietorial interest. Although Syria looked to the Soviet Union for economic and military assistance, Syria also regarded France as its window on the West.

Shortly after the American Committee of Concern got off the ground, Alain Poher, president of the French Senate, visited Clay. Poher was the second most powerful political figure in France and was politically at odds with President Charles de Gaulle. In contrast to de Gaulle, who was actively courting Arab favour, Poher, with a large Sephardi Jewish population in his southern France constituency, was widely regarded as soft on Israel and a hard-liner on human rights abuses in Arab states. When approached by members of the French Jewish community to lead a committee similar to that of Clay, he did not hesitate.[21] As a first step in furthering the cause of Jews in Arab lands, he and Clay agreed to organize an international conference in Paris.

In early 1970, the International Conference for the Deliverance of Jews in the Middle East, presided over by Alain Poher, convened in Paris. Representatives from twenty-five countries participated, including several Canadian Jewish Congress delegates, and the conference was well covered in the international press. The most dramatic moment came at a press conference when a recent Jewish escapee from Syria, wearing a face mask to protect her identity and the safety of family she left behind, spoke to the press and delegates about the horrific conditions in which Syrian Jews lived. However, despite extensive deliberations, the conference did not produce any easy solutions. Delegates agreed that it was critical to keep the plight of Jews in Arab lands, and those in Syria in particular, in the Western eye. To this end, the conference established an international committee headed by Poher and mandated to encourage the organization of active Committees of Concern in all Western countries. It was understood that these committees would be most effective if their membership included highly respected non-Jewish community and political leaders.[22]

Keeping non-Jewish participation up front, if only a name on a letterhead, was important so that the Committees of Concern would be viewed as distinct from Israeli interests and therefore Arab leaders would not be able to dismiss committee members as Israeli stooges. Israel also recognized the value of these committees in keeping attention focused on the plight of Syrian Jews, and used its leverage to encourage Jewish communities worldwide to organize Committees of Concern with strong non-Jewish participation. Shortly after the Paris conference, the Israeli embassy in Ottawa started prodding the Canadian Jewish Congress to organize a Canadian Committee of Concern. Congress was unusually resistant to this request, cautious about the role such a committee might play and concerned about who would control it. What if independent-minded committee members opted for a form of protest that was not in keeping with Congress's approach—quiet diplomacy? What is more, a Committee of Concern might undermine any Congress intervention on behalf of beleaguered Jews. In the Syrian case, Congress was convinced that the best course was to use personal contacts to gently but firmly press the government to help resolve the problem.

Congress was already in contact with Canadian officials on behalf of Albert Elia, the former secretary general of the small Lebanese Jewish community who, in September 1971, had been kidnapped in Beirut. Elia was widely acknowledged to have helped fellow Jews escape from Syria through Lebanon, and it was assumed that the

Muhabarat, Syria's secret police, had whisked him off to prison in Syria to warn Lebanese Jews to stop assisting Syrian Jews.

Elia had two adult children living in Canada. Supported by Congress, Elia's children requested that External Affairs intercede with the Syrian government on behalf of their father.[23] External Affairs agreed to contact Lebanese authorities but cautioned Congress to refrain from accusing the Syrian government of involvement in the kidnapping. The minister of External Affairs requested that Congress also refrain from publicizing the Syrian Jewish problem so that External Affairs would be seen as an honest broker rather than acting under pressure from Canadian Jewish interests. Putting Elia or Syrian Jewry into the spotlight, External Affairs warned Congress, might lead to Elia's death. Satisfied that Canadian diplomats would make every possible effort on Elia's behalf, Congress and Elia's family agreed to remain silent.[24]

Unfortunately for Elia and his family, discreet Canadian inquiries and expressions of concern went nowhere. The Lebanese denied any knowledge of the kidnapped man's whereabouts. While suspicions of Syrian involvement in the kidnapping were rife, reliable information about where the older Elia was being held, his condition, or even if he was still alive was impossible to get. The family lived on rumours. With time passing and no useful feedback from External Affairs, Congress saw nothing further to be gained by silence. Elia's daughter in Canada went public with her father's story. In a press statement, she linked her father's kidnapping to the ongoing oppression of Syrian Jewry. Her cause was immediately taken up and profiled by the Alain Poher group in Paris, and she appealed to UN Secretary General Kurt Waldheim to intervene with the Syrian government. It was to no avail. While the campaign for the safe return of Elia generated a momentary media flurry and spotlighted the plight of Syrian Jews, Elia was never seen alive again.[25]

Early in 1971 Congress leaders in Montreal cautiously revisited the notion of forming a Canadian Committee of Concern, and Saul Hayes, Congress executive director, approached former prime minister John Diefenbaker, asking him if he would lend his name "to the distinguished list of committee members who are in the main non-Jewish."[26] Soon Congress was again having second thoughts. The organization might have responded to grassroots pressure from the rank and file to organize a committee, but there was no such pressure, not even from the growing Sephardi community in Montreal. Much of that community was relatively new to Canada, having arrived directly from North Africa or from North Africa via Israel. While their numbers swelled the ranks of the Montreal Jewish community, they were not yet major players in the Jewish political arena. Few, if any, were from Syria and they had no first-hand experience of the conditions there.

And what would a Committee of Concern in Canada do anyway? It was unlikely that it could organize a campaign on behalf of Syrian Jews on a scale comparable to the campaign for Soviet Jewry. There was no significant contingent of Syrian Jews in Toronto or Montreal and there was no visible Syrian government presence—no embassy, no airline offices, no Syrian anything. And they couldn't protest Canadian government inaction on the issue because Congress had already been assured that the Canadian government was onside.

In contrast, the cause of Soviet Jews offered a smorgasbord of options for Jewish community activism. Deep historical and family connections existed between Jews in Canada and Jews in the Soviet Union. There were also Soviet diplomatic, institutional, cultural, and business connections that stood as ready targets of protest. Even if Canada was supportive of detente, in the Cold War climate of the day the Soviet Union was still the enemy of the West, Jews were hostages in the enemy camp, and much of Congress's energy went into publicizing the oppression of Soviet Jews.[27]

But the Syrian committee idea refused to go away. In November 1971, the influential Toronto rabbi Gunther Plaut wrote a short column in the *Canadian Jewish News* about the terrible situation of Syrian Jews. He applauded the campaign on their behalf by Committees of Concern in the United States and France and supported the creation of such a committee in Canada. In a letter to Alan Rose, Congress assistant executive director, Plaut volunteered to help set up a committee "along the line of the American and

French Committees which involve high level Christian leadership."[28]

Rose and other Congress officials were still concerned that a high-profile Syrian Jewish campaign endorsed by Congress might "hamper the steps being taken by External Affairs in Syria at the moment," and told Plaut to hold back. In response to yet another Israeli request that a Canadian Committee of Concern be established, one Congress spokesperson hinted that a Congress-directed campaign on behalf of Syrian Jewry would only be possible under the tightest Congress control.[29]

For all its reservations, Congress officials knew they could not appear to be indifferent to initiatives on behalf of Syrian Jews by world Jewish organizations. And if Congress did not take the lead, might that not leave open the door to less responsible community elements, like the JDL? As a result, Congress joined in setting aside the anniversary of the 1969 execution of eleven Jews in Iraq as a Day of Solidarity with Jews in Arab Lands. Rabbis across the country were urged to dedicate their Sabbath sermons on the Saturday proceeding the Day of Solidarity to the plight of these Jews.[30]

The Day of Solidarity also marked the opening of the Second International Conference on Jews in Arab Lands held in Paris. In the weeks leading up to the conference, there was a small flurry of activity focusing on Syrian Jewry. The American Committee of Concern under Clay issued a statement detailing the repressive conditions under which Syrian Jews lived. This was followed by a call to action on behalf of Syrian Jews by the influential Anti-Defamation League of the B'nai Brith and press coverage in the widely read *Jerusalem Post* and other major newspapers, including *Le Monde* and the *Christian Science Monitor*. A rally protesting the oppression of Syrian Jews was held in front of the UN building in New York, while inside the Israeli ambassador to the United Nations addressed the General Assembly on the issue. In Jerusalem, one thousand protesters paraded in a driving rain to shout their condemnation of Syria's treatment of its Jews.[31]

The Paris meetings attracted delegates from seventeen countries, including a representative of the Canadian Jewish Congress who attended as an observer. Alain Poher declared that in the past, "a virtual wall of silence has fallen upon this little community, which finds itself totally isolated from the outside world."[32] The conference was designed to break that silence. At one key event the press, reported the *New York Times*, was allowed a "peek through the wall" that kept the plight of Syrian Jews out of public view. Two Jews, a man and a woman, were introduced as recent Jewish escapees from Syria. Again, to protect their families left behind in Syria, they were disguised and no photographs were permitted. In a packed ballroom of the Paris Hilton Hotel, they spoke through a translator and described how the Syrian Jewish community members were kept prisoners in their own homes, subject to arbitrary arrest, torture, and denial of even the most basic human rights. In the previous month, the two had presented evidence to an Independent Commission of Inquiry. Transcripts of their testimony were distributed.[33]

Conference organizers were disappointed that the French press did not give them much coverage, but the meetings were featured prominently in foreign papers, including the *New York Times* and in the international edition of the *Jerusalem Post*. At the end of the conference, Syrian Jews were promised that their cause would be taken up by international human rights organizations and become the centrepiece of the world Jewish agenda. This pledge turned out to have a hollow ring, but through January and February 1972 the Syrian Jewish cause was the subject of a joint action plan put forward by the Conference of Presidents of Major American Jewish Organizations and the World Conference of Jewish Organizations. That same year, Syrian Jews were the topic of a widely reported debate in the Israeli Knesset and an address by the Israeli minister of police to the 28th World Zionist Congress in Jerusalem. One press report optimistically claimed that the plight of "Jews held captive in Syria" was finally moving out of the shadows to become a major international humanitarian concern.[34]

With Syrian Jews now very much in the Jewish public eye and the Israelis continuing to put considerable pressure on the Canadian Jewish Congress to publicize this matter, Congress officials again debated how to proceed. All agreed it was necessary to support the international Jewish outcry on behalf of Syrian Jews, but the organizational problems had not changed. There was still no focus for anti-Syrian protest in Canada and Congress officials concluded that organizing a major protest in Canada would not be worth the effort. It was better to continue the campaign on behalf of Soviet Jews, where the Canadian voice was more likely to have impact. This, some Congress officials argued, was not a case of favouring Soviet over Syrian Jews, but a case of making a positive contribution where possible.

Others disagreed. If Syria was not the Soviet Union, neither was it Iraq. There had been no tangible payoff for remaining quiet about Syrian Jews. Maybe it was time to go public. Publicizing the Syrian Jewish problem was better than doing nothing. And if it also helped Israel in its battle of images with the Arab states, so much the better.

Alan Rose still had reservations about Congress taking a higher-profile position on Syrian Jewry, but he could not deny that his advocacy of quiet diplomacy had not yielded results. With Jewish organizations worldwide issuing statements deploring the treatment of Syrian Jews, Congress could not be an exception. The organization agreed to take the lead among Canadian Jewish organizations and issue a public statement outlining its concern for Syrian Jewry and pledging to do all in its power to assist them. However, Rose cautioned that the statement should be vetted by "Mr. Mitchell Sharp [External Affairs] in view of our understanding with him." Before it was released, the Congress statement on Syrian Jews was sent to External Affairs for review. The department requested that two paragraphs dealing with the inquiries that the department had made at the behest of Congress be deleted. This was done.[35]

Rose might have believed the deletions were requested to avoid accusations that the department was the handmaiden of Canadian Jews, but the truth is that External Affairs wanted any reference to Canadian intervention with Syria removed to ensure accuracy. The statement claimed that in response to discussions between Congress and External Affairs, the Canadian government had conveyed its concern to the government of Syria over that country's treatment of its Jews. But Canada had only made general inquiries regarding Syrian Jews; it had never made any formal representations to

Syria. With regard to Albert Elia, in spite of what Congress officials believed, Canadian officials had never actually discussed his kidnapping with Syrian officials. They had only explored the Elia case with Lebanon, where Elia was a citizen. Canada had given the Lebanese assurances that it would be willing to accept Elia into Canada, the home of his children, if that would expedite his release, but nothing came of the offer. The Canadian government was concerned about the fate of Syrian Jews, but External Affairs held to the view that any direct approach to Syria might make the situation even worse for the Jews and undermine Canada's ability to intercede on their behalf.[36]

So different were External Affairs' and Congress's understandings of their discussions that it is hard to believe they had been talking to each other. And as Congress in Montreal cautiously edged toward a major public statement on behalf of Syrian Jewry, it would soon find that it no longer held a monopoly on the issue in Canada. While Congress dragged its heels on organizing a Committee of Concern, Rubin and Judy Feld decided to organize their own committee in Toronto. Despite Congress's self-declared monopoly on Jewish political action in Canada, they went about staking their own claim to the cause of Syrian Jewry.

CHAPTER THREE

The Task at Hand

RUBIN AND JUDY FELD knew nothing about Canadian Jewish Congress discussions of Syrian Jewry. They were removed from Congress's centre in Montreal, and they had also accepted Meir Kahane's populist line that the Jewish establishment did not care about the Jews of Syria. Writing in the New York right-wing *Jewish Press*, Kahane charged Israeli and Diaspora leaders with hiding their inaction behind "expert advice" that protest "against the Syrians would lead to retaliation against Syrian Jews."

> By this I [Kahane] mean that, just a few years ago the world and most Jews, for that matter, were totally ignorant of the plight of Soviet Jews and it was this ignorance—a product of Jewish silence—which was responsible for any action to save them, so today is there another silence, ignorance and, consequently, a failure to make significant progress on the question of Syrian Jews. By this I mean that just as a few years ago the desperation of Russian Jewry was not alleviated by the fears of what might happen in case of Jewish militancy, so today will there be little tangible salvation for the oppressed Jews of Damascus and Aleppo so long as Jews in the world fear to react.

Kahane drew three telling conclusions from his comparison of the Soviet and Syrian situations:

> 1) Silence and tepid respectable efforts that are timid and only occasional do not help in any great measure.

2) Only a campaign which publicised the problem will lead to the awakening of people and their organizing to free the Syrian Jews.

3) Militancy does not hurt, but rather, is the swiftest and most effective way to spotlight the problem.[1]

His attack on the Jewish establishment struck a responsive chord with Rubin Feld, but Rubin did not see himself leading a campaign in support of Syrian Jews. There was, however, no existing movement in Canada that he could join.

When Rubin read Rabbi Gunther Plaut's 1971 *Canadian Jewish News* article applauding the efforts of the Poher and Clay Committees of Concern and calling on the Canadian Jewish community to organize a committee along the same lines, he wrote to the rabbi, offering to enlist. Rabbi Plaut replied encouragingly that a Canadian Committee of Concern was in the planning stages, and "you can rest assured that when it is established it will be brought to your attention." Unfortunately, after the Canadian Jewish Congress in Montreal advised him of the need to favour quiet diplomacy over protest, the rabbi put his plan on hold.[2]

Unaware that Congress had poured cold water on Rabbi Plaut's suggestion, Rubin Feld grew impatient and, after a few weeks, phoned the rabbi to renew his offer to help get a committee up and running. Rabbi Plaut explained that he now believed a special committee on Syrian Jewry was unnecessary and insisted that the Canadian Jewish Congress had the issue well in hand. While Rubin's obvious concern and offer of assistance were appreciated, there was nothing that needed to be done.

Rubin was taken aback by what he regarded as a don't-call-us-we'll-call-you brush-off. He could not understand how Rabbi Plaut could say that the Canadian Jewish Congress had things in hand. Where were the protest demonstrations, the boycotts, the petitions? Where was the outcry on behalf of Syrian Jews? Rubin heard only silence. Kahane was obviously right. The Jewish establishment was all talk and no action.

If Rabbi Plaut and the Congress crowd were reluctant to lead, Rubin concluded that he would have to. Jews were in distress. He was morally obliged to do all he could. The problem was what to do.

At least he could
days of the campaig
ner to her husband.
played a quiet second
characterized not so much
in style. Rubin was quiet, eve
analyzed issues carefully, often
tions. Like a gently flowing river,
obstacles. Judy was outgoing, impuls
pushy. She had a high energy level a
consultation and discussion. When anyt
plowed through it or pushed it aside. She fo
in a committee or to share authority with ot
could count on as loyal to her cause. Judy was so
in a china shop, but she had the drive and energy ne
things happen. The Felds made an oddly balanced t
quiet and often calming manner belied his passion for Sy
and he was effective in keeping Judy's zest for action focuse
goal. Once she was committed to the cause, Judy Feld could n
deterred from moving it forward. The two were united in their c
viction that Syrian Jews needed them, that Syrian Jews were being
left out in the cold by the callous indifference of mainstream Jewish
leadership.

But how to get started? Seeking practical advice, Rubin Feld
called the Israeli consul in Toronto. Once the consul heard that the
Felds were interested in Syrian Jewry, he agreed to see them. Israeli
diplomats in Canada were still getting nowhere in pressing Congress
to mount a public campaign. There was no harm in finding out what
Rubin and Judy Feld had in mind and encouraging them if they had
anything to offer.

In late December 1971, Rubin and Judy Feld met with the consul, who decried the lack of any Canadian Jewish initiative on the
issue. He applauded the Felds for their enthusiasm and sensitivity
and encouraged them to *shri gevalt* (scream horrors) on behalf of
Syrian Jewry. But the Felds did not get the tangible support and concrete ideas they were hoping for. The consul encouraged Rubin and
Judy to go ahead and organize a committee, but otherwise he offered

with only a renewed conviction
 Canada on behalf of Syrian Jews
THE RE e chances were that nobody would.
 g to have to be their own.[3]

them y find the ideas and help they needed?
tha small circle of like-minded friends, some
a rifted out of the Toronto JDL following the
ation. Several were prepared to lend a hand in
 adian Committee for the Rescue of Jews in Arab
 Rubin as chair, planning meetings were held at the
 A core circle of less than ten people soon grew to about
 cluding a number with no previous JDL links. None of
 new much about Syrian Jews, but they began with two
 mptions: the Jews in Syria were oppressed and mainstream
 wish leaders were ignoring their plight.

The group who met in the Feld home volunteered time, energy, and a little money. They quickly realized that it was important to position the cause of Syrian Jews as a human rights crusade. They needed to raise awareness of their fledgling committee both inside and outside the Toronto Jewish community and give it a non-sectarian, humanitarian profile. To accomplish this goal, they brought non-Jews on board, especially Christian clergymen and academics. Rubin recruited several local clergymen and others he knew through his medical practice. If these non-Jews who kindly lent their names to the committee's letterhead were not the mainstays of Toronto's religious, academic, or social establishment, at least they gave the committee the appearance of being non-denominational. And since none of them wanted to play an active role in the committee, they would not get in the way.

The core group weighed the relative merits of possible kickoff events for the campaign. They were looking for an event that would not be expensive to organize, that they could pull together quickly, and that would focus media and community attention—Jewish and non-Jewish—on the cause of Syrian Jews. A public demonstration in Toronto was ruled out. The issue of Syrian Jewry was not well enough understood to bring out a crowd, and there was no Syrian diplomatic mission in Canada to serve as a focus. What about organizing a protest outside the Canadian Jewish Congress's offices to draw attention to Congress's do-nothing policy? That too was rejected; the image of Jews attacking Jews on behalf of Jews was far too negative. Nearly out of options, the group hit on the idea of holding a "teach-in" on Syrian Jews. It might not be as splashy an event as a public demonstration, but it would start an information flow—something committee members needed as much as anyone else—and draw in more supporters. A small planning team was soon busy organizing the teach-in for February 20, 1972—arranging logistics, speakers, publicity, and fundraising.[4]

The committee was buoyed by an editorial in the *Canadian Jewish News* endorsing the idea that a campaign on behalf of Syrian Jews comparable to that on behalf of Soviet Jews was past due. Under a headline declaring "World Action Needed to Save Syrian Jews from Destruction," the *Canadian Jewish News* warned, "If Syrian Jewry is to escape another Holocaust, it will come about only by the impact of world opinion backed by positive world action." It was the duty of world Jewry, including Canadian Jewry, to mobilize world opinion.[5]

The Felds, mistaking the editorial for a groundswell of interest, hoped that their teach-in would spark a movement like the campaign for Soviet Jews that the establishment would be forced to take up. Organizing a teach-in, however, posed the problem of locating reliable and up-to-date information on Syrian Jewry. Easier said than done. Rubin and his committee had good intentions but few connections.

The Israeli delegation to the United Nations was a likely place to start looking for information. After some delay, the committee received a copy of the 1971 Israeli statement to the UN General Assembly meetings—useful but not enough.[6] Remembering Rabbi Plaut's praise for the American and French Committees of Concern, Rubin Feld wrote to both General Lucius Clay and Alain Poher for information and program advice, proposing to "co-ordinate" but not "affiliate" his committee's efforts with their own. To Clay, he explained that the newly organized Canadian group took shape "mainly because of Canadian indifference and silence regarding the sad plight of Arab Jewry, especially the imprisoned Jews of Syria." To

Alain Poher, he complained that the problem of Jews in Arab lands "has received virtually no attention in Canada and all Canadians, Jews and non-Jews, are dismally ignorant of the grave predicament of the imprisoned Jewish communities in the Arab States." Rubin offered his committee as a Canadian clearing house for the distribution of information on Syrian Jewry and he requested advice "regarding constructive activities pertaining to our Committee."

Clay's response was cool and read like a form letter. While he applauded Rubin's concern and promised to supply up-to-date information on the Syrian Jewish situation, Clay made no mention of Rubin's offer of a special relationship nor his request for advice. At least Clay replied; Poher did not.[7]

The Felds were disappointed but undaunted. On the advice of Rabbi M. Mitchell Serels, the leader of a Sephardi congregation in Toronto and an early member of the committee, Rubin wrote to the Brooklyn-based Committee for the Rescue of Syrian Jews. Taking a swipe at the Jewish establishment, he complained, "For too long we in Canada have been apathetic and indifferent to the sad plight of Jews in Arab States." The Committee for the Rescue of Syrian Jews was actually the organizational cover for one man, Abraham Dwek. Dwek was an energetic activist and successful businessman of Syrian Jewish origin who, like the Felds, was not allied with any mainstream Jewish organization. Originally from Aleppo and impassioned by the plight of Syrian Jews, he devoted his energy and considerable personal wealth to publicizing the Syrian Jewish cause. Dwek collected any information he could find on the problems of Syrian Jewry and, delighted to have Canadian customers for his material, he put the Felds on his mailing list. Before long, the committee began receiving a constant flow of press clippings, model petitions, letters to politicians, press releases, and press advertisements. Dwek also offered the Felds advice on setting up a committee and developing program strategies.[8]

In the first batch of material from Dwek, there was a reference to initiatives on behalf of Syrian Jews by the American Jewish Committee. Rubin promptly wrote to George Gruen, director of the organization's Israeli and Middle East Affairs and the man seconded to the Clay Committee, who mailed him a kit of background literature and an updated fact sheet on the situation of the Jews in Syria. Gruen also put Rubin's committee on both the AJC and Clay Committee mailing lists for future information.[9]

Rubin and his committee now had enough to pull together an information package for the teach-in. However, they still needed speakers who could contribute to a discussion of Syrian Jewry. Three were hurriedly lined up. Two of them—Donald Keating, a former United Church minister in Toronto who had gained notoriety by openly challenging the alleged anti-Israel and antisemitic bias of the United Church Observer, and Rabbi Mitchell Serels—were not experts on Syria. The main speaker would be Saul Friedman, professor of Middle East and ancient history at Youngstown University. Rubin had run across several articles the professor had written on Jews in Arab lands, but had no idea whether Friedman was a good public speaker or even if he had anything more than a passing academic interest in the subject. Judy still recalls how surprised Friedman was to be invited to Toronto to address a teach-in on Syrian Jews. When he was asked whether he had ever spoken on the issue, Friedman responded that he had never met anyone who was interested in Syrian Jews. He agreed to come.[10]

Publicity got under way. The event was to be held at Toronto's Beth Shalom synagogue. Information was spread mostly by word of mouth, though flyers were also posted in Jewish neighbourhoods and paid advertisements were placed in the Canadian Jewish News and the Toronto Star. The planning committee approached several Jewish community organizations, including local synagogues and the B'nai Brith, to publicize the event. Few did. Invitations were sent to every member of the federal Parliament and Ontario legislature—"leaders of our great nation." None came. The organizing committee compiled a list of prominent Jewish community leaders, and sent invitations to all of them. None came. Letters of regret, primarily from invited politicians, offered perfunctory expressions of concern for Syrian Jewry and other oppressed minorities, requested information, or asked to be kept informed—hardly the kind of massive outpouring of enthusiasm the organizers had hoped for.

The teach-in evening was forecast to be one of the coldest nights of the year. Some members of the planning committee worried that the weather forecast was an omen. They had become disheartened in the days leading up to the event. There were few signs of interest. No high-profile political participants had promised to attend. The *Canadian Jewish News* told organizers that it would not even send a reporter to cover the teach-in. Insiders started lowering their estimate of how many people to expect.

In an effort to encourage Jewish youth to attend, the organizers asked for support from the educational directors of several larger synagogues, including Beth Tzedec. The Felds were members of the Beth Tzedec congregation and Rubin had volunteered to head a synagogue committee on the needs of foreign Jewry. They offered a free dinner at the synagogue before the teach-in to any school age youth who would attend. And remembering the political dictum to always book a room that comfortably holds only half the number of people expected to give the impression of overflowing interest, some organizers wondered whether they should switch the event from the large sanctuary at Toronto's Beth Shalom synagogue to a smaller room. Police security arranged for the event appeared excessive. As the doors opened, nobody knew quite what to expect.

It was a relief when the three main speakers arrived and the first people began drifting in out of the night cold. To the delight of an anxious planning committee, the sanctuary began to fill. To their amazement, when the teach-in began, the sanctuary was packed with more than seven hundred participants. Each person was offered a pin with a yellow star, bordered in red and emblazoned with the words "Free Syrian Jews," a twelve-page pamphlet, and a "Fact Sheet: Condition of the Jews in Syria" containing material pulled together from the international press. Postcards calling on "Syrian authorities to cease their persecution of the Jewish minority, to release those unjustly imprisoned, and to permit those Jews who wish to emigrate to do so" and addressed to Hafez al-Assad, president of the Republic of Syria, were distributed for signatures.[11]

The teach-in got off to a slow start, but interest remained high for a program that was top heavy in speeches and light on opportunities for discussion. Members of Toronto's small Sephardi Jewish community, informed of the teach-in by Rabbi Serels, turned out in deference to their rabbi. For some of them, their concern was not so much an expression of solidarity with oppressed Jews as it was an affirmation of their own past experiences and present fears for their family and friends who were still in Arab lands.

A tiny band of Arab sympathizers also turned out. They saw the campaign on behalf of Syrian Jews as a crass attempt by Zionists to use the alleged mistreatment of Jews in Arab lands to deflect attention from the crisis of Palestinians in the West Bank and Gaza and in refugee camps in the countries bordering Israel. As far as the Arab sympathizers were concerned, human rights were not being denied to Jews, who now had their own country, but by Jews, who were denying Palestinians their legitimate political and human rights.

The tension between the two groups was palpable, but the sanctuary venue and the conspicuous presence of uniformed police kept a lid on disruptive behaviour. Rubin Feld welcomed everyone and linked the teach-in to a growing protest movement in Europe, Latin America, and the United States. Even in the Soviet Union, Rubin told the audience, oppressed Jews had petitioned the Soviet government to intercede with Syria, a Soviet client state, on behalf of Syrian Jews. Only in Canada, he lamented, was there no active community engagement with the cause. "Canadians to this date have generally been silent and indifferent." This, he pledged, would now change.[12]

Saul Friedman's brief and pointed remarks on the oppression of Jewish minorities by Arab regimes set off mutterings of discontent among the small group of Arabs. The room was very quiet as the second speaker, Donald Keating, was introduced as a former minister of the United Church who had resigned because of the Church's hostility to Israel. The audience gave Keating a standing ovation as he stepped to the microphone. His condemnation of the United Church's preoccupation with Arab refugees while ignoring Jewish suffering at Arab hands, however, was the last straw for the small band of Arabs and their supporters. Muttering gave way to angry shouts and pro-Palestinian slogans. The outburst was greeted first with silence, then with a return salvo of catcalls. Fearing that the shouting match would turn ugly, the police ushered the most boisterous pro-Arab attendees out of the meeting. Suddenly energized, the crowd greeted every suggestion that Jews in Syria and other Arab lands were innocent victims of deep-seated Arab antisemitism and systematic anti-Israel hysteria with applause and a chorus of support.

As the meeting drew to a close, the participants were encouraged to sign the postcards to Syrian President Assad and take away additional blank cards for others to sign. But anyone who came to the teach-in expecting an action plan was disappointed. Beyond vague promises of future events, there were no concrete strategy proposals.[13]

The organizing committee evaluated the event later that evening at the Feld home. Judging by the unexpected number of people who turned out, the teach-in was declared more successful than the committee had dared hope. The Arab outburst and the response of the gathering was as much proof as anyone needed that the issue of Syrian Jews, like Soviet Jews, touched a nerve. The committee members were convinced they were on to something.

Media coverage, however, was disappointing. The *Canadian Jewish News* ran a story based on an after-the-fact interview with someone in the audience, and the article focused on the disturbance during the teach-in. A *Toronto Star* reporter did cover the event, but the paper only gave it two paragraphs buried on the inside pages. Even worse, the article was run under the headline "Six Arabs Ejected from Synagogue." Rubin Feld responded coldly to the article in a letter to the editor: "I cannot help but feel that, if the situation were reversed, and a group of Jews disrupted a lecture series in a mosque, the occurrence would have received front-page treatment by the *Toronto Daily Star*."[14]

Following the teach-in, the Felds continued their efforts. Judy distributed an additional six thousand postcards throughout the community and had another twelve thousand printed. The committee received several requests for the yellow star pins, the teach-in pamphlet, and the fact sheet from Jewish community groups, and made plans to distribute tape recordings of the teach-in. Rubin even received a letter from two young women at Toronto's Jewish parochial high school asking him to help them set up a "student action group for Jews in Arab lands" along the lines of his own group.[15]

There was no obvious next move. The Felds, as disciples of Kahane, were still convinced that initiatives from the Jewish margins, particularly JDL-style activism, had shaken Western Jewish leaders out of their lethargy on Soviet Jewry. Once the JDL had alerted *amcha*, the Jewish people, to the crisis, establishment Jewish leaders had no choice but to take up the cause. What had been done for Soviet Jews now needed to be done for Syrian Jews. But how? What was the best way to get information on Syrian Jewry out to the public and into the media?

Even after the teach-in neither of the Felds was particularly well informed on Syrian Jewry. In spite of the material they had compiled from the press and from advocacy groups, they remained largely in the dark about the day-to-day situation, about Congress's earlier efforts on behalf of Iraqi Jews, and about ongoing discussions with External Affairs on behalf of Albert Elia and Syrian Jews. What was needed, they believed, was to give the issue of Syrian Jews a higher profile. A postcard campaign had proven effective in highlighting the Soviet Jewry issue. It made sense to do the same for Syrian Jewry. In the Soviet case, tens of thousands of postcards were signed by individual Jews in the United States and Canada and mailed to refuseniks (Jews who were refused exit visas) in the Soviet Union. Soviet officials might not have allowed the cards to reach them, but the authorities were made aware that the international community knew about the refuseniks and was concerned.

The Felds and their committee had no idea if there were any Syrian refuseniks, but they knew where to send the protest on their behalf—to President Assad. With thousands of newly printed postcards in hand, the small band of activists fanned out into the Jewish community to circulate postcards wherever they could—at community events, Jewish parochial schools, and synagogues. Everywhere individuals were asked to read the card and sign. No stamp was necessary. The committee purchased $1,300 worth of stamps with the proceeds from selling the Free Syrian Jews pins.

The postcards were collected at the Feld home and stored in the basement in plastic garbage bags, and soon there were more than ten bags stuffed with signed postcards. In early March 1972, with a radio playing in the background and empty soft drink cans and pizza boxes scattered around, the small group stamped postcards, tied them in bundles of a hundred, and packed the bundles back into plastic garbage bags. When the process was done, and with the media on hand, two cars were loaded with the stuffed bags and a caravan made its way to the central post office in downtown Toronto. Judy remembers that the postal clerk on duty was overwhelmed by the sight of thousands and thousands of cards being piled up at his wicket, but that the chief postal clerk was accommodating. He offered to ensure that the postcards stayed together to be forwarded on a single flight. A short story on the "Postcards of Hope" appeared in the local news section of the *Toronto Star* Saturday edition under the headline "Help asked for Syrian Jews."[16]

Postcards were not the only items that the Feld committee mailed to Syria. The Toronto group managed to initiate a fragile thread of communication and an airlift of religious articles to Syrian Jews. It was to become a lifeline. Direct contact began on the telephone with another idea borrowed from the campaign for Soviet Jews. As information on individual refuseniks had leaked out of the Soviet Union, activists in North America placed person-to-person long-distance calls to the dissidents—sometimes with media covering the event. Often Soviet authorities did not allow the calls through. But each call still represented a victory. If the activists did speak to a refusenik, the conversation gave support to the cause on both sides. If the call was not put through, it validated accusations of human rights violations against Jews in the Soviet Union. North American activists also knew that, as in the postcard campaign, with each call Soviet authorities were served notice that a caring outside world was watching.[17]

The four Toronto activists that gathered on a cold Sunday afternoon in the office of the Sephardi synagogue soon learned that phoning Syria was not like phoning the Soviet Union. Both Judy Feld and Rabbi Serels remember that they only had the vaguest idea of whom to call. Rabbi Serels had gotten the names of a rabbi and a Jewish school in Damascus from a CBC French-language radio interview with the rabbi and one other member of the Jewish community. As Rabbi Serels dialled the international operator, Judy and Rubin Feld and an Arabic-speaking Egyptian member of Rabbi

Serels's congregation sat around the desk or listened on extensions. Rabbi Serels told the operator in Montreal that he wanted to speak person-to-person to a Rabbi Hamra in Damascus. No, he did not have a telephone number. No, he did not have an address. No, he was not sure of the exact spelling of the rabbi's name. All he had was the rabbi's name and the name of a school.

The Canadian operator said she would see what she could do. She dialled through to an operator in Rome who, in turn, patched the Toronto call to an operator in Damascus. Speaking in English, the Rome operator asked to be connected to a Rabbi Hamra, a functionary in the Jewish community. For a moment, the Syrian operator was silent. Then, in very slightly accented English, she said that this was impossible. There was no listing for a Rabbi Hamra.

The group in Toronto did not believe her. How could Rabbi Hamra have no telephone? He was, they protested to the operator, an important rabbi. Surely he had a telephone. The Egyptian Jew in Toronto asked in Arabic to be connected to the Jewish school or any other Jewish institution, even the Jewish cemetery. Rabbi Serels, interviewed years later, suggested that using the word "Jew" in Arabic might have posed something of a linguistic problem for the Syrian operator. The word commonly used for Jew in Syria might have had a derogatory connotation. Another word used for Jew was a derivative of "Israeli" which, because of its identification with the Jewish state, might also have been problematic. The call was obviously going nowhere, and they could hear a building aggravation in the voice of the Syrian operator. After one last protest that there was no listing for a Rabbi Hamra, Syria disconnected.[18]

What now? The Canadian operator awaited further instructions while the Toronto group discussed what had just happened. She offered to try dialling Damascus again, but this time she and her colleague in Rome could not get through. With the Canadian operator still on the line, the group in Toronto again discussed their options. The operator suggested that the Toronto group give up for the moment and try again the next day. She volunteered to serve as their operator and gave them her number and work schedule for the next week. The group reassembled several times, and each time they failed to reach anyone in the Jewish community.[19]

They decided to give it one last try. This time the same Canadian operator, patching the call through Rome, connected to a male operator in Damascus. When asked to look up the telephone number of the Jewish school, he hesitated. The Egyptian Jew, frustrated and angry, took the phone. Speaking in Arabic, he demanded to be put through to someone in the Jewish community immediately. There was a momentary silence, then, almost beyond belief, a telephone rang somewhere in Damascus. The group in Toronto were so prepared for another failure that they hardly knew what to say to the voice at the other end of the line. They had been connected to the Jewish school. The Egyptian Jew asked for Rabbi Hamra. Rabbi Hamra was not there. To reach him, the callers would have to call a second number.

A second phone rang. Eli Bellas, at home in Damascus, came to the telephone. The Toronto group tried to remain calm. They told Bellas in Arabic that this was a call from the Jewish community in Canada and asked him to put someone on the line who could speak for the Jewish community in Damascus. Bellas begged the operator to call back within the hour. He hung up and immediately ran next door to fetch Rabbi Hamra.

Bellas's neighbour, Rabbi Ibrahim Hamra, had just been appointed assistant to the aging chief rabbi of Damascus. At the time, Rabbi Hamra had no telephone of his own. As Bellas excitedly explained about the strange telephone call from Canada, Rabbi Hamra took for granted that the Muhabarat, the Syrian security police, had listened in on the call. Foreign calls to Syria were routinely screened by the Muhabarat, and the Jewish community in Damascus assumed that all their telephone calls were closely monitored. A telephone call to the Jewish community from abroad was going to demand an explanation.

Rabbi Hamra, interviewed in Toronto almost twenty years after that first eventful call, clearly remembers that day. The telephone call from Canada had put him on the spot, but he knew the ground rules. Instead of going next door with Bellas to await the return call from Canada, the young rabbi rushed off to the headquarters of the Muhabarat's Jewish section, only a few doors from his own home. Rabbi Hamra knew that was what the Muhabarat expected when they allowed the Canadian call to be routed through to Bellas in the first place.

Rabbi Hamra was no stranger to the Muhabarat. Its Jewish section oversaw all activities in the Jewish community, and Rabbi Hamra dealt with them on many matters. He had often visited their offices and knew the local security personnel well, but there were still procedures to be followed and a game to be played. Pretending that he did not know the Muhabarat had been listening in on the line, Rabbi Hamra reported the call and requested guidance on how to respond to the return call. The security agents in turn acted as if Hamra's report was a surprise to them. They suggested that he take the next call and find out what the Canadians wanted.

Shortly after Rabbi Hamra entered the Bellas house, the telephone rang. Knowing that Muhabarat officers were listening, he answered, speaking in Arabic to Rabbi Serels. Their conversation lasted less than a minute. Rabbi Serels explained that he represented a Canadian Jewish group who were hoping to enhance the spiritual and educational life of the Syrian Jewish community. Would the Syrian Jewish community welcome religious books and articles? Before Rabbi Hamra could answer, Rabbi Serels asked for the address and telephone number of the Jewish school in Damascus so that they might telegraph Rabbi Hamra there. Rabbi Hamra gave the information. The two rabbis said goodbye and they, and the Muhabarat, hung up.[20]

Rabbi Hamra immediately rushed back to the Muhabarat to report on his telephone conversation and advise them that a follow-up telegram was likely. Meanwhile, in Toronto, the group fell strangely silent. It was as if getting the telephone call through had been an end in itself. The call had established communication with the Jewish community in Damascus, but it had been so short and almost too businesslike, with no hint of the excitement that the Toronto group felt. Who was Rabbi Hamra, and what would he make of the call? Nonetheless, they had offered assistance to the Jewish community in Syria and further contact was possible.

That day the Toronto committee sent a telegram to Rabbi Hamra in French, asking him what Jewish religious articles the community needed. Taking their cue from the rabbi, they kept the telegram businesslike. Unsure of the Syrian community's financial situation and wanting to encourage a response, Rubin prepaid a reply telegram. The wait for an answer began. Little did they know the route their telegram would take over the next ten days. Before the telegram was approved for delivery to Rabbi Hamra, it was read by the Muhabarat. When the telegram was delivered to the rabbi, he immediately reported to the Muhabarat that he had received a telegram from abroad, and requested their advice on how to respond. He was given permission to reply. Rabbi Hamra telegraphed Rubin Feld in French that the Jewish community would welcome religious articles and he listed a number of books that he would find useful. But the telegram was a test of the sincerity of his would-be benefactors in Canada on the one hand, and a test of the Muhabarat on the other. Would the security police allow him to receive communications and religious items from abroad and, even more important, would they allow him to maintain some level of contact with Western Jews?

The Felds and their committee bought religious and educational materials, including the religious books Rabbi Hamra had requested, and mailed the first shipment to Damascus. They had purchased the material with money collected from their Toronto supporters, but many of the books and religious articles posed a problem. Some of the books were published in Israel. Others contained maps of Israel or were decorated with Israeli symbols. The group reasoned that the Syrians would not permit the delivery of material published in Israel or depicting what might be seen as Israeli national symbols, like a Star of David or an outline map of Israel. A razor was used to carefully remove the title page and any other indication that a book was published in Israel. Illustrations that might be regarded as pro-Zionist were also excised. Each book was then hand inscribed in French with the phrase "A gift to the Jewish Community of Syria from the Jewish Community of Canada."

A second parcel containing *tallisim*, prayer shawls, and other religious articles posed similar headaches. It was difficult to find inexpensive *tallisim* that did not have decorations that might be identified with Israel—often Yerushalyim, the Hebrew name for Jerusalem, or other Jewish symbols were imprinted on the silk cloth or sewn on the corners. When the marks were only on the corners, volunteers carefully removed the offending segments and replaced them with plain silk cloth.[21]

Rabbi Hamra assumed that each shipment from Toronto had been opened and carefully examined by the Muhabarat before he was notified that a parcel had arrived at the Damascus post office. Nevertheless, as soon as he had collected the parcel, he carted it over to the Muhabarat office for inspection. As far as he was able to judge, nothing was ever removed or withheld from the packages. He was allowed to telegraph Toronto, acknowledging receipt of the shipments. The only problem Rabbi Hamra had was with the *fact* of the shipments. After the second parcel arrived, the Muhabarat advised him that it was not appropriate to develop relationships with persons abroad, especially with those suspected of Zionist sympathies. Rabbi Hamra responded that he knew nothing of anyone's sympathies, nor was he in a relationship with the donors. There was no communication, just the generous supply of religious items and educational materials. That was all.[22]

But that was not all. In the telegrams and letters from Toronto telling the rabbi that a parcel was on its way, or from the rabbi acknowledging that a package had been received, or in notes of greeting that were placed in the boxes of religious items, the correspondents began a guarded dialogue. They used a code that had been devised by Jews during the Spanish Inquisition, inserting into their letters and telegrams apparently harmless references to passages of religious text that spoke of hope and redemption, of the reunification of the Jewish people, or of freedom from oppression. In one telegram, Rubin Feld and Rabbi Serels referred to Psalm 122, verse 2 ("Our feet stood inside your gates, O Jerusalem"). Rabbi Hamra responded with a reference to Psalm 121, verse 1 ("I turn my eyes to the mountain; from where will my help come?"). When the Toronto group referred to Psalm 126, verse 5 ("They who sow in tears shall reap with songs of joy"), Rabbi Hamra replied with Ecclesiastes 3, verses 1–8 ("A season is set for everything, a time for every experience under heaven"). The Muhabarat questioned Rabbi Hamra about the scriptural references, but the rabbi responded that the passages were merely used as traditional Jewish greetings.[23]

These small phrases spoke volumes. In the early 1970s, Syrian Jewry was cut off from Jews in the outside world. These few stolen words pierced that isolation. For the Felds, the secret exchanges confirmed their worst fears. The question was how to communicate this to others. Rubin believed that if people understood the crisis of Syrian Jewry, there would be a massive outcry. Even the Syrians would have to bend before outraged world opinion.

The Felds knew they would need more resources and more allies to galvanize a mass protest on behalf of Syrian Jews. But it was not easy to join with others working to the same end. The Poher and Clay Committees of Concern had connections and status; the small Toronto group did not. The Felds' first efforts to ally themselves with these two important committees had not been reciprocated. The Felds' JDL experience had left them with little use for the Canadian Jewish Congress, but the Congress voice still carried weight in both the Jewish and non-Jewish communities. On the plight of Syrian Jewry, however, the voice of Congress was still silent. Would Congress grant the Felds and their small band of supporters licence to speak on behalf of the Canadian Jewish community regarding Syrian Jews? If they did, Congress would have a public profile on the issue and the Felds and their supporters would have increased credibility.

Congress did not see it that way. In March 1972, the chair of the Ontario Region Foreign Affairs Committee reported to the Congress Regional Executive that the teach-in had been a success, but for someone else rather than for Congress. There was now a danger that the event's organizers might attempt to speak for Canadian Jews on other issues as well. This was not acceptable. What would happen to Congress's position as the political voice of Canadian Jewry if others were allowed to run off with parts of the Jewish political agenda? Congress had to regain command or risk losing control in other areas.

The Ontario Region Executive learned that the National Office of Congress was very much involved in the issue of Syrian Jews behind the scenes. But working behind the scenes was obviously not good enough if a non-Congress group could publicly champion the cause and leave the impression in the Jewish community that Congress was doing nothing. As a first step to developing a higher profile for Congress on the issue, the chair of the Ontario Region Foreign Affairs Committee announced that the plight of Syrian Jewry would be the subject of the next meeting, and he would invite leaders of the small Toronto Sephardi community to attend "because of their particular concern."

A Feld sympathizer on the executive sent Rubin a copy of the confidential minutes of the Congress meeting. Rubin did not feel threatened. He was fiercely protective of his independence of action, but he wanted to forge alliances with others who were committed to his cause. If Congress officials were sincere, he would also welcome a partnership with them. If he could speak to the leadership of Congress, perhaps he could ignite in them the passion that fired his activism on behalf of Syrian Jewry. He requested and received permission to attend the upcoming meeting of the Foreign Affairs Committee.[24]

Unfortunately Rubin Feld came to the May 18, 1972, meeting with two strikes against him. He knew little about the institutional culture of Congress and nothing about the understanding between Congress and External Affairs on strategy regarding Syrian Jews, but some members of the Foreign Affairs Committee already knew him by reputation. They remembered him as one of the JDL leaders of the anti-Kosygin demonstration that had upstaged the Congress demonstration. Now, apparently oblivious to the steps already taken on behalf of Syrian Jewry, Rubin and his small group of followers had the audacity to believe that they should be given licence to set the community agenda on the issue.

Rubin and Judy Feld's reception at the meeting was cool. They found themselves being lectured on the responsible limits of community activism. Behind guarded hints of covert diplomatic activity at the highest level, a Congress official from Montreal insisted the assembled group take its cue from the National Office and proceed with caution. And what was Montreal doing? The national spokesperson hinted that Congress's National Office was in the process of organizing a national Committee of Concern on Syrian Jewry, placing newspaper ads, planning a visit with the Syrian ambassador to the United Nations, and sending a delegation to Ottawa to discuss the plight of Syrian Jews with Canadian government officials. But no mass protest was planned.

The committee welcomed a suggestion to add Rabbi Serels to the Ottawa delegation as a voice of Sephardi Jewry. They discussed ways to feature the cause of Syrian Jewry alongside that of Soviet Jewry. In the spirit of co-operation, Rubin Feld offered to make his fact sheet on Syrian Jewry available for distribution. But he felt like an unwelcome guest at the meeting. The Ontario Region members seemed only too pleased to be told by the National Office that the Syrian Jewish issue was well in hand and no more needed to be done.

After the meeting adjourned, Rubin fell into a private, and, for him, unusually rancorous exchange with a Congress spokesperson. Rubin was warned that any precipitate action by his committee could do irreparable damage to the cause of Syrian Jewry—the blood of thousands could be on his hands.

The Felds were shocked but not surprised by the warning. As far as they were concerned, Kahane was proven right yet again. Congress was just being Congress—doing little and proud of it. The Felds would continue doing what they decided needed to be done and hoped that the more action they took, the greater the likelihood that they would shame Congress into taking up the Syrian Jewish cause. But that was a long way off.[25]

The Felds' first priority was to ensure that communication with the Jewish community of Syria remained open. Accordingly, it was important to keep filling Rabbi Hamra's shopping lists of religious books and articles. It was also important to forge links with other groups who might provide suggestions for programs and up-to-date information on the condition of Syrian Jewry, have influence in the international community, or have influence with Syrian authorities. Rubin sought the co-operation of groups as diverse as the National Union of Israeli Students, the Israeli Council for Jews in Arab Lands, and Amnesty International. But he felt some bitterness that in spite of his committee's efforts, the high-profile Poher and Clay Committees of Concern still commanded all the attention. Rubin wrote to both a member of the Israeli Knesset and a reporter for the

Jerusalem Post who had written an article on the Poher committee's activities to complain that important as the Poher committee was, there were others working on the issue as well.[26]

Rubin Feld also sought platforms in and around Toronto. He addressed synagogue men's clubs, brotherhood and sisterhood breakfasts, service organization meetings—almost any audience that would have him. He was soon at ease delivering what became his stock speech, "Syrian Jewry—The Jews of Despair." Much of his talk was compiled from press clippings and news releases, but the tone was all his own. Evoking images of horror and despair reminiscent of the Holocaust, he demanded that his listeners not let themselves be found wanting in the case of Syrian Jews, as their parents had been when the doomed Jews of Europe cried out for rescue. He ended his speech with a warning: "We must not abandon those Syrian Jews, for if we abandon them, their blood will be on our hands. We must not forget these Jews of despair."

After each talk, Rubin distributed copies of his fact sheet and sold his yellow star pins. In most cases, his hosts made a financial contribution to his committee, distributed postcards, and allowed the group's or synagogue's name to be used to petition Ottawa, the United Nations, or the government of Syria. But few synagogue brotherhoods matched the enthusiasm of the Shaarei Shomayim Brotherhood in Toronto. After Rubin addressed the group, its president mailed protest letters to Prime Minister Pierre Trudeau, the minister of External Affairs, Mitchell Sharp, a number of MPs with large Jewish constituencies, and dispatched a telegram to President Assad. He received several polite, noncommittal responses from Canadian politicians but nothing from Assad.[27]

While the Felds worked in Toronto, the Congress head office in Montreal put forward its own long-awaited public agenda on Syrian Jews. The organization declared May 1972 Syrian Jewish Solidarity Month and requested meetings with Syrian diplomatic officials in New York and with Mitchell Sharp in Ottawa. Topping the list of activities was a decision to set up a Committee of Concern. In March 1972, a number of prominent Canadians, Jewish and non-Jewish, were invited to join and John Diefenbaker agreed to be committee chair.

Nothing went as hoped. A Congress delegation was granted a meeting with Sharp. However, the planned meeting was blindsided by one of the Felds' efforts to raise public consciousness of the Syrian Jewish situation. Rubin had written to a number of prominent members of the government enclosing his fact sheet and requesting that each of them sign a petition protesting "the circumstances in which the Jewish population of Syria is forced to live." The petition urged the government of Syria to "repeal the specific legislation it has enacted to contain its Jewish communities, to release Jewish prisoners unlawfully detained, to stop this unwarranted persecution and to end barbaric maltreatment and harassment of Jews residing in Syria, and to permit the Jews in Syria to leave."

One cabinet member, unsure how to respond to the request that he sign the petition, sent the material to External Affairs for review. The department hastily checked the accuracy of the claims made in the fact sheet, judged them to be outdated and misleading of the current situation of Jews in Syria, and advised against any member of the government signing the petition.[28]

External Affairs also sent the fact sheet to the Canadian embassy in Beirut so that officials could validate or correct specific points made in it. The embassy consulted a contact in the United Nations High Commission for Refugees who was regarded as particularly knowledgeable on the situation of Syrian Jews. A dispatch sent back to External Affairs in Ottawa noted that while several points had some basis in fact, other points were outdated, wrong, misleading, or deliberately inflammatory.

A point-by-point review of the fact sheet was passed on to the minister's office in preparation for his June 5, 1972, meeting with the Congress delegation. The accompanying assessment from External Affairs officials asserted that while the situation of Syrian Jews was fluid and needed to be watched, there was nothing that called for a change in Canadian policy or demanded that Canada speak out publicly on the issue.[29]

The department briefing note on "The Situation of Jews in Syria" stated that in the previous three or four months the circumstances of the Syrian Jewish community had not worsened. On the contrary, things seemed to be getting better. One of the key improvements was the lifting of several restrictions on Jewish activities, including a prohibition on Jews' travelling outside their immediate neighbourhood. According to the note, this restriction was initially imposed to stamp out Jewish attempts to illegally escape from Syria. The author of the memo conceded that since Jews were not allowed to leave Syria legally, any attempt they made to leave was illegal. Most Jews held in Syrian prisons had apparently been involved in illegal emigration and currency export schemes, a preliminary step to escape. Jews and Jewish institutions were subject to restrictions and surveillance but the restrictions facing Jews were only worse by degree than those experienced by other Syrians in a totalitarian state. The recommendation was that the minister should hold to the line that any unilateral Canadian intervention was neither necessary nor advisable.[30]

The June 5 Congress meeting with Sharp was cordial, much like a chat among old friends. But the Congress delegation was unaware of the hands-off tone of the briefing note that Sharp had received from his officials. Alan Rose was convinced that External Affairs was onside in the case of Syrian Jewry, as it had been in the case of Iraqi Jews. Congress leaders conceded that the situation of the Jews of Syria might have improved somewhat, but argued that their situation was still far from satisfactory. They remained subject to state-imposed discrimination and no one expected this discrimination to let up. Their only hope was to leave Syria, but emigration was not allowed. Saul Hayes asked if the Syrian government might consider a third-party initiative on emigration similar to the Iraqi proposal. If so, here was a role for Canada. Congress asked the minister to use his good offices to secure the release of "persons unjustly imprisoned and to permit the departure of those Jews who wish to do so." The minister responded that the Canadian government would be sympathetic to applications by Syrian Jews who wanted to emigrate to Canada, especially if the applicant had family there. Beyond that, the minister offered Congress delegates his concern and co-operation, but no specific commitments.[31]

A second Canadian Jewish Congress delegation travelled to New York and received a far less sympathetic hearing from Dr. George

Tomeh, Syrian ambassador to the United Nations. Congress requested the meeting with the ambassador and, to the surprise of the Congress delegates, he agreed, as long as the parameters of their discussion were decided before the meeting. He foreclosed some lines of discussion by asserting that any restrictions on the freedom of Syrian Jews were not the fault of Syria. Jews were part of the "polyglot peoples of Syria." In the past, he claimed, all Syrians "grew up in a family atmosphere in which Christians, Jews and Muslims mixed and lived together like brothers, as Almighty God wants us to be." Any problems that Syrian Jews faced were a result of wilfully removing themselves from the Syrian family by flirting with a separatist Zionist ideology. "Unfortunately," the ambassador wrote, "it is only after the advent of some ideologies that feelings of differentiation have been imposed upon us." With his letter, the ambassador enclosed several articles copied from the international press—including interviews with members of the Syrian Jewish community—contending that the situation of Syrian Jewry was far better than was alleged.[32]

Even with the conditions, Congress still welcomed a meeting, which was held at Syria's UN Mission Offices in New York on the morning of June 9, 1972, several days after the meeting with Sharp. The Canadian delegation stated its concerns and then listened to a short, dismissive lecture arguing that in Syria all Jews were equal before the law. When Congress delegates suggested that Syrian Jews held in prisons were guilty of nothing more than wanting to leave the country, the ambassador responded that Jews, like others in prison, had violated Syrian law. If they were guilty of attempting to leave illegally, they had to be punished. He rejected any suggestion that there was discrimination in Syria on the basis of race or religion, and offered himself as an example. He, the Syrian ambassador to the United Nations, was a member of the Syrian Christian minority.

The ambassador rejected as unnecessary a Congress proposal to send an observer on a fact-finding mission to meet with Syrian Jewish community members. If Congress wanted to know what Syrian Jews thought about their status in Syria, he would supply the organization with the name of a "distinguished member of the

Jewish Community" who might be contacted for his views. Asked for information about Albert Elia, the Lebanese Jew who was kidnapped and reportedly imprisoned in Syria, the ambassador was evasive. He did suggest that requests for reunification of individual Syrian Jews with family in Canada "would be given sympathetic consideration" by his government. The ambassador welcomed the opportunity to discuss Congress concerns again as the need arose. The Canadian Jewish delegation was ushered out empty-handed.[33]

The rank and file of the Jewish community might regard Congress as a powerful organization, and it was treated respectfully by government, but the two delegations had been given a lesson in the limits of Congress's power to instigate change. However, Congress knew how to put on a good show and announced a major Montreal rally on behalf of Syrian Jewry in a manifesto issued to the press six weeks before the event. The manifesto, titled "A Cry from the Night," also ran as a paid advertisement in several Ottawa and French-language Montreal newspapers. The ads called on Canadians to "add their voice to the wave of world-wide protest. Even a cynical world seemingly immune to suffering cannot deny this cry from the night. Syrian Jewry is a claim on the conscience of all mankind." The ad closed with a quote from Isaiah, "Is this not the task that I have chosen? To loose the bands of wickedness, to undo the heavy burdens, and to let the oppressed go free, and that ye break every yoke?"[34]

On June 27, 1972, the rally on behalf of Syrian Jews drew several thousand to the ballroom of Montreal's Bonaventure Hotel. The main speaker, the American black civil rights activist Bayard Rustin, demanded that Syrian Jews be allowed to emigrate. "We're merely asking for the human equation," said Rustin. "Let our people go where they want to go, in the name of human democracy and human freedom." The rally shouted its approval of a resolution urging Syria to "release those Jewish prisoners, whose only 'crime' is their desire to leave the country."[35]

The Montreal rally was a singular success. But instead of being the high-profile kickoff for a continuing campaign on behalf of

Syrian Jews, it was a one-shot affair. There was little follow-up. Several Jewish organizations under the Congress umbrella—the Canadian Zionist Federation, the National Council of Jewish Women and Hadassah-Wizo—chimed in with their own resolutions, statements of concern, or telegrams to Canadian, United Nations, and Syrian officials. Rabbis delivered the occasional sermon and the Canadian Jewish press carried articles about the situation of Syrian Jews. This was a pale imitation of the high-profile campaign on behalf of Soviet Jewry.[36]

In truth, Congress officials did not expect their efforts to lead to any breakthrough. Were its efforts doing any good where it counted—in Syria? Some said yes. In a memorandum to members of the Governing Council of the World Jewish Congress, a WJC official applauded the diplomatic and other pressures as contributing to the "slight improvement in our fellow-Jews' situation in that country."[37] Congress leaders, however, privately concurred with reports that Syrian authorities were slowly loosening some restrictions on its Jewish population for its own domestic reasons. An External Affairs official who met informally with Alan Rose shortly after the Congress delegation met with the Syrian UN ambassador was left with the feeling that Rose "personally was reasonably satisfied with the present position of Jews in Syria." Nonetheless, he added, "Mr. Rose said that the main thrust of his group's representations [to the Syrian ambassador] have been that it should not be a crime to want or try to leave a country and that the Jews in Syria should be allowed to do so."[38] But there was nothing in the Syrian Jewish cause to turn it into a campaign comparable to that on behalf of Soviet Jews. In the end, Congress's foray into Syrian Jewish activism dead-ended.

In Toronto, while the Felds continued their efforts to build interest in the cause, they still had to balance their work for Syrian Jewry against the demands of family and professional life. They couldn't do it all, but the Felds were determined to do all they could. The breakthrough opening of communication to Syrian Jewry through Rabbi Hamra was exciting, but it had to be kept covert. Their efforts at community education—lectures, articles, letters to the editor—

had not forced the Syrian government to let even one Jew leave. Rubin continued to ask Canadian politicians for a humanitarian intervention on behalf of the Jews, but polite replies were all he received.

When Alan Rose was quoted in the *Canadian Jewish News* as saying that Syria was the Arab state "most impervious to pressure" and that he questioned whether "continued intervention by the world community would bring any results," Rubin was furious. In a letter to the *Canadian Jewish News*, co-signed by Rabbi Serels, Rubin protested that there were always those who declared impossible what they did not want to do in the first place. International protest, he declared, did work.

> Four years ago, Soviet Russia seemed impervious to world opinion— yet tens of thousands of Jews have been allowed to leave. In January 1969, when eleven Iraqi Jews were hung in Baghdad's Liberation Square in a festival atmosphere before television cameras in full public view, the Iraqis seemed impervious to world opinion. Nevertheless, most Iraqi Jews have been issued exit visas.[39]

Congress officials reacted angrily to the letter. Sol Kanee, president of Congress, dismissed it as a cheap shot "verging on slander," and charged that Rubin did not hold a monopoly on caring. Rabbi Serels had been part of the Congress delegation that had met with Mitchell Sharp and knew how deeply concerned Congress was. He also knew Congress would seize any opportunity to secure the freedom of Syrian Jews as it had in the case of Iraqi Jews—a story that could not yet be made public. Kanee protested, "It is much easier to criticize others in the Jewish press than effect the emigration of hundreds of Jews from Iraq."[40] But despite Rubin Feld's bravado and Kanee's anger, the reality was that neither campaign on behalf of Syrian Jews—that of the Felds' committee or that of the Canadian Jewish Congress—was exactly creating a firestorm of public interest.

In May 1973, Rubin and Judy Feld returned to Israel. Rubin attended a medical convention, but while they were there they found time to travel—Rubin made the strenuous early-morning climb up the twisting path to the ancient fortress of Masada in the

Judean Desert overlooking the Dead Sea. The Felds also met with Haim Cohen, a justice of the Israeli Supreme Court who headed the Israel Council for Jews in Arab Lands. Judy remembers that Cohen was more intrigued by the work that the Felds were doing in Toronto than he was informative about the state of Syrian Jewry. He encouraged the couple to continue their efforts and helped arrange a briefing for them with an Israeli Foreign Ministry official who was well versed on the situation of Jews in Syria.[41]

The Felds returned to Toronto still convinced of the rightness of their adopted cause and determined to redouble their efforts. But that was not to be. On the evening of June 7, 1973, just a few days after they got back, Rubin Feld, who had just turned forty, suffered a heart attack while he played with his youngest child. Judy found him dead on the floor of the family home. He had no history of heart disease, nor had he complained of illness.

Among those touched by Rubin Feld's death was Rabbi Hamra in Damascus. He was informed of the death by the Muhabarat, who called him into the security police offices after monitoring an Arab-language program on Kol Yisroel, the Voice of Israel, the Israeli broadcasting network. Justice Haim Cohen, whom the Felds had met in Israel, commented on Diaspora concern for Syrian Jews and mentioned Rubin Feld and his Canadian initiative. The Muhabarat connected the Feld mentioned by Cohen with the Feld who had phoned Damascus and sent parcels to Rabbi Hamra, and questioned the rabbi about his relationship with Rubin. He explained that he only knew Rubin Feld through the boxes of religious items sent from Canada. The Muhabarat official showed Rabbi Hamra photocopies of the telegrams he had sent to Toronto thanking Rubin Feld for the packages and referring to the Psalms. The rabbi again explained that the references were affirmations of faith and were offered in thanks for the parcels, nothing more. The Muhabarat let him go with a word of caution about keeping the authorities informed of all his future dealings with foreigners. However, the Muhabarat must also have made inquiries in Toronto. Although the Kol Yisroel broadcast did not mention that Rubin Feld had died, the Muhabarat informed Rabbi Hamra of his death.

Realizing how closely the Muhabarat were monitoring his every communication with the outside world, Rabbi Hamra stopped including biblical references in his telegrams or letters sent from Syria—with one exception. On the occasion of the Jewish New Year, Rosh Hashanah, and with the permission of the Muhabarat, he sent a telegram of greetings to the Feld home in Toronto. In the telegram, Rabbi Hamra referred to the Haftorah reading for the second day of Rosh Hashanah—Jeremiah 31:2–20. Judy Feld read the passage and wept.[42]

> Thus said the Lord: A cry is heard in Ramah—wailing, bitter weeping—Rachel weeping for her children. She refuses to be comforted for her children, who are gone.
>
> Thus said the Lord: Restrain your voice from weeping, your eyes from shedding tears; for there is a reward for your labor—declares the Lord; they shall return from the enemy's land. And there is hope for your future—declares the Lord: your children shall return to their country.[43]

CHAPTER FOUR

Be Strong and of Good Courage

THE TORONTO-BASED CAMPAIGN on behalf of Syrian Jews should have ended with Rubin Feld's death. The formal organization was more letterhead than reality. Judy and a small group of supporters who shared Rubin's concern for Syrian Jewry and deep mistrust of established Jewish community leadership had all relied on him for direction. Rubin had regarded Judy as a partner, critical to everything he did, but she had left it to him to set the course.

There was little to show for two years of work. Rubin had organized programs and given lectures. His committee had shipped off thousands of post cards to the president of Syria and other world leaders. He had pressed fellow Jews to share his concern, sent letters to editors, and repeatedly written to Canadian government officials and MPs, resigning himself to the "I share your concern" replies. But Rubin's hopes of reshaping the Canadian Jewish agenda to include a sustained campaign on behalf of Syrian Jews were not realized. His most important breakthrough was opening a line of communication into the Syrian Jewish community. When he died, Rubin Feld left behind a legacy of concern but not an organization that could carry on without him. There was no plan of action, no working alliances, and no grand design.

The plight of Syrian Jews was not Judy's first priority when she started to pull her life back together. Her husband's death had been so sudden, so unexpected. He had been young and vital. One minute he was alive, active and tanned from his trip to Israel. The next, his family was sitting shiva, the week of ritual mourning following burial. There had been no goodbyes and no time to think about the future. No one else in her circle of family or friends had been widowed at such a young age. Friends rallied around, but they did not know how to help her and her three young children reconstruct their lives.

On the final morning of the shiva, Rabbi Serels came to the Feld house to pay his respects. The two of them talked, or rather Judy talked and the rabbi listened. She spoke of her inability to make sense of what had befallen her and her children. On the spur of the moment, she asked Rabbi Serels to drive her out to her husband's grave. She wanted see the mound of dirt where he was buried. She had to make herself realize that he was gone forever. At first the rabbi refused, but Judy persisted, protesting she would go without him if necessary. He reluctantly agreed. They drove out to the graveyard and stood by the freshly turned earth. When they returned home, Judy showed the rabbi a telegram addressed to Ronald Feld that had arrived during the shiva. It was a simple acknowledgement from Rabbi Hamra that the second box of books had arrived safely. Judy Feld and Rabbi Serels looked at one another and cried.[1]

Judy would have to figure out a way to earn a living. Rubin's tangled business affairs would have to be sorted out and wound down, and his mother would need to be cared for. Judy fell back on her music training, teaching high school music during the day, and giving private music lessons in the evening.

What of the campaign on behalf of Syrian Jewry? Judy Feld sent letters to a number of politicians whom her husband had lobbied, notifying them of her husband's death and letting them know that she was taking up where he had left off: "Because my husband has been so involved for almost two years with the situation of the Jews remaining as hostages in Arab lands, I shall continue his efforts to have these people liberated."[2]

Judy had intended to only tie up the loose ends of the campaign, but she gradually found herself getting more and more deeply involved. The cause gave her life structure, a reason to be active and engaged, and a focus outside her own pain. It gave her an opportunity to build a living memorial to her husband. And it gave her perspective on her own problems: no matter how heavy her own burden, there were those whose load was far heavier than hers.

To begin with, however, she only did the bare minimum.[3] She could scarcely make ends meet or find time for herself and her children. What right did she have to steal time for Syrian Jewry? She credits others with encouraging her and making it impossible for her to turn her back on the cause. In response to a letter from Judy telling him of her husband's death and promising him that the work would continue, Haim Cohen replied, "I am full of admiration for the way in which you carry on your husband's good work and in particular, your life in general, and I wish I could show you how deeply I feel with you and how much I would like to be of some help and give you some comfort."[4] Friends whom Rubin and Judy Feld had met at the Beth Tzedec synagogue were most instrumental in convincing Judy to take on the campaign for Syrian Jews. Several weeks after Rubin's death, a small group of these friends gathered at the Feld home and proposed a fitting memorial to her husband: a fund established in his name and administered at Beth Tzedec. All the money collected would be earmarked for Jews in Arab lands and, in particular, for the cause of Syrian Jewry. The group pledged $5,000 among themselves to start.

Judy believes that these initial contributors were as interested in giving her a creative outlet for her own energies—something beyond caring for her children and worrying about bills—as they were in paying tribute to Rubin. The Dr. Ronald Feld Fund would need a committee to oversee its operations, but everyone assumed that Judy would direct its activities.

The Feld Fund was an innovation for Beth Tzedec, which had no other funds dedicated to this kind work. After some discussion, the board agreed to a proposal that allowed the Feld Fund wide latitude in the charitable efforts it would support.[5]

> The purpose of the fund is to purchase religious articles and books for Syrian Jewry; to communicate with Jews in Syria; to secure their release; to assist their settlement in Canada; to educate the refugee children in day schools and universities in Canada; to publicize the plight of the "Jews of Despair" in an effort to free them.[6]

Beth Tzedec synagogue, Canada's largest congregation and among the wealthiest, was an institutional pillar of Toronto Jewish life. There could be no better host for the Feld Fund, and Beth Tzedec's involvement boosted the cause of Syrian Jews in ways no one could have possibly imagined. As Judy became more and more identified with the cause of Syrian Jewry, so too did Beth Tzedec. She took on Rubin's position as head of the Beth Tzedec's Foreign Jewry Committee. But unlike her husband, she now had a small pool of funds to draw on.

Judy also emerged as a power within the congregation. A battle royal had broken out at Beth Tzedec between long-serving Rabbi Stuart Rosenberg and his followers and a new and powerful group of members who opposed his rabbinic and administrative style. While battles of this kind are the stuff of Jewish political life, the conflict spilled out beyond the congregation and into the community. Rabbi Rosenberg, well known among both Jews and non-Jews, often wrote for the press and was much sought after as a spokesperson on Jewish and public affairs. In the glare of media attention, Rabbi Rosenberg and Beth Tzedec parted ways. Judy was asked to run for a seat on the new board. She agreed, but as no woman had ever served on the board, she did not expect to get elected. To her surprise, she was one of two women who were. She was soon a player in the internal politics of the institution and ensured that the cause of Syrian Jewry remained a priority.

The Beth Tzedec Bulletin, the monthly congregational publication that reached some three thousand members, including many of Toronto's Jewish establishment, soon contained a monthly page updating the synagogue membership on the trials of Syrian Jewry and the work of the Feld Fund. Congress's Ontario Region chairperson, Milton Harris, approached Judy to head a regional Committee on Jews in Arab Lands. Although she still had misgivings about Congress and suspected that the organization was more interested in papering over previous inaction than in actually doing something, Judy agreed to become committee chair. Whatever Congress's agenda was, she had her own. The Congress affiliation gave her the cachet of the widely respected Jewish organization. If it also gave her access to Congress's resources, so much the better.

The appointment of Judy Feld as head of the Congress Ontario Region Committee on Jews in Arab Lands was covered in the local Jewish press. She was interviewed by the *Canadian Jewish News*, and in a reference to her JDL days, the paper headlined its article "'Self-Admitted Disturber' Chosen Head of Body to Help Jews in Arab Lands." Judy complained to the newspaper's editor that she was not a "disturber," but what did disturb her was that "many Jewish organizations were not doing enough to help this unhappy people, the Jews forced to remain in Syria." The effort to save Jewish lives, she protested, was not a disturbance but a *"humanitarian gesture"* and the "fact" that the newspaper's editor did "not consider the saving of Jewish lives to be a decent humanitarian gesture, *disturbs* me the most."[7]

According to one longtime Congress insider, Judy Feld demonstrated little organizational grace and no aptitude for institutional politics. Playing her cards close to the chest, she made almost no effort to court Congress power brokers and refused to play by any rules except her own. As a result, Congress insiders continued to regard her as an energetic but naive outsider, an ineffectual and unpredictable loner, who had only had a "corporal's guard" of supporters on her Congress committee, most of whom were outside the regular circle of Congress personalities. She was not a team player and Congress leaders avoided getting too close to her.[8]

In retrospect, she agrees that she did not play the Congress political game well, but insists that she never intended to play the game at all and was never interested in the rules. She wanted the credibility that came with being chair of a Congress committee; Congress leaders wanted to say they were doing something about the Jews in Arab lands. It was an even trade that served both Judy Feld and Congress well. She disagrees that her committee was only a "corporal's guard." The members were mostly Congress outsiders, but eventually there were eighty of them across Canada, including representatives of many major Jewish organizations. They raised money for the Feld Fund, ran a speakers' bureau, and helped with the hands-on organizational work. Of course, Judy ran a one-person show. Even a close friend and supporter conceded that "to work with Judy, you can never have the illusion that you have any power."[9]

Even with money and organizational backing, Judy was no further ahead than Rubin had been in knowing how to make a difference in the lives of Syrian Jews. Her committee sent out regular information mailings, including reprints of the Syrian Jewry page from the *Beth Tzedec Bulletin*. If given a platform, Judy or one of her supporters was there. An appeal for donations to the Feld Fund and a request that everyone in the audience write to MPs and government officials demanding Canadian action on behalf of beleaguered Jews in Syria were part of every presentation.[10]

Some did write. In July 1973, the minister of External Affairs received a constant stream of letters demanding Canadian intervention on behalf of Syrian Jews. Officials responded that Syria's emigration policy was an internal Syrian affair and Canadian initiatives would only be appropriate on humanitarian grounds. Several applications for family reunification were being actively pursued with Syrian authorities and while no family reunifications had yet been approved, the Syrians appeared to be amenable in bona fide cases. Syria would not, however, allow Jews to emigrate to Israel, its enemy, under the cover of reunification with relatives in Canada. On the whole, officials assured the minister, the situation of Syrian Jews had improved. Canada should monitor the situation and, as long as the position of Syrian Jews did not deteriorate, avoid any action that the Syrians would regard as meddling in their internal affairs.[11]

During the week of the Jewish New Year in 1973, Judy received a telegram from Rabbi Hamra wishing Rubin Feld and Rabbi Serels a Happy New Year.[12] On Yom Kippur two days later, October 7, 1973, Syrian armoured units smashed across the 1967 ceasefire lines on the Golan Heights. They were joined by Egyptian and Jordanian forces who engaged Israeli forces on their respective borders. The surprise attack caught Israel off guard, and in the first critical hours, its very survival seemed in doubt. The Israeli military was finally able to push back the united Arab onslaught, but Israeli self-confidence, inflated during the 1967 Six-Day War, took a beating.

In the wake of the war, Syria's small Jewish community lived on the razor's edge. Haim Cohen informed Judy Feld, "...in the first week of the war, all Jewish males in Aleppo had been arrested.

Other than the telegram to the late Dr. Feld no news has come from Damascus or Qamishli.... There are too many precedents from previous wars to justify any illusion that cheap revenge will not be taken on the civilian Jewish population."[13] Even before receiving Cohen's report, the Toronto committee had sent a telegram to UN Secretary General Kurt Waldheim, asking him to intercede with Syrian government officials to ensure the safety of their Jewish citizens. They also sent telegrams to External Affairs Minister Sharp and other Canadian political leaders asking that Canada do the same, as well as requesting specific information on the safety of Rabbi Hamra and several other individuals.[14]

Sharp assured Judy that he shared her concerns, but reiterated that beyond the applications for family reunification, Canada's "ability to assist in this matter is limited."

> The Jews of Syria are citizens of Syria, and the matter of their emigration is an internal Syrian matter. We must be very careful that our efforts on behalf of the members of the Syrian Jewish community are not seen as interference in the domestic affairs of Syria by the authorities. Otherwise, our work could produce results contrary to what we had intended.[15]

However, Sharp did instruct the Canadian ambassador to Lebanon, also accredited to Damascus, to make inquiries through his contacts. In late December 1973, External Affairs told Judy that the ambassador had consulted people who "are well acquainted and have frequent contact with the Syrian Jewish community," and Canadian embassy staff were reassured that there had been "no deterioration in the community's situation generally either as a result of the war or for any other reason." Nonetheless, External Affairs cautioned that "it was difficult to obtain reliable information from Syria in the aftermath of the war," including information on "the particular circumstances of those people about whom you have asked." The department would continue monitoring the situation.[16]

To keep her post–Yom Kippur War lines of communication into Syria open, Judy Feld airmailed two parcels of religious items to Rabbi Hamra on the eve of the Jewish festival of Chanukah. Rabbi

Hamra sent back a telegram acknowledging receipt of the two parcels with a request for a specific set of religious texts. When Judy mailed them to Damascus with religious items associated with the coming Purim festival, she slipped several references from the Psalms in with the shipment—Psalm 31, verse 25, "Be strong and of good courage, all you who wait for the Lord," and Psalm 20, verse 2, "May the Lord answer you in time of trouble, the name of Jacob's God keep you safe."

The biblical quotations did not go unnoticed by the Syrian authorities, who carefully checked each parcel twice. The following year, Judy again sent two boxes just before Purim. In one she enclosed a note again quoting Psalm 31, verse 25; in the other the reference was to Psalm 20, verse 2. But this time she deliberately misidentified verse 2 as verse 3. Rabbi Hamra recognized the error and understood the message. ("May He send you help from the sanctuary, and sustain you from Zion.") But did the Muhabarat? Again they questioned the rabbi, letting him know that the security police were watching his contacts with the outside world. Mindful of the warning but eager to maintain his communication with Canada, Rabbi Hamra telegraphed Toronto thanking Rubin Feld for the Purim parcel and requesting "more religious books and financial help" for those in need.[17]

Judy and Rubin had once before sent money to Syria, to help a Jewish boy named Simon Khabas. Simon, the youngest of six children of the *shamus* (sexton) at Rabbi Hamra's synagogue in Damascus, suffered from a congenital heart disease. Syrian medical authorities advised Simon's parents that if he was to have any chance for a normal life, he would need drugs and medical treatment unavailable in Syria. For eight years, the Khabas family pleaded with authorities to allow their sick child to seek treatment abroad. For eight years, they were refused.

The first information on the sick little boy reached the West in 1971, and his story was widely publicized by the American Jewish Committee and the Clay Committee. Adverse publicity in the West failed to move Syrian authorities. Simon and his family grew increasingly desperate. In the winter of 1972, with hope of legal exit from Syria fading and his health continuing to deteriorate, Simon and one of his brothers attempted to escape into Lebanon by posing as returning Lebanese travellers. They were caught. Simon, just a child and in failing health, was detained for a day, then released. His older brother was not so fortunate. He was jailed and severely beaten. After several months, the family made another attempt to get Simon out of Syria. Money raised in the community was paid to a smuggler to take him into Lebanon. At the border, the smuggler betrayed him to the police. Again, Simon escaped punishment but his brothers and sisters were accused of organizing the escape attempt, arrested, held without trial for two weeks, and tortured.

Rubin Feld was particularly taken with the story of the sick child. In the months before his death, he approached students at the Community Hebrew Academy of Toronto, the Jewish community high school, and asked them to become the sick boy's advocates. The students organized a fundraiser and student rally in Simon Khabas's name at Toronto's City Hall square. During the rally, several students carried a coffin to symbolize the Syrian response to the boy's illness. The Canadian media covered the rally and a press release was picked up by the Jewish Telegraphic Agency. News stories were run in Jewish papers around the world.[18]

Rubin Feld sent several telegrams to Rabbi Hamra inquiring about Simon, but the telegrams went unanswered. Rubin never knew if they had been received, but he wanted the Syrian authorities to know that the Khabas case was important to the outside world. In a more direct effort to help Simon and his family, Rubin reached into his own pocket to top up money collected by the Toronto students. He sent Rabbi Hamra a money order with a note saying that the money should be used by "any sick child who needed help." The rabbi understood that it was for Simon Khabas and passed it on to his family.[20]

The money was used in yet another abortive attempt to buy Simon out of Syria. One of his brothers, bypassing the local Muhabarat, succeeded in buying an interview with a high-ranking Syrian official. Simon's brother again asked permission for Simon to go to Beirut for treatment. Because he was Jewish, the Syrian official demanded $3,000 as security. But the local Muhabarat agents were angry at being cut out of the graft. Not only was an exit visa denied, but for circumventing them, the authorities picked up Simon's brother and beat him.[20]

In Canada, Rubin continued to press Simon's case. Why not bring him to Canada? Rubin petitioned Mitchell Sharp to intervene on behalf of the sick boy. Rubin also approached several MPs from Toronto ridings with large numbers of Jewish voters asking them to approach External Affairs on Simon's behalf. Several did speak to Sharp, who again explained that there was very little Canada could do. Nevertheless, he promised that Canadian officials would look into the case. External Affairs asked the Canadian embassy in Lebanon to check with its contacts at the UN High Commission for Refugees office in Damascus and advise Ottawa if there was any room for a Canadian initiative. The results were not encouraging. Embassy officials concluded that Simon's case remained an internal Syrian matter; Canadian interference would benefit neither Simon nor the Syrian Jewish community as a whole.[21]

Despite the discouraging response from External Affairs, Rubin Feld believed that there must be a way to bring Simon to Canada for treatment. In the spring of 1973 he arranged a meeting with the president of the Canadian branch of the International Red Cross to talk about the case. Rubin died a week before the meeting. When Judy received an inquiry about the case from Israel after Rubin's death, she confessed to being at a loss as to how to proceed. Would the Red Cross listen to a doctor's widow, a music teacher? They couldn't expect much help from "the [Canadian] government and the establishment Jewish organizations which do nothing except say that there is nothing that can be done." But because Simon Khabas was so desperate and his case had been so important to her husband, Judy pledged to do what she could.[22]

Syrian officials were apparently prepared to let Simon die. But suddenly, in February 1974 they relented and granted him permission to go to Beirut for one month of medical treatment. The Kahabas family had only to post a $400 bond against their son's return. But Simon had to go alone.

Once in Beirut, Simon, now seventeen years old and very weak, contacted the local Jewish community. After a preliminary examination in a local hospital, he was transferred to the American University Hospital. Test results were disheartening. Too much time had passed without appropriate treatment. Simon was deteriorating rapidly, and his condition was diagnosed as inoperable. Doctors agreed that he should seek another opinion and suggested that he go to Paris.

Simon's family in Syria applied for an exit-visa extension and passport. The application included a $1,200 advance against the cost of issuing the necessary passport and extended exit visa. The application was denied. Syrian authorities demanded Simon's return at the end of the month when his exit visa expired.[24] Desperate, Simon fled to France and, with the help of French Jewish officials, he was secretly taken to Israel. Simon's case was taken up by Haim Cohen's Israel Council for Jews in Arab Lands and he was soon in hospital in Tel Aviv. But again the medical diagnosis was bleak. With luck and appropriate medical care, he might have ten more years to live. Remembering all that Rubin Feld had done, Cohen wrote to Judy Feld informing her of his situation. "The poor boy is in a terrible state of depression, particularly as he is separated from his family." Simon's attending physician in Israel suggested that doctors in Canada might be able to do something more for Simon. Judy was asked to revisit the possibility of bringing him to Canada for treatment.[24]

She and the Feld Fund moved into action. Several doctors in Toronto volunteered their time and skill. Consultations began. For several months during the spring and summer of 1974, doctors in Israel and Toronto exchanged letters and medical records. As doctors considered medical options, students at the Beth Tzedec Congregational School took up Simon's cause. They raised nearly $1,400 to help defray some of the medical costs and allow him small comforts. Judy flew to Israel with two of her children. She had previously arranged the trip as a chance to rethink her situation and earn a little money. She took a short-term job teaching music education, and rented a third floor walk-up apartment in Jerusalem. While she was there, she met with Haim Cohen and others in Israel involved in the Syrian cause. She also met Simon Khabas. Simon insisted on making the trip from Tel Aviv to Jerusalem to visit Judy in her apartment. Difficult as it was for him, he slowly climbed the three flights of stairs to her door, determined to make it on his own. He was winded from the strain but obviously excited when he reached her.

This young man was the first Syrian Jew that Judy had met. Whatever image she had in her mind, Simon did not fit it. The frail and slight Simon was blond and blue-eyed, hardly the olive-skinned, dark-eyed boy she expected. The two talked, with Simon's doctor serving as translator. Simon's obvious sadness on being told of Rubin's death touched Judy. She asked the young man to fill in the details of his life and his efforts to get out of Syria. She felt a chill when, in his homesickness and loneliness, Simon began calling her "Mother" and confessed his fear of dying. When the visit drew to a close, Judy gave him the money raised by the students in Toronto. She promised to see him again soon. She never did.

When she returned to Toronto in the late summer, the medical news was bad. Cardiologists advised her that after reviewing Simon's medical records, they agreed with their Israeli colleagues—"in essence, inoperable situation."[25] There was no more to be done.

In early December 1974, Simon's doctor contacted her. An Israeli cardiologist who had just returned from studying at the Mayo Clinic had reviewed the case. He felt that, with new surgical techniques, Simon might have one slim chance if an operation was performed right away. It was taking a big chance, but Simon wanted the procedure. Legally, he was still too young to authorize the operation himself. His family in Syria could not be notified that he was in Israel. If Syrian authorities found out, the family would be severely punished. Simon had named Judy Feld his guardian without her knowledge or permission. Now Simon's cardiologist was asking her to authorize the operation.

She consulted doctors in Toronto, the Israeli consul, and several rabbis. They all told her that she had no choice. She had to sign. The necessary papers were sent to the Israeli consul in Toronto by diplomatic pouch. Judy, still hesitant, took the papers home, but in the end she signed. She returned the documents to the Israeli consul, then went home and downed the better part of a bottle of gin. The next day she wrote Simon an upbeat letter, promising they would soon be together again in Israel.

In early February 1975, Simon underwent open-heart surgery. He did not survive. His doctor sent Judy Feld a copy of the surgeon's report:

> With great sorrow I would like to inform you that the operation of Salim [Simon] Shabas was unsuccessful, and he never got off the open heart lung machine...[analysis of the operation] indicates that he had no chance whatsoever, and without the operation he could not survive more than another year or two....We were all moved by the whole case, but we feel that he was treated properly and as I said before he belonged in that group of Patients who have no chance.[26]

Additional money raised by the students at Beth Tzedec Congregational School covered small costs associated with his funeral in Israel. But who would sit shiva for him? Since there was no safe way to let Simon's family know about his death, Judy mourned him on their behalf. She had lost someone else's child. The following Saturday, Simon Khabas's death was announced from the pulpit at Beth Tzedec. The entire congregation stood as one and recited the Kaddish, the Jewish prayer spoken by immediate family during the period of mourning.[27]

The death of one teenage boy had brought home to Judy the human face of Syrian Jewry's plight, but it was the death of four young Jewish women—three sisters, Mazal, Laura, and Farah Zebac, and their cousin Eva Saad—that aroused anger and protest across the Jewish community. On March 4, 1974, the bodies of the four women had been found raped, robbed, murdered, and mutilated in a cave near the town of Asfura on the Syrian side of the border with Lebanon. According to a *New York Times* story, the finger of one of the young women had been cut off in order to remove a ring. On the Sabbath before the festival of Purim, celebrating the defeat of a genocidal plot to murder the Jews of ancient Persia, the girls' bodies, bundled in sacks, were returned to their parents for burial.[28]

Syrian authorities appeared to be less interested in uncovering the truth than in damage control. After disclaiming any responsibility for the murders, they set about finding a scapegoat. The story released to the diplomatic community and the media was that the victims had hired smugglers to take them across the border into Lebanon. The smugglers had driven the four women out of Damascus as planned, but once the smugglers learned that the women were carrying jewels and other valuables, they had taken them to the cave near the border.

The horror of the deaths shook the Damascus Jewish community. Immediately following the funeral, Jewish women staged an unprecedented protest march. In anger and pain, one thousand Jewish women paraded out of the Jewish quarter, where they had remained in virtual detention since the Yom Kippur War. They made their way through the busy streets into the middle of the city, and were joined by a number of Syrian Christian women. The demonstrators demanded that they be permitted to leave Syria, and that they be allowed to put their case before President Assad. Syrian police were taken by surprise but quickly recovered and dispersed the demonstrators. Some of the women were shaken up but otherwise unhurt. There is little doubt that had the demonstration involved Jewish men, the police would have used far less restraint. Arrests and beatings would have been the order of the day.[29]

Syrian authorities moved swiftly to prevent the dead girls from becoming martyrs and to deflect accusations that the Syrian authorities were implicated in the murders. The minister of the Interior announced that four men had been arrested for the crime—two smugglers and two Jewish men from prominent families. The four men were alleged to have been a gang specializing in organizing the flight of wealthy Jews from Syria. They were said to have persuaded the young women to escape and later shared the booty.

Jewish community leaders worldwide were outraged. The idea that the two Jewish men "would go to a cave in the mountains to participate in the robbery and murder of four girls from their own community, is an insult to the intelligence of the enlightened world and a slap in the face of justice and human decency." Any confessions could only have been extracted by torture and were designed to conceal the true "facts." As far as Jewish observers were concerned, Syrians officials were as culpable as if they had themselves raped and murdered the women. By denying Syrian Jews the most basic of human rights, devaluing their lives, and keeping them virtual prisoners, the government was inviting desperate Jews to escape. Syrian authorities might just as well have been in the cave with the smugglers.[30]

Western diplomats in Damascus agreed that charging the Jewish men in the murders was a crude effort to deflect attention from Syria's mistreatment of its Jews. A high-ranking External Affairs official dismissed as unlikely in the extreme that any Jews would have been involved in the murder. The Canadian embassy informant on the Jewish community in Syria, however, again advised the embassy that the situation was not nearly as bad as world Jewish community leaders made out. The two Jews were not arrested for actively participating in the murder, but for being in league with the smugglers.[31]

Rabbi Hamra was adamant that this was untrue. The two Jewish men might well have helped the four young women to make contact with the smugglers. The women had left a note for their parents telling them that they were escaping and that the two men would know where they were. But, the rabbi insisted, the Jewish men did not initiate the escape attempt. The young women were desperate to leave Syria, and if the men had not helped them to contact smugglers, the four would have turned to others or gone on their own. By dealing with the smugglers for them, the two men erroneously thought they were protecting the women.[32]

Other young people attempted to escape despite the extreme dangers. One young man who succeeded was Shlomo Kaski. In 1973, just before the Yom Kippur War, Kaski, only eighteen, was determined to leave Syria. Several false starts in negotiating with shady inter-city taxi drivers who he hoped would spirit him across Syria's border with Lebanon had left Kaski poorer but no further ahead. Finally, he located a smuggler with a proven track record. Unlike rough-and-tumble smugglers who guided their clients across the frontier by foot in the dead of night, Kaski's smuggler was a white-collar worker with government connections, who was, for a price, able to arrange false identification papers with typical Christian-Arab names. The smuggler and a driver drove Kaski to the border and told him to stay quietly in the car while the smuggler showed

Kaski's newly minted identity papers to the Syrian border police. The smuggler returned to the car. Money had passed hands. The driver was waved forward across the border and the smuggler produced the same documents for the Lebanese border police. They joked, and the smuggler promised a gift when he passed through on his way back. They drove on. Kaski was out of Syria.

He was still not safe. If he was caught in Lebanon, he would likely be sent back to Syria and punished. The car reached Beirut too late for Kaski to be discreetly dropped off near a synagogue where he might find temporary sanctuary. Instead, he was delivered to the home of an old Arab woman who put him up for the night. Early the next morning, she walked him to a street corner and pointed to an unmarked door that she said was a safe house. Hoping that nobody was watching, Kaski knocked on the door, and when it opened a crack, he identified himself as a Jew from Damascus. A hand reached out and pulled him in quickly. "There are police everywhere."

Kaski and two others were hidden for ten days. They saw almost nobody and were told nothing about what was planned for them. On the tenth night, the three were told to collect their things. A truck pulled alongside their hiding place, stopping only long enough for the three Syrian escapees to scramble into the covered truck bed. Seven others were already sitting on the floor. The truck was normally used to carry animals and stank. No one in the back dared look out as the truck pulled away, nor did any of them know where they were headed.

Several hours later, the truck reached a Lebanese fishing port some distance from Beirut. Still in the dark, the Syrian Jews were taken one by one onto a small fishing boat. Two of the fishermen whispered to each other in Hebrew, but there was no doubt that the Arab crew was in charge. As soon as all the passengers were on board, the small boat set out to sea.

The fishing boat eventually stopped. As it bobbed about in the sea, signal lights pierced the blackness and an Israeli naval vessel pulled alongside. The ten passengers were tossed like sacks of potatoes onto the deck of the ship several feet above the fishing vessel. As the Lebanese boat headed off, the Israeli vessel charted a course for Haifa. There, the passengers disembarked, washed, ate, and were taken to Lod, site of Israel's international airport. They met with Israeli authorities, who gave them immigration and identification papers, made arrangements for their housing, and the Syrians began their integration into Israeli society. All of them were cautioned not to tell the details of their escape to anyone, especially about the rendezvous at sea. Any information leak to Syrian or Lebanese authorities would jeopardize similar operations in the future and put Israeli operatives in Lebanon in grave danger. Kaski's aunt in Israel took him in and he began building a new life.[33]

In the early spring of 1974, Judy Feld was busy as the head of both the Feld Fund and the Congress Ontario Region Committee on Jews in Arab Lands when the Israeli consul in Toronto invited her to his office. Israel thought Canada might be willing to take a more outspoken position on the human rights of Jews in Arab lands in light of the recent murders of the four young women in Syria. The Israeli consul also hoped that Canada would join other Western countries in monitoring the trial of the two Syrian Jewish men to ensure they were not made scapegoats. The Israelis feared that the men would be subject to a show trial and public lynching like the Baghdad hangings. International concern might give the Syrian Jewish community some protection against further punishment.

The consul asked Judy to meet with Mitchell Sharp and go over the situation of Syrian Jewry with him. The consul was sure that with an election in the offing and many Jews in his electoral riding, the minister would grant her request for a meeting. Judy was taken aback. She might be a Congress chair and active at Beth Tzedec, but she still thought of herself as the music teacher from Sudbury. Even her supporters would not rank diplomacy as her strong suit. Judy felt out of her league, but allowed herself to be flattered into thinking that she could do the job. With coaching from the consul, she wrote to Sharp on Congress letterhead and requested a personal meeting to discuss Syrian Jewry. A few days later, she received a call from Sharp's executive assistant, asking her to join the minister for a breakfast meeting at the Park Plaza Hotel in midtown Toronto. The consul briefed Judy on Israel's concerns, and coached her on diplomatic niceties.

Judy winces when she tells the story of the meeting. From the moment she was ushered into the minister's hotel room, she knew that she was in over her head. She assumed that Sharp was more concerned with firming up his Jewish support in the coming federal election than he was with the plight of Syrian Jews. Judy spoke at length of the situation of Syrian Jews, about the murders in Syria, about Amnesty International and the trial. At one point Sharp's executive assistant interjected that Judy sounded like "Queen Esther trying to save the Jews."

The minister asked what Judy would have Canada do. She replied that she wanted Canada to recommend that Amnesty International be present to monitor the trial in Damascus. The minister explained that any public statement might undermine Canada's ability to work with the Syrians on cases of family reunification. Syria already saw Canada as pro-Israel and, before Canada could do anything, he would need more facts. The Jewish community could rest assured, however, that Canada would continue to monitor the situation. He promised to raise the Syrian Jewish issue with the American secretary of state, Henry Kissinger, at an upcoming meeting.[35]

Sharp thanked Judy Feld for coming and rose to show her to the door. Sensing that she was about to leave empty-handed and insulted by what she took to be a patronizing dismissal, Judy lost her temper. She told Sharp that to mark Israel Independence Day, she would be chairing a community-wide public gathering at Beth Tzedec. Israeli Supreme Court Justice Haim Cohen would address the gathering on the situation of Jews in Arab lands. She insisted that the minister give her a statement of Canadian government concern about the impending Damascus trial that she could read to the audience. If he did not send a letter, she would announce that he had personally refused to make such a statement. Sharp protested that he was being blackmailed, but Judy pressed on, telling him that she planned to write two speeches for the gathering. Which one she delivered would depend on whether she received the statement. She demanded to hear from him, one way or the other, by 4:00 p.m. on the day of the meeting. Judy then turned on her heel, opened the door, and stormed out. She went to a pay phone and called the

Israeli consul. She explained what had happened. He angrily accused her of ruining everything. She went home dejected.

The minister might have been angry, but he was a politician and there was an election coming up. External Affairs put out feelers for information on what role Amnesty International was prepared to play at the trial of the two Jewish men and what role Canada could play. The Canadian embassy in Beirut reported that Amnesty International had not sought a role at the trial. Canada should tread very cautiously in anything having to do with Syrian Jews or the trial.[35]

At four o'clock on the day of the event, Mitchell Sharp called Judy. The minister tersely read her a prepared statement that she could relay to the community gathering. The statement might have been less than Judy wanted, but she still feels it was more than Sharp intended to deliver. She listened and thanked him, and then asked that the written statement be delivered to the office of the Beth Tzedec rabbi in time to be read to the meeting. That evening, after Justice Cohen finished his speech, Judy Feld read the telegram.

> The government shares the concerns of many Canadians arising out of the news reports regarding the situation of Jews in Syria and particularly the arrest of four persons following the murder of four Jewish women recently. I have asked for a full report from our embassy in Beirut, which is also accredited to Syria. As well, a number of other diplomatic soundings are underway in an effort to ascertain the facts. The nature of the charges against the four persons, the locale and timing of the trial and the nature of the trial itself are unclear at the moment. If, as has been reported, Amnesty International is seeking Syrian acceptance of foreign observers at the trial, we would urge the Syrian government to give a positive response. To date it appears that no such representations have been made by Amnesty International.[36]

A copy of the telegram was sent to Amnesty International's office in Paris. Amnesty International did monitor the trial. In the glare of international attention, charges against the two Jewish men were reduced. They were sentenced to six months each for complicity in the escape attempt. Judy Feld never met with Mitchell Sharp again.[37]

In the aftermath of the murders, all was quiet. Once again, there was no focus for mobilizing a campaign on behalf of Syrian Jewry. Judy Feld and a close friend and supporter, Kayla Armel, were going over the problem at lunch when they hit on an idea. Why not hold an annual memorial service for the four young Jewish women murdered in their attempt to escape from Syria? It could be held as part of regular synagogue services on the Sabbath nearest the women's *Yartzeit*, the anniversary of the death of a loved one traditionally observed with the lighting of a memorial candle and the recitation of the Kaddish prayer. According to the Jewish religious calendar, *Yartzeit* for the four young women would fall on the Sabbath before Purim. Judy approached the rabbi at Beth Tzedec, J. Benjamin Friedberg, with the idea. He not only approved but also explained that the Sabbath before Purim was called *Shabbat Zachor*, Sabbath of Remembrance, named for the Torah portion read on that particular Sabbath.

Judy and her committee arranged to symbolically unite the two streams of Jewish tradition, the western Ashkenazi and eastern Sephardi, the religious tradition of the Jews of Syria, in the prayer service for that day. The cantor at Beth Tzedec shared the *bimah*, the podium, with a Sephardi cantor from Brooklyn. The Torah readings and other portions of the service were delivered alternately in Sephardi and Ashkenazi melodic traditions. Even the traditional post-service *kiddush*, a congregational sharing of cake and wine, was replaced that week by a sampling of Middle Eastern treats. Members of Toronto's Sephardi community were encouraged to attend. The vast Beth Tzedec synagogue was packed.

Professor Saul Friedman, who had been part of Rubin Feld's original teach-in several years earlier, was invited back to Toronto to deliver the sermon on Jewish refugees from Arab lands. At the close of services, the rabbi drew the congregation's attention to the fact that in Damascus, the parents of the four women would that day be standing to recite the Kaddish. In solidarity, several thousand people in the Beth Tzedec sanctuary rose and, as they had for Simon Khabas, joined together in reciting the Kaddish.[38]

The moving *Shabbat Zachor* service was widely covered in the Jewish press. Before long, Judy Feld received requests for information on *Shabbat Zachor* from congregations across Canada and the United States. This was a breakthrough. The *Shabbat Zachor* service created an annual focus for Jewish community concern for the Jews of Syria. That was no small achievement, and one that would continue year after year for the next twenty years.[39]

Not long after the murder of the four women, two incidents in the American media showed how far the campaign on behalf of Syrian Jews had yet to go in educating the general public. *National Geographic*'s April 1974 edition featured a story titled "Damascus, Syria's Uneasy Eden." The article left the impression that while the Jews of Damascus might be subject to minor inconveniences, often as a response to Israeli military actions in the Middle East, Syrian Jews lived generally normal lives under a Syrian administration that maintained a watchful but tolerant and supportive attitude toward its Jewish citizens. Rabbi Hamra was quoted in the article as saying, "Today we have rights like any other citizen." The rabbi conceded that Damascus Jews need a permit to leave the city and were not free to emigrate, but that this was largely to prevent them from emigrating to Israel where "each new settler...is the potential bearer of a gun pointed at a Syrian soldier."[40]

The response of the Jewish community in the United States was swift. Calls lit up the National Geographic Society's switchboard, and letters poured in complaining that the article not only misrepresented the oppression of Syrian Jews but also sanctioned that oppression with the good name of the National Geographic Society. A delegation from the American Jewish Congress met with *National Geographic*'s editor-in-chief and his staff. How could they be so naive? Didn't the magazine realize what would happen to Rabbi Hamra if he had spoken the truth? Although the editor admitted that the article was flawed and the society had sent letters to that effect to all those who had complained, he refused to publish a retraction.

Not satisfied, the American Jewish Congress members from Washington picketed the National Geographic Society's headquarters and issued a lengthy press release challenging the accuracy of the article and the intellectual honesty of the society. They asked all

American Jews to write letters to *National Geographic*, particularly if they were subscribers to the journal.[41]

In a break with eighty-six years of publishing tradition, the November 1974 edition of *National Geographic* added an editor's column to reply to the National Geographic Society's members. In this first column, the editor acknowledged that as the April issue rolled off the presses

> ...reports from Damascus of the barbaric murder of four Jewish women focused world attention on the plight of Damascene Jews. Many of our Jewish members sharply criticized us for not delineating in greater detail the harsh conditions under which that small community has been forced to exist since 1948. We began to wonder if we had unwittingly failed to reflect the true situation. Now after months of carefully reviewing the evidence, we have concluded that our critics were right. We erred.[42]

Only a few months later, CBS's *60 Minutes* broadcast a segment on Syrian Jews. The piece included portions of a conversation Mike Wallace had with a wealthy Jewish merchant from Damascus in the presence of three Syrian "officials." The merchant claimed that life was good for Syrian Jews and that the Syrian government did not distinguish between Jewish and non-Jewish citizens. If there was any public antipathy to Syrian Jews, it was the result of Israeli actions on the Golan Heights, which Syrians regarded as deliberately provocative and illegal.

The *60 Minutes* segment brought on another storm of protest from American Jewish leaders. Did Mike Wallace honestly believe that any Jew would dare to jeopardize his or his family's safety by telling the truth about Jewish life in Syria? Why not talk with Syrian Jews who had risked their lives to successfully escape? Jewish leaders accused *60 Minutes* of compromising its journalistic integrity, and allowing itself to become a mouthpiece for the Syrian regime. Arab spokespersons in the United States welcomed the propaganda that *60 Minutes* offered. The National Association of Arab Americans issued a publication titled *On Syrian Jews* that used the *60 Minutes* report to refute charges of discrimination against the

Jews of Syria and dismiss the allegations as nothing more than Zionist propaganda.[43]

Four months later, 60 Minutes rebroadcast the piece with some changes. Wallace added a commentary conceding that one needed to be skeptical of interviews conducted in Syria. But ever balanced, he added that President Assad had made a "calculated decision" to end any mistreatment of Syrian Jews.

The rebroadcast unleashed another angry response from Jewish organizations. What "calculated decision" was Wallace talking about? Syrian Jews were still singled out, subject to harassment and arbitrary arrest. They were still refused the right to travel abroad, the right to emigrate. And, by the time the program was rebroadcast, Wallace must have known that two of the merchant's own family had fled Syria and that other family members had been interrogated for a month in a Syrian jail. Two American Jewish organizations filed official complaints with the National News Council, a non-profit organization that investigates accusations of media misconduct.[44]

60 Minutes revisited Syria to prepare a longer segment dealing with Syrian Jews. This time, while Wallace pointed out "signs of greater normalization in the life of Syrian Jews under President Assad in such matters as education, employment, and travel within the country," the broadcast was also careful to acknowledge that "Syria is a police state," and that life was appreciably worse for Jews than it was for other Syrians. The report also included an interview with an escaped Syrian Jew, his name withheld and face in shadow lest his comments bring reprisals on his family. Repression might be less severe under President Assad than it had been under his predecessors, he acknowledged, but his escape, at great personal risk, should be seen as testament to the intolerable conditions under which Jews in Syria were still forced to live.

Jewish organizations were satisfied. At least 60 Minutes' second segment did not exonerate the Syrian regime and the media attention might force Syrian authorities to ease up. "One wonders whether it was purely coincidental," a spokesperson for the American Jewish Committee noted, "that only two weeks before the scheduled return to Syria of the CBS team, the Syrian authorities finally began to issue new identity cards to Syrian Jews without the distinctive red marking *Mussawi* (follower of Moses)."[45]

It was still not clear how to translate concern for Syrian Jews into concrete action. The Canadian Jewish Congress was still largely silent on the issue. In the summer of 1975, a small group tried to rekindle interest in a Quebec Regional Task Force on Syrian Jewry. The group included McGill law professor Irwin Cotler, who had recently been part of an academic tour of the Middle East that included a stop in Damascus. He had visited the Jewish quarter, but was not granted free access to Jews. A guide, whom he took to be a Muhabarat agent, was present at all his conversations with Jews. Nevertheless, through the translations and the positive talk about life in Syria, it was impossible to mistake the fear that still gripped the Jewish community. When Professor Cotler returned to Montreal, he was so convinced that something had to be done that he assembled a planning group for a campaign on behalf of Syrian Jewry. A Congress staff person, working with the fledgling committee, contacted groups already involved in Syrian Jewish protest, such as the American Jewish Committee, seeking information and advice. Judy Feld gave the group a briefing.[46]

But nine months later, the Montreal group had little to show for all its discussions. Once-enthusiastic committee members drifted away. One jaded member of the planning group was not even sure if Congress had committed itself to an all-out campaign on behalf of Syrian Jewry at the national level. He

> opened the [Committee's] meeting by asking about the position of [Canadian Jewish Congress] National Chairman, Rabbi Plaut. He was concerned that people have been asking questions concerning Syrian Jewry, and nothing is being done. He asked what policy existed on a national level concerning Syrian Jewry.
>
> It was noted that the Israeli Ambassador or a government representative will be asked what the official position is of the Israeli government or Israeli representatives abroad, regarding this question.[47]

In October 1975, Judy Feld was invited to speak on the issue of Syrian Jews at the Second World Congress of Jews from North

Africa held in Tel Aviv at the end of October 1975. Because of the growing political importance of North African and Sephardi Jews in the Israeli political scene, the meetings turned out to be a who's who of Israeli leaders. Judy Feld stood out in the largely male, Sephardi, and politically charged gathering. She was a single, enthusiastic, and committed Ashkenazi woman, unschooled in the political gamesmanship that dominated many of the meetings. She was also continually sought after, invited out to dinner or to local nightclubs. Most invitations were politely turned down.

Judy did not allow herself be distracted from advancing her cause. Her formal presentation to the gathering was well received. More important, she made a number of high-level contacts who would become increasingly useful to her. Brash and assertive and oblivious to formal diplomatic niceties, Judy Feld held candid one-on-one conversations with key players in the Israeli and international Jewish scene. She discussed the Syrian Jewish plight with Israel's president, prime minister and foreign minister, with the president of the World Jewish Congress, with Mordechai Ben-Porat, deputy speaker of the Knesset and newly elected head of the World Organization of Jews from Arab Counties, with the American Congressman Stephen Solarz, whose Brooklyn Congressional District included many Jews who had left Syria in the years immediately following the Second World War, and with any number of Knesset members and spokespersons for Sephardi communities the world over. By the end of the meetings, Judy Feld was recognized as an articulate advocate for the Syrian Jewish cause. Doors she had not previously known existed were slowly opening to her.[48]

CHAPTER FIVE

Carrying Their Fears With Them

JUDY FELD WAS GAINING prominence in Jewish circles but some Canadian public servants still regarded her as a "special interest" pain in the neck. They also regarded her expertise as suspect. In early 1975, External Affairs updated its report on Syrian Jews for Allan MacEachen, who had replaced Mitchell Sharp as minister. The department assessment still contradicted the dark picture Judy Feld painted. Although the situation of Jews in Syria was always precarious, they said, there was no evidence that Jews were being persecuted. The Syrians continued to regard Jews with suspicion because of their links to Israel. Canada's capacity to help Jews leave Syria was "limited." The government could do nothing more to convince Syria to approve the applications for family reunification, but Canadian Immigration officials said they would respond sympathetically to Syrians Jews who managed to escape. Were any of the Syrians who entered Canada the previous year Jewish? External Affairs did not know. Canada did not tabulate immigration or visitors landings by religion.[1]

Judy insisted that, despite External Affairs' assessment, the situation of Syrian Jews was alarming. Others in the Jewish world agreed. A confidential memo from the head of the World Jewish Congress to a select group of Jewish leaders warned that, contrary to "false propaganda which was recently spread in the U.S. by some Congressmen who came back from Syria with untrue information on the condition of the Syrian Jews," the actual situation of Syrian

Jews remains "very bad." There were reports that President Assad was willing to ease the plight of Syrian Jews and even "allow some to leave the country discreetly, but this is for the time being only a speculation."[2]

In May 1975, American senator George McGovern met with Syrian President Assad and Assad offered to permit Jewish emigration to the United States "on condition that the U.S. enacted a law forbidding these Jews from ever going to Israel." The media reported this as a softening of Syria's hard line on Jewish emigration, but both Assad and McGovern knew that this condition, plainly in violation of the American Constitution, rendered Assad's offer meaningless.

Judy Feld had little patience for guessing what President Assad meant when he hinted at possible Jewish emigration. Why not take him at his word, she argued, and see what happened. Any Syrian offer to let Jews leave, "even with qualifications," represented a breakthrough and was worth pursuing. She wrote to MacEachen requesting that Canada "make available necessary visas for that Jewish community of approximately 4,500 individuals" and ask Syria to let the Jews emigrate to Canada.

Assad's qualifications were as impossible for Canada to accept as they were for the United States. How could Canada prevent any Syrian Jew who might become a Canadian citizen from going to Israel? Judy's request received a polite—"let me affirm the Canadian Government's concern for this issue"—reply from the minister. He did not mention her suggestion that Canada set aside 4,500 visas for Syrian Jews under Assad's conditions, and it was obviously never considered.

Judy was convinced that the Canadian government could do more for Syrian Jews if it had the political will. She slammed the government for being "evasive and at times even obstructive" on the admission of Syrian Jews, even on applications for family reunification. Whenever she was given a microphone and a sympathetic audience, Judy asked her listeners to join her in protesting the lack of government action. Many did. The prime minister's office and the departments of Immigration and External Affairs received numerous letters from Canadian Jews who demanded an explanation for Canadian inaction on the persecution of Syrian Jewry.[3]

It is hard to believe that Judy Feld could find time for a private life, but she was also a young and attractive woman. Whoever wanted to build a serious and lasting relationship with her, however, would have to be prepared to make room for her three children, a financially dependent mother-in-law from her first marriage, and her firebrand commitment to Syrian Jewry.

Enter Donald Carr. A lasting relationship between Judy Feld and Don Carr was an unlikely prospect. He was, and still is, a stalwart of the Toronto Jewish establishment. A successful lawyer and founding partner in his own law firm, he was the quintessential insider, a *macher*, a doer, a member of the inner circle of Canadian Jewish political life. If Don Carr was not the very personification of the do-nothing Jewish leadership that Judy Feld had dismissed for years, he stood at their right hand.

But they shared many similar life experiences. Don Carr's first wife died after a long battle with cancer, leaving him to parent three children. And while his and Judy's political affiliations were widely divergent—Don Carr, for example, had no use for the JDL or its leader, Rabbi Kahane—the two shared a mutual commitment to community, passion for Israel, and concern for the continuity of Jewish life.

It was their children who brought them together. Don Carr's son, Adam, and Judy Feld's son, Gary, attended the same Jewish day school and became close friends. Don first met Judy when he dropped by her house to pick up Adam. He had seen her at a Beth Tzedec picnic because both families were congregation members. The two single parents had never had a real conversation, but Don Carr was drawn to Judy Feld. He remembers looking over at her from across the sanctuary in synagogue and thinking to himself, I'm going to marry that woman.

Don Carr had been out of the dating scene for years. In the spring of 1976, he set his doubts aside and asked Judy out to dinner. The usually confident Don felt awkward and nervous when he arrived at her home. They dined at the hotel where, several years earlier, Kosygin had stayed and the Jewish community had held its anti-Soviet protest. It didn't take long for nervousness to pass and for the two of them to relax and enjoy each other's company. The next day, roses arrived at the Feld home with an attached note of apology. Don Carr asked forgiveness for dominating the previous night's conversation with talk about his first wife. They spoke on the telephone later in the day and agreed to go for a walk that evening. By the time they returned home, they were engaged to be married. In keeping with Jewish tradition, they waited until the ritual eleven-month period of Don's mourning had passed before they married. They sold their separate homes and moved into a large house in Toronto's Forest Hill neighbourhood.[4]

Now the couple took on a new challenge—making a blended family with six children work. For the children, the excitement of change was tinged with the apprehension of finding their place in a new house, of being part of a restructured family unit, learning to get along with a new set of siblings and, of course, testing boundaries with a new parent. Most of the children adapted well to their new environment, but one or two found adjustment more difficult and were less ready to embrace a new parent or new siblings. Adapting was particularly difficult for Judy's oldest son, Alan. He was a teenager when the new household was taking shape and remembers a sense of being emotionally dislodged. His father's death had left him feeling responsible for his household, and ceding this role to a new father was not easy. Alan credits his stepfather's patience and unconditional love with helping him to work it out.[5]

How did Judy Feld Carr's continuing work on behalf of Syrian Jews affect the new household? Her children had been brought up with the Syrian Jewish campaign as part of their routine. But although Don and his children were no strangers to Jewish organizational life and his first wife had been active in her own right, none of this was as consuming as Judy's involvement with Syrian Jewry. She was, according to her son, a "woman who struck a balance between life as mother and life as activist." There were constant meetings, long-distance telephone calls, secret visitors, cryptic telegrams, covert trips abroad, boxes in the basement packed for shipment, and piles of documents to be sorted. Whatever else was going on in the home, however, the children knew there were rules and order. Dinnertime, especially Friday-night dinner, was set aside for family, a refuge both from Don's office matters and the cause of

Syrian Jewry. The children were expected to be there.[6]

Judy had found love and companionship for the second time with a man who shared her Jewish commitment and encouraged her activism. And although Judy had managed to put most of her financial woes behind her, marriage provided her and her children with security. It also provided her an entree into many of the Canadian Jewish community's most influential people. Don Carr's position in the Jewish community shielded Judy from public attack by her detractors. He acknowledged that he was not a front-line activist, but happily endorsed his wife's hands-on activities.

Don Carr's considerable influence enhanced her community profile even before they married. One evening, the two of them went to dinner with Syd Harris, then national president of the Canadian Jewish Congress. Don Carr and Syd Harris knew each other well. Don Carr had supported Harris's bid for Congress president, and though the two men were not business partners, their two firms shared office space.

Predictably, dinner conversation turned to issues of Syrian Jewry. Syd Harris already knew about the religious articles being sent to Syria and the covert line of communication into the Jewish community of Damascus. He asked how Congress could help her. Judy blasted Congress national officials in Montreal for not giving the problems of Syrian Jews a national profile. She requested that Harris create a national Congress committee parallel to the committee working on the Soviet Jewry campaign.

Syd Harris agreed that a national committee on Jews in Arab Lands was a good idea and at the next National Executive meeting he sponsored a resolution setting it up. The resolution was approved and Judy was appointed chair. As chair of a national Congress committee, she would also be a member of the National Executive.[7]

Judy was delighted. Her appointment would go a long way toward ensuring that Syrian Jewry was given prominence on the Canadian Jewish agenda. What is more, her new title gave her a platform to reach government and media. Given that the Clay and Poher committees were seldom heard from, and even the committee in Israel was largely moribund, the Canadian committee could become a world leader.

In truth, Judy was not prepared to burden herself with the minutae of running a national committee: supervising support staff, preparing detailed budget proposals, and accounting for the budget from Congress. With little patience for administrative trivia and the politics of group decision making, she wanted the national chair's position only for the added credentials. She assumed that same core group she worked with would continue as her "nucleus with a different title." It would be business as usual with a more impressive letterhead. She welcomed new members who would support her work, raise money, write letters, and help organize *Shabbat Zachor* in local communities across Canada. She wanted her committee members to speak out on behalf of Syrian Jews within their own synagogues and organizations. But if they wanted formal meetings and a share in the decision-making process, they had better look elsewhere. She had no budget to bring people from across Canada together for meetings. As far as Judy was concerned, she did not need meetings—she knew what had to be done.

This headstrong style was costly. Judy attended National Executive meetings, but she failed to cultivate support among other executive members. She also received little financial and staff support from Congress's National Office. She interpreted this as indicative of the low priority that the National Office gave to issues of Syrian Jewry, but in fact, they were open to being convinced.[8] Judy never did that. She remained a Congress outsider despite her marriage to Don Carr. Her reports on her Syrian activities were often bracketed by warnings that much of her work was covert and even the Congress executive had to be kept in the dark. Some of the executive may have been intrigued by the cloak-and-dagger talk, and as a result, Judy was tolerated. Most of the time this was all she needed. When she required money for her Syrian work, she could use the Feld Fund. What was most important to her was that she was now included in Congress delegations that met with the minister of External Affairs and senior public servants.[9]

In April 1976, Judy Feld Carr, as part of a Congress delegation, asked Allan MacEachen to press for Syrian approval of the applications for family reunification that had been sitting cold for almost four years. The minister promised to have the Canadian ambassador in Beirut again raise the outstanding applications with Syrian authorities, but he told Judy not to blame the Canadian government for dragging its feet. In one case a sponsoring family had sabotaged its own application by indicating on the form that the Syrian family intended to resettle in Israel. Canada, he warned, could not serve as a back door for immigration to Israel without jeopardizing Canada's credibility with Syria and the rest of the Arab world.[10]

In the autumn of 1976, Moshe Chazan, an elderly Jew from Damascus, was the first Syrian Jew in twenty years to be allowed to emigrate "legally carrying a Syrian passport and an American visa." The mechanics of his emigration remain a mystery. Moshe Chazan had a daughter in Toronto, Esther Green, who had left Syria shortly after the end of the Second World War. She had not seen her father for over thirty years. Her family were simple folk—her father was a craftsman. After his wife died in 1975, the elderly Chazan felt desperately alone. He wrote to his daughter that he had nothing left in Syria and wanted to be with his family in Canada. Mrs. Green was unsure how to proceed and approached both the Jewish Immigrant Aid Service in Toronto and her local MP for assistance.

After receiving a discouraging prognosis by JIAS, Esther Green was directed to a travel agent in Toronto who dealt extensively with travel to and from Arab countries. Mrs. Green pre-purchased a Damascus–New York round-trip ticket for Chazan. He, in turn, applied for a Syrian passport and posted a cash bond of $9500 against his safe return, should his passport application be approved. For a time nothing was heard from the Syrian authorities, until Esther Green received a telegram in French from Damascus signed by her father stating, "Send me $2000 very quickly in order that I can come to visit you in ten days." She arranged for the money to be sent to a bank in Damascus. Chazan was issued a Syrian passport stamped with an exit visa and an American tourist visa and told to pack his bag.

The official fiction remained that Chazan would be returning to Syria, but both he and the Syrian officials knew this was not the case. His cash bond would be forfeited, his return ticket would never be used, and the tiny house and personal effects he left behind—

even the picture frame that had held his precious family photograph—would eventually become state property. He arrived in New York with no money and one suitcase containing a few items of clothing, some personal papers, including his Syrian identity card stamped in red with the Arabic word *Mussawi*, his family photograph—without its frame—his late wife's comb, his *tallith* and *tefillin*, and because of his fear of violating Jewish dietary prohibitions during his lengthy journey, some home-cooked kosher food items.

When Chazan passed through American Customs and Immigration inspection, his daughter and son-in-law were waiting. The reunion was joyous. But Canadian consular officials were caught unaware when Chazan and his daughter came to arrange a Canadian entry visa. Nobody had informed them that Chazan was arriving in New York from Syria en route to Canada, and as far as the officials were concerned, no one could just walk in off the street and be issued a Canadian visa. There were forms to be filled out. It would take time to process the application. They needed medical examinations, financial guarantees.

Chazan's family had expected to return to Toronto with the tired and confused Moshe Chazan. Expecting a visa to be issued over the counter, the family was instead advised that the process might take a week or more, and there was no guarantee that Chazan would get a Canadian visa. What was to be done? The Green family could not stay in New York, and the old man could not be left on his own. Sending him back to Syria was unthinkable. Fortunately, someone in Ottawa went out on a limb and, before the end of the day, Chazan was issued a Canadian entry visa and the family flew home.

Esther Green had run across Judy Feld Carr's name while she was trying to bring her father to Canada. She called after returning to Toronto and invited Judy to her house. Esther Green translated as the elderly Chazan tried to give Judy a picture of Jewish life in Damascus. In particular, he spoke of the bleak future for the unmarried Jewish women who greatly outnumbered eligible Jewish men. He explained that many young men had escaped across the border into Lebanon. Others dreamed of leaving Syria, and refused to marry lest a wife and family make escape impossible. To be single in a community where women traditionally marry young and status is tied to marriage robbed these women of a Jewish future. Jewish leaders had to do something for these young women, he warned, or more would try to escape and end up like the four murdered women who had put their trust in smugglers. Toward the end of their talk, the old man confided his one lingering fear: as he sat in the safety of his daughter's living room in Toronto, he remained terrified that he would be sent back to Syria, which he referred to as "hell."

Judy could not figure out why the Syrians had let the old man leave. The Syrian government had refused to budge on several Canadian applications to sponsor the immigration of family members. But there was one oddity in Chazan's story: he knew nothing about the telegram in French that had been sent to his daughter requesting additional money. Chazan did not send it. He did not even know French. Perhaps officials in the Syrian regime had pocketed that payment. If so, this was an important lesson for Judy about the commerce of emigration. Money talked. It might also open doors, pay for documents, and make the impossible possible.[11]

Through the 1970s, as the Syrian administration began to ease its tight grip on Jewish life, a few Jews were permitted to travel outside Syria on business, for medical attention, or to visit relatives. Some, like Chazan, did not go back. Like Chazan they left healthy deposits behind. But unlike Chazan, they were also forced to leave a wife or children behind as a guarantee of their return. In one case, a married couple was allowed out for two months to visit two of their children in the United States. There was no question that the couple would return to Syria. They left eight other children behind.

This couple knew about Judy's shipments of religious items and, while they were in the United States, they got in touch with her. She invited them to Toronto but they were terrified that Syrian authorities would find out they had gone and punish them. Assured that a visa to Canada could be arranged quietly without their Syrian passports being stamped, they agreed to come. They were very concerned about secrecy, fearing the long arm of the Muhabarat. Judy had to promise that she would not speak publicly about their visit and never reveal their names. They wanted no follow-up communication sent to them in Syria because the mail would be read by the authorities. Even her assurances of secrecy did not completely ease their anxiety. They "constantly felt great fear they were being followed and were terribly frightened when they saw a Toronto policeman."

The Syrian couple were hesitant about meeting at Judy's home. And she too was inclined to be cautious—not of the Muhabarat, but of her Syrian visitors. A couple allowed out by Syrian authorities might have too cozy a relationship with the secret police. Judy did not want to invite them into her home until she was sure of their loyalties. The initial meeting, which took place in the rabbi's study at Beth Tzedec synagogue, lasted six hours. The couple described every aspect of the situation of Syrian Jews and gave details on how the money and religious articles sent by the Feld Fund were being distributed. Here were prominent members of the Damascus Jewish community who had first-hand experience of living in terror of arbitrary arrest, of beatings, of having their property confiscated. They feared that their children would be denied an education, that their daughters would not find Jewish husbands, and that the only option for the young was to attempt a dangerous escape, for which the price was imprisonment and torture if escape failed, and imprisonment and torture of family members left behind if escape was successful.

Judy understood how they would carry these fears abroad with them as surely as they carried their passports. Convinced that they were not agents of the Muhabarat, she invited them to lunch at an informal coffee house. The meal was anything but relaxed. The Syrian couple shifted about uncomfortably, their eyes darting here and there, looking for anyone who might be watching them. Before they left Toronto, they again implored Judy not to communicate with them in Syria. However, she could contact them through their family in New York. Judy rejoiced in establishing yet another connection to Syria.[12]

In May 1976, the American Jewish Committee issued a four-page summary of available information on the status of Syrian Jewry. President Assad had removed many of the discriminatory regulations that confined Jewish life and hinted that further liberalization might be in the offing.[13] But the sweeping powers of the Muhabarat to oversee all aspects of Jewish life had not changed. Their every move was subject to review. The Muhabarat was a hands-on presence whose hands often reached into Jewish pockets. Baksheesh— bribery—was part of life in Syria, but the Muhabarat regarded Jews as particularly ripe for the picking. The ban on Jewish emigration also remained unchanged.

The Syrian regime was anything but secure in the mid-1970s. Would the liberalization survive a new regime coming to power? One American observer doubted it.

> ...many in the Jewish community believe—as do other minorities in Syria, that the present improvement is attributable largely to the personal policy of President Assad. They fear that these gains could all be undone overnight if President Assad were to be replaced or if the Syrian regime encountered economic problems or if renewed conflict erupted in the area. The continued existence of a powerful and pervasive Syrian internal security apparatus, without controls by any democratic institutions, raises the ominous danger that the hostage Jewish community may be used as a convenient scapegoat by any extremist political regime that may come to power.[14]

In the meantime, however, reports of liberalization continued. In January 1977, fifteen American Jewish women, members of Hadassah, visited Syria as part of a tour of the Middle East. The women were allowed to speak to members of the Syrian Jewish community, but always in the prsence of a Syrian official, presumed to be a Muhabarat agent.[15] Despite this, the Hadassah spokesperson also reported an easing of the regime's restrictions on Jews.[16]

President Assad issued a decree reinstating civil parity to Syrian Jews in February 1977—except in the area of emigration.[17] Temporary travel abroad was now easier, but only with stringent guarantees that the individual would return. Any travel to Israel was still prohibited. Syrian authorities were apparently more open to humanitarian applications for family reunification, but there was no sign of action on the Canadian applications. Despite the case of Moshe Chazan, External Affairs reported that "no immigrants have come to Canada under such circumstances."[18]

When an editorial in the *Canadian Jewish News* approvingly noted the changes in Syria, Judy Feld Carr wrote a stinging rebuke. The *Canadian Jewish News* "completely misses the point." What proof was there that the Syrians had implemented anything more than cosmetic change? Anything Syrian authorities or Syrian Jewish leaders said to visiting politicians or Diaspora Jewish leaders was suspect. All contacts between Syrian Jews and visitors were monitored, and Jews knew the price exacted from them and their families if they told the truth. Syrian Jews outside the country worried that they were being watched and remained guarded about what they said and to whom. Rather than being taken in by a Syrian facelift, she argued, Diaspora Jews should keep up the pressure.

> What rejoicing can there be even if repression, reminiscent of Nazism, is only alleviated somewhat? The time to rejoice will come when and only when, the Jews of Syria are allowed to emigrate. Until the world sees that, our efforts will continue, and our voices will cry as loudly as possible.[19]

In one of those anomalies that characterizes the Syrian Jewish story, President Assad personally approved the departure of fourteen Jewish women for the United States in the early summer of 1977. Press reports of their departure credited the intervention of Stephen Solarz, whose Brooklyn congressional district included many of the estimated 25,000 Syrian Jews in the United States. Congressman Solarz publicly championed the cause of the some five hundred Jewish women who had little prospects for marriage.

Stephen Solarz first became aware of the problem during a visit to Syria in 1975. Working with Stephen Shalom, a Brooklyn businessman with connections in the Syrian community, Solarz pressed the American administration on the issue and tried to persuade Damascus to allow the women to leave. The timing was auspicious. The Syrian authorities had just liberalized regulations regarding Jews and suggested that they might approve their emigration in humanitarian cases.

Before a meeting between President Assad and American president Jimmy Carter in Geneva scheduled for May 7, 1977, Solarz and Shalom hammered out a plan with Carter that might circumvent Syria's ban on re-emigration to Israel. They would ask Assad to allow a number of unmarried women to emigrate to the United States where, by arrangement, they would marry eligible American Jewish men. The argument was that once the women were married to Americans, they were unlikely to move to Israel. At the meeting in Geneva, Carter raised the issue "and got a favourable response from Assad."

President Assad delivered. He cut through the red tape and gave his personal order for the issuing of migration permits to unmarried Jewish women whose names were supplied by the Damascus Jewish community. But there was a catch. The government would not approve permits allowing single women to join men they intended to marry; all the women authorized to emigrate had to be married according to Syrian law.

One of the women was Lulu Hulabi. In 1977 Lulu was a twenty-five-year-old teacher in a Damascus Jewish school. In a community where girls often married in their early teens, she thought she was destined to remain single. One day, after she arrived home from school, Lulu received a message asking her to come to Rabbi Hamra's office. When she walked in, she was told that she was getting married.

On July 19, 1977, members of the Damascus Jewish community gathered at a synagogue to witness the marriage of two couples—veiled Syrian Jewish brides marrying American Jewish men who had come to Damascus. As well, they witnessed the proxy marriages of another fourteen Syrian women, including Lulu, all dressed in white and gathered under the traditional marriage canopy. Unlike the two other brides, the fourteen wore no veils. As Syrian officials looked on, a senior member of the Jewish community stood in for the fourteen absentee bridegrooms and the rabbi performed the marriage ceremony. The proxy marriages were duly registered and recognized as legal in Syria. The women, all now wearing wedding rings, left Syria.[20]

Proxy marriages are not binding in the United States. The women were not handed over to husbands but assigned to private homes in the Jewish community. Only after each couple met and agreed to the marriage was another Jewish marriage ceremony held, and the couple married according to American law. If the couple did not hit it off, there was no pressure for them to marry. The women, who entered the United States under special authority of the attorney general, were free to go their own way and free to remain in the United States.[21]

Lulu did not marry the man selected for her. After living with a Jewish family in Brooklyn for nine months, she fell in love with and married Solomon Sasson. Some years later, thirteen of the women married on that 1977 summer day in Damascus were located. Only one was single. All but one lived in Brooklyn, and among them they had a total of fifty children.[22]

The departure of the fourteen women made barely a dent in the number of unmarried Syrian Jewish women. The problem continued to fester, and it was only with great tact and liberal doses of baksheesh that Jewish leaders were occasionally able to get permission for a few more of them to leave Syria.[23]

With the exception of the "brides," the Syrian government remained uncompromising on the release of Syrian Jews. Sometime after Judy Feld Carr was appointed head of the Congress National Committee on Jews in Arab Lands, she received a call from Hannah Cohen, who explained that she was originally from Aleppo. In 1945, Hannah, age twelve, and her mother left Syria for Palestine. Her brother, a rabbi in Aleppo, stayed behind. With the 1948 declaration of the state of Israel, Hannah lost contact with her family in Syria. She eventually served in the Israeli army and married an Israeli. Together they moved to Toronto, where, now Canadian citizens, they ran a gasoline station. Hannah re-established contact with her family in Aleppo with the help of the Canadian Red Cross. Several letters passed between her and her brother, Rabbi Eliahou Dahab, the community *shochet* (ritual slaughterer). After thirty years' separation, she had applied to visit Syria, and to her surprise, her visa application was approved. She would be leaving soon to visit her brother and his family in Aleppo. Hannah had heard about the Feld Fund and the packages sent to Damascus. Would Judy Feld Carr be interested in sending similar packages to the Jewish community in Aleppo?

The two women met in the tiny, cluttered office of the gasoline station. The setting was typical of Hannah Cohen, a no-nonsense woman who brushed aside Judy Feld Carr's caution that she might be risking her safety by visiting Syria. Hannah had not told the Syrians that she had once lived in Israel, let alone served in the Israeli army. Judy worried that if the Muhabarat got wind of her past, Hannah's Canadian passport would not be enough to protect her. But Hannah concluded that the Syrians would not be concerned with a middle-aged Canadian woman visiting her elderly brother. Judy outlined the system of sending packages, telegrams, and letters that she had developed with Rabbi Hamra and Hannah volunteered to make the necessary connections in Aleppo. Judy gave her $500 from the Feld Fund to give to the Jewish leaders for their community work.[24]

Hannah Cohen was as good as her word. Through her brother, Rabbi Dahab, and his son-in-law, Rabbi Henri Farhi, she arranged for the distribution of religious items and money from Canada. But the visit of a Jewish outsider to family in Aleppo, even a Canadian citizen with a valid Syrian visa, prompted the local Muhabarat to investigate. Hannah knew they would be watching and carefully avoided doing or saying anything publicly that would create a problem. On the day she was leaving, however, with photographs and several sensitive letters in her shoulder bag, including a letter to Judy Feld Carr that she intended to smuggle out of Syria, Hannah was picked up and taken to Muhabarat headquarters in Aleppo for questioning.

For three hours, clutching her bag the whole time, she was interrogated about her history, her family, and her connections to Israel. Her interrogator showed her copies of family photographs that she had mailed from Toronto to her brother in Aleppo. Who was in the photographs? What did her husband do? Her children? How had she reconnected to her family in Aleppo? Had she ever been to Israel? The questions were endless and menacing. Replying to every question in Arabic, she denied any interest in Israel. No, she had never been to Israel. She invented a fiction about going to Canada in 1945, directly after leaving Syria. She was a little girl and did not recall all the details. Yes, she enjoyed her visit to Syria and hoped to come again.

Hannah avoided going to the washroom lest the authorities use the opportunity to rifle through her bag. If they found the letters or photographs, not only would she be in trouble, but so would her family and all those who had trusted her to take letters out of Syria. Rabbi Dahab had been imprisoned for three months each time one of his three sons escaped. On the last occasion, three years before his sister's visit, he was confined to a small cell, denied toilet facilities, and severely punished whenever he relieved himself. During those three months he developed a bowel infection and severe kidney problems, which prison authorities left untreated.

Hannah Cohen was lucky. Her interrogator was satisfied, and at last she was allowed to leave, her shoulder bag hanging unopened at her side. Hannah is certain that because her married name was Cohen, Syrian authorities were concerned she might be connected to Eli Cohen, an Israeli spy who years earlier had infiltrated the highest ranks of the Syrian regime before he was detected. Satisfied that she had no relationship to Eli Cohen, they let her go.[25]

Hannah grabbed an inter-city taxi and made for the airport in Damascus. Later that day, she boarded a flight for London. Once there, she did not continue on to Toronto the way she was ticketed. Instead she bought a ticket for Cyprus, where she connected to an El Al flight to Tel Aviv. From the airport she went directly to her elderly mother's home and soon found herself surrounded by her nieces and nephews, including Rabbi Dahab's three sons. She brought them letters and photographs from their parents.[27]

Judy Feld Carr now had contacts in Aleppo and its approximately fifteen-hundred–strong Jewish community. Using Hannah Cohen's connections, she sent parcels of religious articles. For Hannah, however, this was not enough. She wanted to get her family out of Syria. Through JIAS in Toronto, she made an application to sponsor the immigration of eleven family members. She also turned to Judy Feld Carr for help. After all, Judy was a Congress committee chairperson, a member of the National Executive. Like many in the Canadian Jewish community, Hannah Cohen believed the Canadian Jewish Congress was a force to be reckoned with. Didn't Judy Feld Carr meet regularly with high-ranking Canadian government officials? Surely it should be nothing for her to arrange an exit visa from Syria.

Judy did not want to disappoint Hannah, but she did not have anywhere near the influence Hannah imagined. Still, there was something in Hannah's request that intrigued her. Might it actually be possible to get someone out of Syria? Making an application through JIAS or directly to Canadian Immigration authorities usually meant years of frustration. But Moshe Chazan's family had bypassed both JIAS and Ottawa and somehow got their elderly father out. Had they inadvertently stumbled on a way to get people out of Syria? Judy didn't hold out undue hope, but she promised Hannah Cohen she would work on it.[27]

First, however, she had to firm up her new contact with the Jews of Aleppo and start the flow of packages and small amounts of Feld Fund money "to help teachers and for anyone else who is in need."[28] On the home front, Judy hoped that the April 1977 trip to Syria by the minister of Defence, Barney Danson, might bring the cause of Syrian Jews some much-needed publicity. Danson was scheduled to visit Canadian troops serving with the UN peace observation team on the Syria-Israel armistice line in the Golan Heights. Judy pressed the minister, a Jew, to do more. She asked him to visit the Damascus Jewish community, attend a synagogue service in the Jewish quarter, and talk with President Assad about the emigration of the Jews. She sent an information package on Syrian Jewry to be included in the minister's briefing materials. In the end he did none of the things she suggested. Judy was disappointed. When the minister was quoted in the *Toronto Star* as saying his schedule was so tight that it did not permit him time to visit the Jewish community, yet television coverage of his visit showed him exploring archeological excavations, Judy Feld Carr became enraged.

At the Ontario Region Congress executive meeting in Toronto Judy raised the issue of the minister's apparent lack of interest in Syrian Jews. "This does not show concern for the Jewish people; the least he could have done was not to make a public statement [to the press]. We, as community leaders, must learn from history and get off the fence, not worry about politics at such occasions...." The committee members cautioned Judy not to jump to conclusions about a minister who had an enviable record of service in the community. But she would have none of it; she wrote to Danson, demanding an explanation and warning him that he would feel the sting of community anger at the upcoming Congress plenary in Montreal the following month.[29]

Danson replied that during official visits like the one to Syria his time was not his own. Every part of his itinerary was laid out in advance and, to a great extent, reflected the wishes of his hosts. They knew that he was Jewish and he had used the opportunity to discuss issues of Jewish concern with Arab leaders, including President Assad. In veiled language, the minister suggested that issues specific to the Jews of Syria were not forgotten.

> There were other aspects more germane to your specific concerns which have some hope of success, rather than publicity which might give me short-term satisfaction, but would prove counter-productive to the real matters which concern you and I. The matter was, however, not neglected.[30]

Judy was not satisfied. What matters outside that glare of publicity was he referring to? She asked him to meet her before the Congress plenary meetings in Montreal. Danson declined. The line between public duty and community interest is a difficult one to draw, but he felt he had served both well. He had said all he was going to say on the subject. Judy backed away from further public confrontation.[31]

When the minister returned to Ottawa from the Congress plenary, he requested up-to-date briefing information on the situation of Syrian Jews and Canadian policy respecting them. The report he received was once again at odds with the portrait painted by Judy and her committee. The briefing notes described a mistrusted populace at the margins of Syrian social, economic, and political life, but not a community in danger for their lives. The solution to the Syrian Jewish emigration issue was not in Canada's power to shape, but was dependent on the resolution of the Israeli-Syrian standoff.[32]

In the meantime, Hannah Cohen's application to bring her family to Canada was going nowhere. Judy asked a Congress official in Toronto to write a letter to Canadian Immigration in support of her application, asserting that Rabbi Dahab would be a valuable asset to the Toronto Jewish community.

[He] is a strictly observant Jew, a most learned person, a Hebrew scholar and a highly qualified ritual slaughterer. We, in Canada, have difficulty in obtaining functionaries of this calibre, particularly ritual slaughterers, and therefore we would have a post available for Reverend Dahab when he emigrates.[34]

Months, then years, passed with no apparent action. The documentation had been forwarded to Canadian officials in Beirut, then on to Damascus for Syrian government review. Hannah Cohen's application went no further.[34]

Syrian officials not only refused to approve the application, they also obstructed the process. The would-be immigrants had to sign a Canadian document stating that they wanted to come to Canada, and they also had to complete medical forms. However, Syrian postal authorities would not deliver the necessary forms. Canadian Immigration routinely sent the documents, but they always got lost in the mail. This made the Syrian Jews very nervous. How many would actively court the wrath of Syrian officials by stating their desire to emigrate? Such a statement did not guarantee permission to leave so much as it guaranteed that Syrian officials would make the applicant's life miserable. Canadian Immigration authorities nonetheless remained unbending in their demand that the paperwork be signed and submitted.

The Department of External Affairs and this Department [Immigration] have been concerned with the plight of the Jewish minority in Syria for several years. As you know, we have expressed to the Syrian government our concerns about the immigration of those Syrian Jews having close relatives in Canada. However, the Syrians are reluctant to allow free immigration of their citizens. It is the negative attitudes of the Syrian government to the emigration of their nationals, not Canadian immigration requirements, which is the greatest obstacle in the path of Syrian Jews wishing to join family in Canada.[36]

Judy Feld Carr warned Immigration officials that sending the forms by mail was not only a waste of time but was also dangerous. It fingered specific Jewish families to the Muhabarat. If Canadian

Immigration needed the forms filled out, she urged that they be hand delivered to Syria by Canadian embassy officials in Beirut.

> You may be aware that the Syrian government does not allow its Jewish citizens to travel outside the confines of their own cities without special permission from the police, and therefore they especially are not allowed to visit Lebanon for any reason.[36]

The only way for the families to receive the application forms would be for a Canadian official to bring them personally when he visited Syria.

According to Judy, Canadian ministers of External Affairs had promised to authorize Canadian embassy personnel in Beirut to do just that. But immigration authorities claimed to know nothing about it. One official warned, "I remain as convinced as my predecessor that any attempt at direct contact by Canadian officials might have adverse effects." However, he said, "that the [Canadian] Employment and Immigration office in Beirut will continue to monitor the situation closely and will take all necessary steps which may be practical and feasible to bring about the processing of the applications."[37]

External Affairs and Immigration authorities came up with what they hoped would be a workable compromise. The Canadian embassy in Beirut would send the necessary medical forms to the British embassy in Damascus, where Canada maintained a small office for the use of Canadian diplomats. One of the prominent Aleppo rabbis in Hannah Cohen's family was often authorized to travel to Damascus on community business and for medical care. He could make a quick stop at the British embassy to pick up the necessary forms. On a subsequent visit, the completed forms could be returned the same way. In the meantime, Canadian Immigration agreed that Hannah could fill out the individual forms on behalf of family members in Aleppo.

Of course, even if the plan worked, Canada could only issue immigration visas for entry to Canada. "The issuance of exit visas is entirely within the responsibility of the Syrian government. We [Canada] have no jurisdiction in this area, and we are not able to make representations on behalf of intending immigrants." Nonetheless, Hannah still welcomed the chance to have her family fill out the necessary medical forms and have Canadian visas issued in their names.

An Aleppo Jewish businessman who secretly visited Judy Feld Carr communicated the arrangement for the document pickup at the British embassy in Damascus. As arranged, the rabbi, at some personal risk, applied for special permission to visit Damascus—ostensibly on Jewish community business. Hoping that he was not being followed, he detoured to the British embassy to pick up the papers that had been sent from Beirut. To his shock, the British knew nothing of any forms or papers and suggested that the family travel to the Canadian embassy in Beirut. "As you know," he reported to Judy, "it is impossible for us to travel to Beirut."[38]

Embarrassed, Ottawa officials could not figure out what went wrong and twisted this way and that for an explanation.

> It could be that the family did not explain to the Embassy officials that arrangements had been made for them to pick up the forms. If they generally asked for the forms for immigration to Canada, they would have been advised that they should contact the Canadian officials, who, of course, are located in Beirut.[39]

Whatever the reason for the foul-up, it was evident that Syrian authorities were unwilling to entertain any request for emigration. This foreclosed legal exit for all but the old and infirm. Even in these cases, a stiff bond against return was often prohibitive. Faraj Sasson, father of Rabbi Jacques Sasson, was not encouraging in a letter he wrote to Judy from Brazil.

> By way of Rabbi Eliahou Dahab and his family, I have to tell you that it is almost impossible for one whole family to leave Syria. It might happen that one single person might leave with difficulty against a deposit which amounts to $12,000 American dollars and with much effort because the government had made restrictions recently following the escape of a good number of persons.

How had Faraj Sasson and his family been able to leave together?

> One of the greatest reasons which helped our departure, it is that we are two old people with a very young child, it is not the same thing

113

when it concerns young people.... I do not have to hide from you this it was necessary to sacrifice my finances of a century of work in our school as a principal and as a teacher, my indemnity, my pension and yet more gifts which I received from my old students scattered in all corners of the world. With that I am actually in debt of more than $3,000.00 to my friends who are still in Aleppo.[40]

Despite his financial situation, Faraj Sasson considered himself blessed. At least he, his wife, and a child were out of Syria.

While there was no progress on immigration, through 1978 and into 1979, Judy Feld Carr and her supporters sent more than $20,000 worth of religious books, along with articles and cash donations to assist the neediest Jews in Damascus and Aleppo. The process had become routine. At the request of either Rabbi Sasson in Aleppo or Rabbi Hamra in Damascus, Judy purchased religious texts, prayer shawls, *tefillin*, and leather straps for the repair of *tefillin* using money from the Feld Fund. Syrian authorities allowed the packages from Canada through, although parcels mailed from the United States sometimes went undelivered or were returned to the sender. In one case, American senders were notified that their parcel had been rerouted from Damascus and ended up in a post office in Calcutta. Several American supporters began to contribute money to the Feld Fund.[41]

Rabbi Sasson and Rabbi Hamra acknowledged receipt of each shipment by letter or telegram. Often the acknowledgment was effusive in its praise for Judy Feld Carr and her assistance to the Jews of Syria. The effusiveness reflected a style of writing commonly used in that part of the world to express gratitude, but the praise was also from the heart. Perhaps none was so flowery as a letter written to Judy Feld Carr in French by Rabbi Sasson after he received a box of religious articles and $1,000 to distribute to the needy Jews of Aleppo. Even from the awkward English translation that was hastily done for her, it is easy to understand why Judy Feld Carr was embarrassed at the extent of the flattery.

We have received your kind letter with your subsidy and have been very grateful. Many thanks to God who sent us a merciful mother, the queen of good and benevolence. We don't know what does express this generous name "Judy Feld"? Does it express a normal person who lives in Toronto? Oh no and thousands of no. Indeed, this lovely name expresses an angel sent by God. This angel who gathers all means of good and humanity holds a pure heart beating with affection for religion and Torah.

Thirty years have passed of our life and we ignore that there is such generous personality in the world whose first and last aim in life is to think about her brothers in Aleppo, to worry about our situation, troubles, and to fulfil our wishes and inquiries. She always offered kindness and good deeds. Therefore, we have now known a lot about your pure personality and we feel that you are living in our heart for ever. We shall never forget as long as we live your kindness. Every body of our families and students participate with us in our great affection to you and everybody of your esteemed community.

We have a good knowledge about you from your good deeds and correspondence, but your photograph was lacking for us. We want your photograph to hold it day and night, to put it in our hearts and inside the holy books you sent so to bless you.[42]

But for all the praise, for all her efforts over eight years, Judy Feld Carr's most important goal still eluded her. She had yet to deliver a single Jew out of Syrian captivity.

Deliver Them Out of Syria

I N DECEMBER 1978, world leaders gathered at the UN headquarters in New York to mark the thirtieth anniversary of
the Universal Declaration of Human Rights. Alain Poher,
president of the French Senate and president of the International
Council for Jews in Arab Countries, was not there. He sent a letter
to UN Secretary General Kurt Waldheim demanding that the UN
condemn Syria for its violations of the Universal Declaration. The
human rights of Syrian Jews, Poher reminded Waldheim, were subject to daily abuse and "repeated appeals to the Syrian Government
for the abolition of the discrimination and persecution of the Jewish
community have been in vain."

> Therefore we have decided to appeal to you once again to intervene
> for the improvement of the situation of this community. By its behav-
> iour in respect to Jews living in its territory, Syria constantly and
> methodically violates the International Charter of Civil and Political
> Rights of 1966 to which she adhered on 21 April 1969. The 4500 Jews
> of Syria, residing in Damascus, Aleppo and Kamishli, are treated as
> hostages and cannot leave the country even for medical treatment.
>
> In special cases, a small number of Jews receives permission to leave
> Syria for limited periods, after having deposited a guarantee of at least
> 25,000 Syrian pounds and leaving in Syria members of their families
> as hostages. This behaviour constitutes a violation of the above
> mentioned Declaration and in particular of Paragraph 12 (2) which

stipulates that every man is free to leave any country he resides in, including his own.

The international community cannot remain silent in face of the refusal of the rights of free exit and freedom of movement.

We ask for your urgent intervention with the Syrian authorities in order to secure permission to any Jew, who so desires, to leave the country and in particular to join members of his family, if any, who reside abroad.[1]

Poher's letter didn't made a ripple at the United Nations. And the Syrian regime was determined to show that it would not tolerate interference in what it regarded as its domestic affairs. This protest by Poher must have smacked of Israeli-engineered propaganda that was designed to discredit Syria while diverting world attention away from Israeli actions in the West Bank and Gaza. Syria was not prepared to yield to the protester's demands; Alain Poher's letter would change nothing for the Jews of Syria.

A month earlier, Judy Feld Carr had secretly met with a Syrian Jew in Toronto. He was an import agent who was allowed out of Syria on short-term exit visas. Encouraged by Rabbi Hamra, he contacted her from New York, and identified himself as a friend of the rabbi. Judy was suspicious and questioned him carefully. Satisfied that he was not a Syrian agent, she convinced him to visit Toronto. At first he was reluctant, worried that if the Syrians discovered that he had visited Canada, he would be punished. He had seen the inside of a Syrian prison more than once. In his youth, he had twice tried to escape into Lebanon. Twice he had been imprisoned and tortured.

Judy reassured him that his visit could be kept secret and he agreed to come. But still afraid that the Muhabarat would find out that he was in Canada, he spent all three days sequestered in the Carr house. He was Judy's first clandestine Syrian visitor, but not the last. Over the years, there was a long line of mysterious strangers who huddled in conversation with Judy as the routine of the household flowed around them.

This visitor was especially well connected through his business and other associations. He knew who in the Jewish community was reliable. He knew how the Syrian regime worked. He knew how to play the angles and what went on at the margins of Syrian society. He knew where to get a fixer and how much it would cost. And he shared this knowledge with Judy Feld Carr. Over the years she relied on him for information and turned to him as a sounding board for her ideas. When he returned to Syria from business trips abroad, he served as a courier for her. Even after he left Syria permanently some years later, he ensured that the money she sent to Syria made its way into the right hands.[2]

The value of his information was in its details—names, addresses, dates, prices, relationships, chronology. He was a walking, talking reference guide to the Muhabarat section that dealt with the Jews and to the aspirations of the beleaguered Jewish community. As she always did when she talked to any of her sources, Judy kept careful notes. After her guest left Toronto, she compiled a confidential report and gave it to the Israeli consul on the understanding that it would be forwarded to the appropriate officials, including those in Israeli intelligence.

This confidential report opened a long and often fractious relationship between Judy and Israeli intelligence. What must Israeli intelligence have made of her—a Toronto mother of six with a master's degree in music education who had put together her own network of informants in Syria? She was an amateur. Could her information be trusted? Could she be trusted? Some of the information that Judy supplied to the Israelis was new, and they did not want to discourage her. They decided to proceed cautiously, acknowledging her assistance without letting her know how critical her material sometimes proved to be. When Judy passed on the report from her visitor, Israeli officials minimized its usefulness and even told her that some of her facts were wrong.[3]

Six months later, Judy was in Israel and a government contact offered to set up a briefing on Syrian Jewry with the Foreign Office. She accepted. The Foreign Office official cautioned her that what he was about to tell her was privileged, but to her amusement, much of what he said sounded very familiar. "I looked at his desk and there was my report in my typing and with my signature. They even had the *chutzpa* to send this so-called wrong report marked

'Confidential' to all the Israeli embassies and ambassadors throughout the world."[4]

How could she put her information to work for Syrian Jewry? In one respect, Alain Poher had been wrong in his letter to Kurt Waldheim. Syrian authorities were allowing some Jews to leave Syria for business purposes or to seek medical treatment abroad. For those who were sick, it was often a grudging permission granted only in the late stages of an illness, after much pleading and greasing of official palms. Such permissions were rare—witness Simon Khabas—but there was a precedent for Syrian authorities to grant humanitarian leave.

The Khabas story, despite its sad ending, encouraged Judy to think that it was possible to "legally" get Jews out of Syria if officials understood or, more to the point, could be paid to understand that medical treatment abroad was necessary. She considered this possibility as hope faded of getting the Syrians to approve Hannah Cohen's application to bring her family to Canada. Why not use the Khabas precedent to get her family's ailing patriarch, Rabbi Eliahou Dahab, out of Syria for medical treatment? Rabbi Dahab suffered from cancer and, according to Hannah Cohen, he was receiving only minimal treatment. Doctors in Aleppo said they could do little more for him. A humanitarian case could be made that Rabbi Dahab needed medical treatment abroad.

The Syrian president himself had opened the door to humanitarian appeals when he eased restrictions on Syrian Jews in the mid-1970s. Of course, Assad did not decide individual cases personally.[5] His officials were responsibile for judging what was a humanitarian need. In a society where officials regularly sold indulgences, why not a stamp in a passport? The question was seldom whether a case was truly one of humanitarian need. The question was how much it would cost. As Syrian Jews knew from their day-to-day experience, there was often room for haggling. But negotiations were not always simple. It wasn't enough to fill out an application, dangle a few gifts in front of officials, and wait for them to process the forms. There still needed to be a legitimizing smokescreen.

Throughout much of 1978, correspondence between Judy Feld Carr and Rabbi Sasson in Aleppo about shipments of religious articles and books included occasional concerned references to Rabbi Dahab's health, designed to catch the eye of the Muhabarat. If the rabbi would apply for humanitarian leave to seek medical treatment in Canada, Judy would be pleased to arrange such care for him in Toronto. Money from the Feld Fund would cover whatever costs were involved. Thanking her, Rabbi Dahab applied for humanitarian leave to go abroad for medical treatment, accompanied by his wife and his older daughter, Olga.

To keep the rabbi's medical condition in front of the Muhabarat, Judy asked for a copy of his medical records to pass on to doctors in Toronto. The records would not be released. She turned to the Canadian representative of the International Red Cross. Its Geneva office requested the records through its representative in Syria. Instead of the records, the Red Cross received a statement explaining, "The person concerned was transferred two years ago to the Damascus Hospital and treated by cobalt; the diagnosis—cancer of the bladder. Rabbi Dahab is presently in the French hospital in Damascus being treated for anemia."[6]

Meanwhile, Rabbi Dahab's family in Aleppo secured a statement from his doctor, countersigned by the local health department and stating that "the patient has been treated here by every possible means available to us without success. Therefore the only possible means and hope existing for the patient to get well is by leaving the country and seeking help overseas." This letter was supplied to appropriate authorities who already knew that the International Red Cross was interested. Money from the Feld Fund was slipped to one official here and another there. Syrian authorities told the family that a temporary exit visa would be granted as long as medical authorities in Toronto agreed to take on the rabbi's case. But the rabbi would have to travel alone. Permission for either his elderly and frail wife or his daughter to accompany him abroad was refused. A subsequent request through the International Red Cross that a nurse be allowed to accompany the rabbi was not acknowledged.[7]

In Toronto, several doctors volunteered to provide free medical services for Rabbi Dahab. Judy and Hannah Cohen sent what medical information they had on the rabbi to several cancer specialists so that they would be ready if and when he arrived. With letters from the doctors in hand, a cash bond posted against his return, and more money discreetly doled out to officials, Rabbi Dahab was issued a passport and a three-month exit visa.[8]

Canada agreed to issue an entry visa, but nobody could guarantee that a visa sent by mail from the Canadian embassy in Beirut would be delivered. Fearing that the rabbi's departure could be held up if he was forced to wait for a Canadian visitor's visa, Judy asked if an alternate delivery route could be worked out. Ottawa approved a plan to send the visa sent to the British embassy in Damascus. Her contacts in Aleppo, however, advised that the plan was problematic. Judy understood this to mean that it was difficult to get permission to travel from Aleppo to Damascus, and a visit to the British embassy was too risky. So Judy approached the minister of Immigration who agreed to make an exception and issue the rabbi a visa upon his arrival in Toronto.[9]

The plan was co-ordinated with Rabbi Sasson, Rabbi Dahab's colleague in Aleppo. Judy prepaid an open round-trip Damascus/Toronto ticket on KLM, booked a flight for the first week of April, made arrangements for kosher food on the trip, and posted the bond against the rabbi's return. She made sure that someone would be on hand in Amsterdam to help the ailing rabbi make his flight transfer there. In the week before his planned departure, she informed Canadian Immigration authorities of the flight plans so that the visa would be waiting at the airport and notified the doctors of his arrival date. Hannah Cohen and her family prepared to welcome her brother. Everything was set.[10]

Without notice or explanation, Syrian authorities suddenly demanded that Rabbi Dahab leave two days early on a Lufthansa flight from Damascus to Frankfurt. The rabbi had no choice and had no way to warn Judy. There was no time to arrange kosher food, so Rabbi Dahab, attached to a catheter, neither ate nor drank during his lengthy journey. Only with the kind assistance of Lufthansa personnel in Frankfurt was he able to transfer to the Toronto leg of his journey.

Several hours before the rabbi's arrival, the travel agent who booked the original KLM ticket called Judy in a panic. The rabbi was already en route to Toronto and would be landing soon. Judy scrambled to rearrange everything. She notified immigration authorities in Ottawa and at Toronto airport of the change in plan. She alerted the hospital. The staff promised to have a medical team standing by and dispatched an ambulance to meet the flight. Somehow everything fell into place. Within an hour of landing in Toronto, Rabbi Dahab, his passport stamped with a Canadian visitor's visa, was being examined by doctors with a Hebrew-speaking nurse in attendance.[11]

The doctors' findings were not encouraging. The rabbi was in very serious condition when he arrived. "The internist who checked him," Judy wrote to an Israeli activist, "told me that he had not seen a body like that since Auschwitz. The poor man was suffering from dehydration and the lack of food, he had sores all around his mouth." Rabbi Dahab's cancer was very far advanced. Doctors would do what they could, but there was little hope.

Rabbi Dahab understood that his time was limited and he made two requests. He wanted to go to Israel to be with his children and have tea with his mother, who was in her nineties. More important, he was worried about his two unmarried daughters still in Syria, Olga and Ava. His second request was that Judy Feld Carr deliver them out of Syria as she had delivered him.[12]

After doing what they could for him, Rabbi Dahab's doctors agreed that there was no medical reason that he should not join family in Israel. But under no circumstances would Syrian government officials countenance the rabbi going to Israel, whatever his health. If they ever found out, they might take it out on his wife and daughters.[13]

Judy and the Cohens devised a charade to prevent Syrian officials from finding out. The rabbi, accompanied by Hannah Cohen's husband, was booked on an El Al flight out of Montreal, under assumed names. Rabbi Dahab could not travel on his Syrian passport because his documentation was needed in Toronto to give the impression that he was still in Canada receiving medical treatment. The Israeli consul in Toronto stepped in. During a visit with the rabbi in hospital, the two men discovered a bond. While posted to Turkey, the consul had issued travel papers for one of the rabbi's sons, who had escaped from Syria. As he had done for the son, he now did for the father. The consul issued the rabbi a *laissez-passer*, authorizing international travel in lieu of a passport. Two weeks after arriving in Toronto, the rabbi secretly left Canada for Israel and a reunion with his mother and his children.

The Carrs travelled to Israel soon thereafter and visited with Rabbi Dahab at the home of one of his children in Tel Aviv. The rabbi, now near death, again made Judy Feld Carr promise to bring his daughters out of Syria. Although she promised, she did not know how she could deliver. A few days later, almost three months to the day after his arrival in Toronto, the rabbi died.

To maintain the fiction that Rabbi Dahab was still alive and receiving medical treatment in Toronto, the family in Israel agreed not to make any public announcement of his death. In Canada, Judy Feld Carr hatched a scheme that she hoped would bring Olga out of Syria. She wrote to Rabbi Sasson in Aleppo and to Rabbi Hamra in Damascus and reported on the rabbi's supposed condition. She also wrote about how lonely he was in Toronto, about the high cost of round-the-clock nursing care, and that the Jewish community could not continue paying indefinitely for it. Was it possible for the rabbi's older daughter Olga to come to Toronto and tend to her father's needs? A telegram was sent to Olga over her father's name, asking that she come to Toronto to take care of him. Rabbi Sasson picked up the cues. With his help, Olga applied for a Syrian passport and exit visa.[14]

When Rabbi Dahab's three-month Syrian exit visa expired his passport was sent to the Syrian embassy in Washington for renewal. His signature on the application was copied from the existing passport but with a shakier hand, as if written by a sick man. Judy took the existing passport photograph to a professional photographer who touched it up to show a sick man—hollow cheeks, less of a smile, eyes with dark circles. Finally, a sympathetic doctor wrote a letter explaining that Rabbi Dahab's medical treatment had to be continued. The renewal application was risky. In due course, however, the rabbi's passport was mailed back to Toronto, his visa extension approved.[15]

Syrian authorities advised Olga that, unlike her father, she would not be issued a passport or exit visa unless she had a Canadian entry visa. American dollars had a way of prompting official action, but in Olga's case, the Muhabarat had put its foot down. She could leave only when she had the Canadian visa in hand. Canadian Immigration officials assured Judy that granting a visitor's visa for Olga would not be a problem.[16] The difficulty was getting it to Olga in Syria. Sending the visa to the British embassy in Damascus was risky because all comings and goings at foreign embassies in Syria were monitored. The previous plan to pick up the papers at the embassy had failed. Judy wanted External Affairs to hand deliver a visa to someone in Damascus who could be trusted to pass it on to Olga in Aleppo. External Affairs officials were skittish. Hand delivery of the visas in Syria involved direct contact between a Canadian official and a Syrian Jew; it was risky for the diplomat and even riskier for the Jew.[17] A Canadian Immigration official advised Judy that the idea had been rejected as reckless and dangerous.

> I remain as convinced as my predecessors that any attempt at direct contact by Canadian officials might have adverse effects not only for the families involved but also for other Syrian applicants. You are, no doubt, aware that there are hundreds of [non-Jewish] Canadians of Syrian origin in this country. They, too, are interested in being reunited with their close relatives who still live in Syria.[18]

Without the co-operation of Canadian officials, they would have to attempt another pickup from the British embassy. Judy decided that under the circumstances, the Syrians should be forewarned that Olga or someone representing her would be going to the embassy for that express purpose. She laid the groundwork in letters to Aleppo and Damascus—Olga was needed by her sick father and it was necessary for her to pick up her Canadian visa at the British embassy in Damascus.

After some delay External Affairs advised Judy that a Canadian official carrying the documents would be at the British embassy, the "post-office" in Syria, for three days in the second week of January. She informed Rabbi Hamra in Damascus and Rabbis Sasson and Farhi in Aleppo of the dates for the pickup. She reiterated in her correspondence that the visa was being issued so "Olga can come to Canada to take care of her very sick father. He is desperately lonely for her and needs her very much."[19]

Olga and Rabbi Farhi's wife were granted permission to travel from Aleppo to Damascus on the appointed day. But they came away from the embassy empty-handed. Rabbi Farhi explained to Judy what had happened.

My wife and Olga travelled to Damascus to the British Embassy on 9 January as you wished to pick up the temporary visa for Olga but that Canadian representative wasn't there and the British Embassy told us that he is in the Hotel and also we didn't find him and he left the hotel in the morning and we have not a passport yet for visa.[20]

Judy was angry with officials for not making good on their promise to be at the embassy and angry with herself for compromising Olga's safety. Instead of attacking Immigration officials, though, she went directly to Ron Atkey, the minister of Immigration, and appealed to him to authorize hand delivery of the visa in Damascus. Atkey agreed to do all he could. He assigned one of his assistants to work with her and External Affairs to get the visa delivered.

They devised a new plan. A high-ranking Canadian official from the embassy in Beirut would take the visa with him on a visit to Damascus, where he would make an unofficial side trip to the Ben Maimoun Jewish Day School. The cover story was that the Canadian official was verifying that the boxes of religious articles mailed from Canada to the Jewish community of Damascus were being put to good use.

The Canadian emissary was to arrive at the school promptly at two-thirty in the afternoon, after the Syrian attendant, a government informant who monitored school affairs on behalf of the Muhabarat, had left for the day. However, the information was incorrect: the Syrian normally left the school at three in the afternoon. Fortunately, that day he didn't feel well and left early. Rabbi Hamra must have felt uneasy when the Canadian arrived at two-thirty. He was too early. Had something gone wrong? Could this be a trap? He breathed a sigh of relief when the Canadian visitor gave the pre-arranged code, "Judy sends regards." The Canadian diplomat handed over the envelope containing the visa and left.[21]

With a Canadian visa in hand and cash supplied by the Feld Fund to cover both the requisite bond against her return and money to prime the Syrian bureaucratic pump, Olga's exit visa application made its way through the system. It took another few months and another few payments, but an exit visa was finally issued. Olga left Syria for Toronto on a prepaid round-trip KLM ticket. When she arrived in Toronto she was told that her father had died. Her safe removal from Syria had been her father's last wish.[22]

Olga's departure from Syria in 1980 was like an adrenaline rush for Judy Feld Carr. She had succeeded in getting Rabbi Dahab to Toronto, but he was sick and needed medical care. The story concocted to bring Olga out had been no more carefully constructed than any of the other family reunification applications that had gone nowhere in the Syrian approval process. As far as Judy could figure, the difference was that the road that brought Olga out of Syria was a toll road. It was pay as you go. Having learned this simple truth, Judy Feld Carr soon became a regular on the route.

Gradually word began to seep out into Syrian Jewish communities that a woman in Toronto, Mrs. Judy, could buy people out of Syria. Those desperate to bring family out of Syria called Mrs. Judy and she listened. Once she verified that a story was true, it was hard to say no. Judy found herself with an expanding case load and worked on many of the files simultaneously. The possibility to rescue Jews from Syria excited her, and she was not going to let any opportunity slip through her fingers.

The case of Rabbi Dahab's other daughter, Ava, was particularly important to her. Judy's strategy was simple and, in Syrian terms, legal. She again concocted a humanitarian case supported by pleas for help from Toronto. For nineteen-year-old Ava, the pretext was a variation on the theme used to bring Olga from Syria. Judy suggested that since Ava's mother, Rabbi Dahab's wife, suffered from a chronic heart condition, she too would benefit from medical treatment in Toronto. As soon as Syrian authorities signalled that they might be induced to let the rabbi's wife to travel abroad for medical care, Judy argued that the woman was both too ill and too frail to travel alone. In a letter to Rabbi Dahab's son-in-law, Rabbi Farhi, Judy went further and invented a legal case for why mother and daughter had to travel together.

I am very concerned about your mother-in-law and Ava. I am pleased that your mother-in-law was accepted, but it will be impossible for her to come here *alone* because she is too sick. The Canadian government has told me that they will have the Canadian visa here in the airport for her as soon as she gets off the plane *only* if she is accompanied by her daughter. This is Canadian law. They want her young healthy daughter to travel with her, in case she becomes more sick on the plane. The visa has been arranged for the two of them to enter Canada temporarily.[23]

Unfortunately, Syrian authorities rejected pleas that both mother and daughter travel together. They were prepared to let the mother leave, but the daughter had to stay.[24] Judy and Rabbi Farhi proceeded on the assumption that this was just a sign that negotiations were not over. Syrian authorities kept finding problem after problem in granting Ava leave to travel with her sick mother, problems money managed to solve. Unfortunately, however, a few days before Rosh Hashanah, the Jewish New Year, Ava's mother died quietly in her sleep.[25]

Judy could no longer argue that Ava was needed to escort her sick mother to Canada for medical treatment, so she wrote to Rabbi Farhi suggesting that Ava might find comfort for the loss of her mother in a visit to her aunt, Hannah Cohen, in Toronto. Syrian officials sensed that they would have to produce an exit visa or see this deal fall through. After almost a year and a half and several more cash payments to iron out an endless stream of "administrative" problems, Syrian authorities accepted a deposit against Ava's return to Syria and issued her passport and exit visa. With assurances from Canadian authorities that Ava would be granted a Canadian visitor's visa on arrival in Toronto, she boarded her flight from Damascus to Toronto.[26]

When the KLM flight touched down in Toronto, the excited Cohen and Carr families were waiting at the airport to welcome Ava to Canada. But after all the other passengers had cleared customs and immigration, Ava still had not appeared. What could have gone wrong? Had Ava been prevented from boarding her flight at the last minute? Has she missed her connecting flight in

Amsterdam? Worried, Don Carr and Ava's uncle, Jeff Cohen, went to the Canadian Immigration office in the terminal. Ava was being detained for questioning by an Immigration officer. Don Carr explained that a Canadian entry visa had been pre-arranged. If there was any problem, he was a lawyer and Jeff Cohen, the passenger's uncle, spoke Arabic. The two men were ushered into the waiting room. There was no problem; the Immigration officer was going through the formalities of issuing Ava her Canadian entry visa. While the official was completing the paperwork, he asked if it was true that Ava was Jewish. Don Carr answered yes with some unease. Canadian Immigration officials had no business asking about religion. The officer suddenly switched into Hebrew and explained that he was a former Israeli. He had not realized that there were any Jews in Syria. A few minutes later, with a parting "Shalom," Ava was legally in Canada.[27]

There were several loose ends to tie up. It was now safe to let Rabbi Dahab to die in the eyes of Syrian officials. An Ontario death certificate required a body, but Rabbi Dahab was already buried in Israel. Different regulations in Quebec made the paperwork easier, so a new fiction was devised. If Syrian authorities asked questions, it would be said the rabbi had gone to Montreal to consult another doctor and died there. As a further precaution, a Jewish burial society in Montreal agreed to erect a gravestone for the rabbi over an empty grave.[28]

And what of Olga and Ava? Once the Syrians knew that Rabbi Dahab was dead, Olga would be expected to return. Ava was also supposed to go back to Syria when her visitor's visa expired. Both women were already in Israel, and neither had any intention of returning to Syria. Ava suggested that Syrian authorities would accept marriage as a legitimate reason for the two sisters not to return, so Judy arranged fictional Canadian marriages for the two sisters. In correspondence with Rabbi Farhi about other matters, she dropped comments that they were being courted by respectable young men in Toronto.

Ava is very happy here. She has gotten used to the cold weather, and has seen Montreal. You do not have to thank me for her new clothes, it was a pleasure to see her look so beautiful, and that makes me very happy. I have spoken to some Rabbis here to introduce her to young men now. Several students from the university have taken her out for parties and dinners, and she has enjoyed them very much. Perhaps, it will happen that she will meet someone that she may love, and get married. Her sister has met someone, and has been going out with him for a long time.[29]

What was only dating in the early spring was serious talk of marriage by mid-summer and weddings by the late summer. A co-operative Toronto rabbi wrote up a *ketuba*, the traditional Jewish marriage contract given to every Jewish bride, for each of the sisters as proof of marriage. Copies were sent to Rabbi Farhi, who presented them to Syrian authorities. By means of a code—"Montreal" was used for Israel and "clothes" as code for travel arrangements—Judy Feld Carr had already let Rabbi Farhi know Olga and Ava were in Israel.[30]

It had taken four years, but an old man's dying wish had come true. His daughters were safely out of Syria and free to begin their lives again. For Judy Feld Carr, redeeming Jewish souls from bondage was exhilerating, but expensive. She paid out many thousands of dollars over the years, sending religious articles into Syria and bribing Syrian officials for exit visas. Judy and a small group of activists, particularly her friend Helen Cooper, used every opportunity to fundraise for the Feld Fund. Money came in from ordinary people who trusted Judy and wanted to help her work.

But some of the ransom money came from deeper pockets. There were no major public fundraising functions, no celebrity dinners, no art auctions, and no plaques for donors or cocktail parties. Donors never knew the details of what Judy was doing, but they were quietly assured that their contribution would make a rescue happen. According to Helen Cooper, the idea of being part of a cloak-and-dagger rescue operation attracted the donors. In many cases, Judy sent individual donors a photograph of the family their money had helped buy out of Syria.[31]

Judy had a short list of repeat donors throughout North America who could be counted on for an emergency infusion of funds. A number of rabbis were willing to approach synagogue members for a donation to the Feld Fund or draw on synagogue discretionary funds if the need was immediate. Trust was important; of necessity a veil of secrecy remained over the money's use.[32] Judy explained this to an Australian Jewish group who volunteered to raise money. Some of the money raised could be used to "ransom" Jews out of Syria, but they could not expect a detailed accounting.

> As your executive wishes, I will send you Xerox copies of each bank draft sent to Syria, under the condition that *never* is it to be made public or discussed outside your immediate executive.
>
> The money will be used *only* when it is possible to ransom someone or to be used for the poor. If you wish, it may pay for religious books to be using in the schools and synagogues. That is your choice. You must understand the secrecy involved in this. If anything should ever by made public, it will be the end of the whole network.[33]

Judy Feld Carr had to straddle the line between secret activity and public promotion. The mandate of the Congress National Committee on Jews in Arab Lands was to inform the community on the plight of Syrian Jews. Publicity was the name of the game and it also helped fundraising. But if Judy was too closely associated with publicity that criticized the treatment of Syrian Jews, it might compromise the very people she was working to help. The Syrian regime presumably had limits to its tolerance. Judy often found herself carrying out the two critical but contradictory aspects of her campaign simultaneously. In late February 1979, while she was working covertly to bring Rabbi Dahab out of Syria, the Carrs hosted a widely publicized gathering for community members to hear firsthand from a recent Syrian Jewish escapee.

"Mr. Albert," was a thirty-seven-year-old Syrian Jew who, with his wife and three children, had struggled through the mountains to a neighbouring country. From there they had made their way to Israel. He was a successful businessman in Syria, but he and his family left with no more than the clothes on their backs. To be caught with cash or jewellery was to court robbery or even murder at the hands of hired smugglers. Mr. Albert, hiding behind a black leather face mask, had held a press conference in New York before coming to Toronto. When the Muhabarat had found out about his escape, remaining family members, men and women, were arrested, imprisoned, and tortured as a punishment and as a warning to others. He told the media that the liberalization of state control of Jews was being rolled back. Restrictions on employment, education, and the freedom to travel more than a few miles from home without permission were again becoming the rule. As the repression increased, more and more Jews were ready to risk everything to cross Syria's borders. With each escape attempt, whether a success or a failure, Syrian repression worsened.

Mr. Albert, again hiding behind his black leather mask, held another press conference in Toronto. Like many Syrian Jews, he said, he had been financially well off before his escape. He had used what cash he could assemble to buy freedom, paying smugglers to get him and his family out of Syria. He gladly left the rest of his property behind. "In Syria, I was 50 per cent a person, in Israel, I can be 100 per cent: I will succeed."[34]

After years of calculated cruelty at the hands of the Syrian state, Mr. Albert had yet to feel secure. He was booked into an upscale local hotel, but when he heard the taxi driver who drove him back to his hotel speaking Arabic, he became frightened. Who was this driver? Would the driver tell anyone where he was staying? He was unable to accept that this was a harmless coincidence, that many taxi drivers in Toronto, one of the world's major immigrant-receiving cities, were new immigrants. He refused to stay in the hotel. Nervous, upset, and fearing for his personal safety, he stayed overnight at Judy's house.[35]

The Toronto press was generous in its coverage of Mr. Albert and his story. Only the *Canadian Jewish News* highlighted the fact that Judy Feld Carr and the Congress Ontario Region Committee on Jews in Arab Lands had invited him to Canada. Syrian intelligence, however, would have connected the woman in Toronto who sent parcels and money to Jews in Syria with all the negative publicity about Syria in the Canadian media. Why they continued to let the packages and money through to Jews in Syria is puzzling. Why did they continue to deliver her letters and telegrams, when those from others were often not received or acknowledged? Why did authorities not clamp down on her access to the Jewish community?

In early January 1980, Judy Feld Carr received a letter from Rabbi Sasson, her key contact in Aleppo. He reported on Olga's efforts to secure a passport and exit visa, and sent along another list of books and religious articles requested by the Jews of Aleppo and Qamishli—"Please don't forget us to send those religious objects."[36] But Judy never got the chance to send him the articles. A little more than a month after receiving the shopping list from Aleppo, another letter arrived from Rabbi Sasson—this time from Israel. Like Mr. Albert, he and his family had escaped across the Syrian border into Turkey. Rabbi Sasson and his family, his brother-in-law's family and "three girls who couldn't marry in Syria" had quietly converted all they had into cash to pay the smugglers. What they could not convert, they simply left behind.

> There were twenty-four of us who escaped from Syria on Friday night. And after we walked for six hours we were sitting in the desert till the following night (Saturday). And then the people who helped us told us to walk. After walking a few hours we arrived at the border. Then the snow and rain started to come down. You must realize that we have nine children with us; my four and five of my brother-in-law from Damascus. The non-Jews who helped us said if the children make any noise at the border all of us will be dead. Therefore we gave them drugs so they will sleep and we carried them. We crossed the border and we walked for about 2 hrs. We rested in the desert and we waited until morning so we could walk during the day. The snow came down heavily. We covered the shivering children with our clothes. They were also hungry and thirsty. We continued walking without food until we arrived at one of the cities in Turkey. They brought us a car and then we went to Istanbul where the Jews welcomed us very nicely. Really, I want to tell you that we had a horrible experience and saw death in each other's eyes in the desert many times. I don't believe we have made it with the children and I really thank God that we made it to Eretz Israel.[37]

Judy had no contacts in the covert and obviously risky activity of smuggling Jews out of Syria, but she knew it was another option for those brave enough, rich enough, or desperate enough to use it. The price paid by the family left behind was very high. As she was reminded every year on *Shabbat Zachor*, the price of failure was higher still.

The situation of Syrian Jews suddenly took a turn for the worse as the decade of the 1980s opened. Syria was torn by internal division and many feared civil war. What if President Assad were overthrown and replaced by a more fundamentalist Syrian regime led by either military dissidents or the radical Muslim Brotherhood? Jews in Syria were convinced that life under a more repressive military regime or strict Islamic regime would be far worse than it already was. As early as 1977 one American Jewish commentator on Middle Eastern affairs cautioned that President Assad's future was anything but certain.

> Moreover, since the recent improvements [in the Jewish community of Syria] are attributed to President Assad's personal intervention, there is the continuing fear that, if Assad were overthrown in one of Syria's periodic military coups, the Jewish community may be used as a convenient scapegoat by an extremist regime that may come to power. Their danger is heightened by the continued existence of a powerful and pervasive Syrian internal security apparatus without control by any democratic institution.[38]

The Syrian regime was grounded in the country's minority Alawi community, a Muslim sect of Shiite origin accounting for only 10 per cent of Syria's population. It was increasingly being challenged by radical elements of the non-Alawi majority, including members of "extremist religious movements such as the Muslim Brotherhood." According to Amnesty International, since 1976 there had been repeated acts of anti-government sabotage and assassination attempts against prominent Alawi leaders, including Assad.[39]

In this political climate, there were grave reservations about the safety of Syrian Jews.[40] Judy Feld Carr felt an even greater urgency to buy out as many Jews as possible, but her one-by-one process was too slow to help all those who were desperate to leave. Jews who were already in the Muhabarat's bad books or were unable to consider leaving family members behind, saw only one option—illegal escape into Turkey or Lebanon. Some smugglers made good on the delivery of their human consignments in the hope of repeat business. Others were not nearly so trustworthy. As some Jews learned, to their pain, smugglers could be in league with the authorities or could indulge in double-dipping, first taking money from Jews, then turning around to sell them out to the authorities.

The Muhabarat would often retaliate by imprisoning and torturing the escapees family. Syrian prison conditions varied from one prison to another and varied according to the social and economic status of the prisoner—money could buy creature comforts. But conditions were usually horrific. A 1979 Amnesty International report on Syria noted that:

> In general the following [prison] conditions prevail: cells are often poorly ventilated and lit and communal cells are frequently subjected to massive overcrowding. Beds are often made of concrete platforms with insufficient bedding. Sanitary facilities of a basic nature are available, showers and laundry facilities being provided on average once a week. Hygiene varies considerably, being of a high standard in Al Mezze [prison] but inadequate in other prisons. Food rations are generally at minimum standard, but vary widely in different prisons.[41]

Torture was all too common in Syrian prisons:

> Consistent allegations of torture in recent years indicate that torture is commonly employed in detention centres and military prisons, where it is used during interrogation in order to obtain "confessions" by detainees. It is also reportedly used in some cases as a means of punishment.
>
> Various methods of torture are allegedly used during interrogation under the supervision of officers of the security forces. There is evidence that different methods of torture are applied in sequence, in increasing order of severity. The following methods are reported to be most commonly used:

- beating by hand or stick for prolonged periods while the prisoner is in a standing position;
- whipping by plastic or rubber hose while forcing the prisoner through a suspended motor-car tyre (*dullab*);
- beating on the soles of the feet while the prisoner is strapped to a table (*fallaka*);
- burning with cigarette lighters and by applying petrol to parts of the body such as the toes which are then set alight;
- simulated executions;
- immersion to the point of near asphyxiation;
- use of electricity on sensitive parts of the body, particularly the genitals.[42]

In late 1979 Judy Feld Carr received a letter from Mordechai Ben-Porat, the head of the World Organization for Jews from Arab Counties about the Albert Shema family of Aleppo. Ben-Porat described the Shemas as "destitute." One of Albert Shema's sons had escaped to Israel in 1972, two daughters escaped shortly thereafter, and another son escaped in 1974. With each escape, the parents and six remaining children were punished, only making them more determined to get out as well. Family members made four more escape attempts during 1978 and 1979. Four times they ran, four times they were caught, and four times family members were imprisoned and tortured.

The last time they tried to make their getaway, the whole family ventured out and all of them, including the youngest, a nine–year–old boy, were caught and imprisoned for a whole month, while police seized their house and belongings and sold all their effects. When some of the members of the family were released in October of 1979, they came back to a house which had been stripped of everything they had in it. The three elder boys, who were detained for another month, were subjected to torture during all that time until one of them fell ill and had to be hospitalized; he has not recovered yet. Albert, the head of the family, is old and ailing and unable to do any work...the family has suffered and sacrificed a great deal—all for their desire to leave Syria and immigrate to Israel. They have shown courage and fortitude and now they are in trouble. It seems very

important to me that they should be helped out of their predicament.[43]

Judy immediately wrote to Albert Shema. She introduced herself as
a friend concerned for his "illness" and offered financial assistance
to help restart the family's business. The offer was accepted and she
sent a cheque for $500 from the Feld Fund.[44] In the next few
months, more cheques and, gradually, bits and pieces of coded information passed between Judy Feld Carr and the Shemas. She learned
that one of Albert's sons, Naim, was also ill and needed medical care
not available to him in Syria. Naim was suffering from the effects of
torture he had endured during his last imprisonment, most pressing
of which were epileptic-like seizures that medication could not control. Albert and Naim had requested humanitarian leave to seek
medical treatment in the United States, where Albert already had a
son. Syrian authorities demanded $10,000 as the price of compas-
sion for their release. Judy asked several donors for most of the
money, then used the Feld Fund for the rest.

She thought a deal had been struck, but in early January 1981,
Syrian authorities delivered only one passport. Only Albert Shema
would be permitted to leave. Much to the family's shock, Naim was
denied exit. Albert was forced to leave his son behind.

What had gone wrong? Were the Syrians bargaining that they
could squeeze another $10,000 out of foreign Jews for Naim? After
his arrival in New York, Albert Shema phoned Judy to thank her for
all her assistance. "God bless you. God will bless you to give you big
favours—we owe our lives to you."[45] But what would become of
Naim? In a subsequent letter, Albert Shema begged Judy to help get
his son out.

> Thank you and the Jewish community's members in Canada, you've
> saved me and now I'm out from Syria.
>
> But my wife and my six children are still in Aleppo, Syria.
>
> My son Naim is sick and needs medical curing and needs to see
> good Doctors out of Syria.
>
> As you know, he became sick when he was in Syrian jail in 1979
> after the arrest of the whole family when escaping to Turkey.[46]

Judy was uneasy about sending more money. Having been duped once by the Syrians, she wanted to be sure that this time they would deliver the exit visa. Judy advised Albert to seek medical care for himself in New York and have the doctor write a letter stating that he was too sick to travel home to Syria. Albert should then submit his passport, originally issued for only two months, to Syrian embassy officials in Washington for renewal.

In the middle of the process, to Judy's astonishment, the president of Israel's office approached her for assistance in dealing with the Shemas. Albert's son Kasem, who had escaped to Israel in 1974, was serving in the Israeli Air Force when his father managed to get out of Syria. Worried for his mother, Naim, and his other brothers, Kasem appealed to Yitzhak Navon, the president of Israel. The president was moved by a soldier's concern for family who had repeatedly suffered imprisonment and torture while trying to escape to Israel. He instructed a member of his staff to see what could be done on their behalf. She got in touch with an Israeli activist who told her about a woman in Canada who might be able to help. Navon's staffperson contacted Judy in the hope that she could "once more perform a miracle." Judy replied that she was very much aware of the family's plight and had already raised $10,000 "ransom" money, which "is how the father got out." She reassured the president's office that "if anyone else, [Kasem's] mother or brothers should be allowed to leave, I would raise the money in Canada, and send it to them. The problem is, of course, that the Syrians are not letting the Jews out at all."[47]

Judy knew that this last line was not quite the truth. Money had bought Albert Shema out of Syria. If she dangled more money in front of Syrian officials and maybe they would let Naim Shema out too. Judy instructed Naim to again apply to leave Syria for medical treatment. The dance of the dollars was repeated. The remaining Shemas in Syria, their business gone and assets depleted, borrowed what money they could to sustain themselves. Family members abroad sent what money they could to help keep the family afloat. Judy also sent money.

With each passing month, Naim's health deteriorated. His epileptic episodes became more frequent and more violent. His condition became so desperate that he was forced to seek hospital care. This was not easy for a Jew who had attempted escape four times and been imprisoned. Judy later learned that no civilian hospital would accept him. Naim was forced to seek care at a military hospital where he was given a bed but offered little treatment. A doctor who refused to take on Naim's case at least examined him, and verified the severity of his condition.

In May 1982, almost a year and a half after his father's departure, Naim was finally given an exit visa to receive medical treatment in New York. In a telephone conversation with Judy after his arrival, Naim told her about his repeated imprisonments, his isolation and daily beatings, his suspension inside a tire hung from the prison ceiling, and of the electrical prods used during torture sessions. He described the punishment inflicted on the entire family, including a nine-year-old child, of the bribes paid to regime officials to get him and his brothers out of prison, and of the ongoing harassment that the family still endured at the hands of the Muhabarat. Free of Syria, Naim was still not free of worry.[48] He begged Judy to understand how desperate the situation was for the remaining family members.

> I am telling you true things very true I want you to really believe my words I am one of the family I know everything they only think to go out they live by themselves they work that's right but a lot of money spending and nobody know We have to pay back the loans that we took three times suffering in the jail ten months giving a bribe the Arab people I am out with my brother and my older brother also they are waiting for me to send them money to be able to go out...I hope you can help us and take my letter with importance and thinking about us if we will be out in the future with God's help we will send you back every penny you help with We will never forget I am a member of the family and I know every very true things that are happening and now if you please can ask us any questions we will answer you I am thanking you a lot and hoping hearing from you soon.[49]

Judy offered what comfort she could. She dared not promise the release of his family. Perhaps Naim's mother might be allowed compassionate leave to take care of her sick husband and son. Perhaps one of the remaining brothers might also be allowed to leave for medical treatment. Perhaps. Everything was perhaps. In the meantime, Judy promised to continue sending financial support to the family in Syria.[50]

Through 1982 reports seeped out of a bloody confrontation between the Syrian military and the Muslim Brotherhood in and around the Brotherhood's stronghold of Hama, Syria's fourth-largest city, 120 miles north of Damascus. To put an end to the insurgency, the Syrian army bombarded the city for three days before beginning a house-to-house search for rebels. Word leaked out of an orgy of indiscriminate killing and a casualty list that topped twenty thousand before the army was satisfied that the Muslim Brotherhood had been broken.[51]

Jews knew that any setback for the Muslim Brotherhood and a firming-up of President Assad's power was better for them. Even so, the horror of Hama offered proof of how far this regime would go to retain power. Jews could only hope they would not be seen as a threat to the state and have the army turned loose on them.[52]

In the same year, Israel launched a massive attack across its northern border to dislodge the Palestine Liberation Organization and other anti-Israel forces active in southern Lebanon. Everyone assumed that Israeli forces would halt their advance after clearing Israel's enemies from a self-imposed security zone on the Lebanon side of the border. Instead, Defence Minister Ariel Sharon exceeded his cabinet authority and ordered Israeli forces farther into Lebanon, claiming as an excuse that Lebanese civil authority had ceased to function and the PLO and its allies had usurped the powers of the state. Israeli forces laid siege to Beirut, bombarding Palestinian strongholds.

The Syrians viewed Lebanon as less as a sovereign state than an adjunct territory in which Syrian power held sway. The Israeli invasion was a direct challenge to the Syrian regime, making a mockery of Syria's claims to be the stalwart of the anti-Israel crusade. In the first days of the attack, Israeli forces attacked Syrian ground-to-air missile emplacements in Lebanon. The Soviet Union warned Israel against any escalation of the conflict. The United States also advised Israel that there were limits to how far it was willing to tolerate Israeli actions before withdrawing its support. Israel's goals were limited; it wanted no confrontation with Syria, nor did it intend any long-term occupation of Lebanon. Nevertheless, tensions heightened between Israel and Syria. If President Assad did not respond, anti-Assad forces, including the bloodied Muslim Brotherhood, might view this as a sign of weakness and challenge him.

The Shemas were frantic, knowing that their family's history of escape attempts made them targets of Syrian government suspicion. Late in 1982, one of the Shema sons in Israel, Victor, phoned Judy. He begged her to finance a scheme he had come up with to smuggle himself back into Syria through Turkey to lead his family's escape. Judy would have none of it. It was a hare-brained scheme that would likely get Victor killed. She would not help him throw his life away.[53]

The notion of smuggling the remaining Shemas out of Syria percolated in Judy's mind. She knew the family was desperate, and that in the political turmoil of the day the Syrians were not going to grant the whole family permission to leave. Smuggling was a high-risk enterprise. If something went wrong in a purchase of freedom, money was lost. In smuggling, lives could be lost. She pleaded with Victor to be patient.

In the spring of 1983, Victor came up with a new plan. He had contacted a smuggler who was trustworthy. For an agreed price, the smuggler would guide the remaining members of the Shema family across the Syrian frontier. Once in Turkey, they would enter an underground railway that ended in Israel. But it would not be cheap. Victor needed money quickly to cement the deal.

Judy hesitated. Shema family members had already tried to escape across the border four times, only to be caught each time. Was it worth chancing another imprisonment and more torture? Yet the Shemas were willing to try again. Could she deny them this chance to reach freedom? Judy promised Victor that she would give him an answer soon. In the meantime, she made discreet inquiries through her trusted network of informants in the Syrian Jewish communities in New York and Israel. Had anyone used this particular smuggler? Was he reliable? If the family made it into Turkey, would the Israelis get them to Israel? Step-by-step, Judy Feld Carr entered the shadowy world of those who covertly moved people across Turkey's borders. She eventually contacted a member of the Jewish community in Turkey who transferred Syrian Jewish escapees from safe house to safe house. Word came back that Victor's smuggler had proven reliable in the past.

For the escape to work, Victor needed $5,000 in American dollars delivered to him in Israel quickly. The money was critical, and the arrangement hinged on Judy's participation. On the eve of the Sabbath, she made up her mind to supply the funds. She notified Victor Shema that she would be at the bank when it opened on Monday morning to withdraw the money and she would send it to him as soon as possible. Victor contacted the smuggler. In Syria, the Shemas were told when and where they would be picked up.

The timing was critical, but fate intervened—Judy's father died. From the time her parents had moved from Sudbury to Toronto, Judy and her father had formed a strong bond. She saw herself as cut from the same cloth as her father, who had taught her to paddle a canoe, hunt, drink, and curse. He was also a warm grandfather, and the family often spent Friday evenings and holidays together. In the spring of 1983, he developed heart trouble and was hospitalized with a coronary. Judy was shocked but not surprised when the hospital phoned at two o'clock on Sunday morning to inform her of his death.

Funeral arrangements became the priority. Jewish burials take place as soon as possible after death, most often the next day if it can be arranged. A service could be held at Beth Tzedec synagogue at ten the next morning, Monday. But through her grief, Judy was also working to another deadline. She knew that in Syria a family was depending on her. Any delay in getting the money together could compromise the Shemas' safety and cost them their only chance at freedom. Ten in the morning was too early. Could the funeral be any later in the day? Monday, April 18, was also Israel Independence Day, and the synagogue was being readied for a celebration. The last possible time to squeeze in a funeral was noon, no later. Judy agreed. Don Carr called a friend and business associate who was flying to Israel late Monday. Would he take a parcel with him to Israel? It contained money having to do with his wife's Syrian activities. The package would be picked up shortly after he arrived in Israel. Pleased to help, the friend would send a courier to collect the parcel late on Monday morning, before the family left for the funeral.[54]

Judy slept badly that night and was up early the next morning. She forced herself to type a letter to Victor Shema, to send along with the money, asking him to acknowledge receipt of the money, and give her a detailed account of the financial transactions, the escape process, including the safe house system in Turkey, and Victor's judgment on the reliability of the smuggler. "I ask this because I may use this for a few more people to escape."[55] In tears and dressed for her father's funeral, Judy set out for the bank. She was the first customer in the door when it opened at ten and she asked for $5,000 U.S. in cash. But the bank did not have that large an amount of American bills on hand. Would an American-dollar money order do? No. Could she wait for a delivery of American cash the bank expected later in the day? No. She pressed the teller on how she could get the money within the hour. After a quick telephone call, she rushed across town to another branch and collected some more American dollars. Still short of the $5,000, she bought the remaining American money at her own bank. She arrived home just ahead of the courier. She put the cash and note to Victor Shema into a manila envelope and handed it to the courier. Just as the family was about to get into the limousine to take them to the funeral, the telephone rang. The courier had delivered the package to the Toronto conduit. Judy quickly dispatched a telegram to Victor Shema in Israel. "Money from me for your mother's trip will be delivered shortly."

Judy remembers the shiva week well. The house was filled with those offering condolences. Prayers were recited morning and evening. But some of Judy's thoughts were elsewhere. All week long, as she waited for the telephone call, she privately agonized over whether she had done the right thing. On the last day of the shiva, the phone rang. As soon as she answered, the voice on the other end said, "The commodity is out." A mother and five of her children were free.[56]

CHAPTER SEVEN

Ransoming the Captives

JEWISH TRADITION holds that it is a holy act, a *mitzvah*, a commandment, to ransom the captive—*pidyon shvuyim*. But what does *pidyon shvuyim* mean in modern times? This is not the dark ages when hostages were ransomed out of bondage for gold. Or is it? Syrian officials dignified the process with passports, exit visas, round-trip airline tickets, and cash bonds against return, but the number of Jews that Judy Feld Carr was ransoming out of Syria by the early 1980s climbed into the hundreds and then into the thousands.

To accomplish this, Judy needed a trusted network of informants to provide reliable and up-to-date information about the people who wanted to leave Syria and about the Syrian gatekeepers—border guards, administrative officials, and Muhabarat agents. Over the years, she worked out codes for communicating with her contacts in Damascus and Aleppo and had collected a wealth of knowledge on life in the Jewish community. She expanded her list of informants by involving several well-connected and trusted Syrian Jewish businessmen who were permitted to travel abroad. She also cultivated ties to people in the Syrian Jewish Diaspora who had their own information pipelines into Syria. And she was often privy to information that Jewish organizations gathered from their own sources, including the diplomatic services of their respective home governments.

As Judy became expert on Syrian affairs, she herself became a valuable source of information. Even the Israelis grew to trust the accuracy and reliability of her information. The Israelis must have had reservations about this Canadian woman who was involved in dangerous Middle East intrigue: at the time, the Americans listed Syria as a state that supported international terrorism. But there was no arguing with the success she had in getting Jews out. The Israeli security and intelligence services co-operated with her, giving her guarded access to their connections, but she was not integrated into their networks. Judy Feld Carr was not willing to let the Israelis control her; they welcomed the information she provided but cautiously kept her at arm's length.

That suited her—Judy was not a team player. She remained something of a loner, at ease only with a few loyal supporters who were mainly occupied with fundraising. She was still chair of the Congress National Committee on Jews in Arab Lands, although her committee did not meet regularly. Few Congress insiders took her seriously. Many continued to see her as energetic but undisciplined, demanding, and needlessly secretive. Congress staff who dealt with her often found the experience exasperating, but most agreed that she was dedicated and knowledgeable. She was also married to an influential community power-broker.[1]

Now that she was deeply immersed in the commerce of rescue, the most important part of Judy's work became figuring out whom the Syrians might be willing to let go, for what price, and who had the final authority to close a deal. How much for a child? For a sickly old man? For a single young woman? For a whole family? If it was not possible to ransom specific Jews out of Syria in the legal market, there were other merchants—smugglers—who could be trusted to deliver the same merchandise for an agreed price.

The security of Judy Feld Carr's rescue attempts depended on maintaining secrecy and a low profile. But she also continued to be a vocal spokesperson for Syrian Jewry and critic of the Jewish community leadership. The cause of Soviet Jews, the "Jews of Silence," was a Jewish priority—what, she demanded at the Congress Plenary in Montreal, was being done about Syrian Jews, the "Jews of Despair"?

> Today, insofar as the organized Jewish Community is concerned, whether in Canada or across the world, the Syrian Jews are the forgotten Jews, and I and those few colleagues who continue the struggle

to make their plight known and to stimulate some overt action, have truly become the Jews of Despair.

The few Jews who manage to get free tell of the horrendous situation of "surviving" with armed Palestinians living next to them in the Jewish ghettos

- of being "protected" by a special group of police so that Jews will not be attacked by the Palestinians
- of having Muslim directors appointed by the government to supervise the Jewish day schools
- of not being allowed to travel to other cities without the permission of the secret police, the Muhabarat
- of having the term "Yahud Mussawi" ("Jewish Member of the Mosaic Faith") printed on their identification card which has normally no place for religion
- of the birth registration stating that a baby was born in the "Mussawi" quarter of the city
- of other restrictive laws, such as not being able to dispose of property unless they can prove that the money is used to purchase a replacement
- of property of families who escape being sequestered by the government
- of censorship of mail and telephone calls
- of frequent house-to-house searches and the military and security personnel who enter private homes with no warrant
- of arrests for trying to escape: the penalty—imprisonment with no trial, and torture by the horrendous methods which were described in the recent bulletin of Amnesty International on the treatment of prisoners in Syria.

Besides the restrictions specifically imposed on Jews, the Jewish community is affected by the general trends within the country. Individual civil liberties disappeared last year as government forces wreaked havoc upon the Muslim Brotherhood stronghold in Hama, Syria's fourth largest city, slaughtering and injuring thousands of residents.

Syrian Jews, Judy told Congress, were "sustained by two things— their religion and their hope." And what was that hope? It was the hope that they would not be abandoned by Jewry in the free world. It was "the hope of rescue and redemption."

She urged Jewish leaders to pressure the Canadian government and the international community to end their silence on Syrian Jews. They must intercede on behalf of Syrian Jews and agitate for their free emigration. "You must make Syrian Jewry, and indeed, the issue of Jews in all Arab countries part of the agenda of all Jewish and human rights organizations."[2] Congress delegates dutifully passed a resolution calling on Syria to live up to its commitments to the United Nations Declaration of Human Rights and allow Jews the freedom to emigrate. The resolution called on the World Jewish Congress to make Syrian Jewry "a priority item" and to "embark upon a program publicizing their plight" in the Jewish and world community.

The Congress motion recommended that Congress enlist a bipartisan group of Canadian parliamentarians into a Committee on Syrian Jewry along the lines of an already existing Committee on Soviet Jewry, which ensured that the issues of Soviet Jewry were on the agenda in official dealings between the Soviet Union and Canada. Judy Feld Carr knew that the level and intensity of contact between Syria and Canada did not match that between the Soviet Union and Canada, but she believed it was still worth the effort. A parliamentary committee on Syrian Jewry could press Syria on its treatment of Jews and give the Canadian Jewish community a stronger position with the government on the Syrian issue.[3]

Most External Affairs officials wanted no part of an intervention with Syria that might strain Canadian-Syrian relations without benefiting the Jews. They were determined to resist Jewish lobbying, but some influential MPs with large Jewish constituencies did succumb to Jewish community pressure. Shortly after the 1983 Congress Plenary Meetings, Judy Feld Carr met with Toronto MP Roland de Corneille who was a member of the governing Liberal Party representing a seat with many Jewish voters. Following her visit, de Corneille rose in the House of Commons to request that Canada take a more active role on behalf of Syrian Jewry, especially in pressing Syria to allow the free emigration of its Jews.[4]

External Affairs officials warned the minister, Allan MacEachen, against any precipitate involvement with Syria on the

146

issue of Jews. To bolster its case, the department again asked its embassy personnel to update Ottawa on the situation and provide information on specific cases of alleged Syrian persecution of Jews.[5] A member of the embassy staff in Beirut went to Damascus, where he found a Syria where fears of civil war and direct confrontation between Syria and Israel over Lebanon had subsided. He spoke to a number of contacts in friendly diplomatic missions and international agencies, and to Jewish informants in Damascus. The resulting dispatch denied that Jews in Syria were subject to any more immediate or harsh persecution than anyone else in the country. "Undoubtedly security police keep their eyes on the community, but no more than on other communities and their schools. (What your [Canadian Jewish] correspondents may not recognize is that Syria is a tightly controlled police state.)"

The Syrian Jewish community, according to embassy staff, was dominated by university-educated professionals who suffered no economic, religious, or educational disabilities. Travel abroad remained difficult for "complete families" but individuals were allowed to travel for business or medical treatment. In an odd twist of logic, the dispatch explained that, according to some Syrians, the travel restrictions were "more through preference than exclusion. Exit deposits and family travel constraints seem to be designed more to constrain exit of professional talent than Jews and the former serves as an emigration tax if the option of permanent departure is chosen." Many Syrians doubted the loyalty of Syrian Jews and suggested that Jews might be a fifth column for Israel. The dispatch concluded that the "community is thus very sensitive to vicissitudes of [the Arab-Israel] conflict and to unwelcome campaign directed on their behalf from abroad."[6]

Had anyone suggested to Judy Feld Carr or other activists that their efforts ran counter to the wishes, let alone the interests, of Syrian Jews, they would have responded with shocked disbelief. They knew that no Jewish spokesperson in his or her right mind would criticize Syrian treatment of Jews in public or even in a private discussion with outsiders. In a state where contact between a Syrian Jew and a foreigner was a reason for the police to bring the Jew in for questioning, the Jews understood that the only truly private thoughts were those that were never spoken.

No one knew this better than Rabbi Hamra, who was often called on to be a spokesman for his community. When the Canadian diplomat asked him for his assessment of the issues raised by Jewish activists, he responded that while he appreciated the concern of Canadian Jews, the attention was unsolicited and as "likely to harm as to help [the] lot of Syrian Jews."[7] Three years earlier, however, Rabbi Hamra had had an opportunity to let Judy Feld Carr know what he really thought. In 1980, he was given permission to travel to New York with his wife and one son. During their trip, the family secretly visited Judy in Toronto.

It was an emotional meeting. The man Judy welcomed at the airport was not at all the elderly rabbi in traditional dress that she was expecting. Rabbi Hamra was youthful, energetic, and very handsome in a casual, short-sleeved shirt. He and Judy had tears in their eyes when the rabbi startled her by giving her a hug. After eight years of guarded correspondence—in which every word was measured—they could speak to each other honestly and openly. He entreated Judy to understand that his public statements were scripted. In truth, he feared for the safety of Syrian Jews and begged her to do all she could to rescue them. The Syrian authorities would continue using him to mask the true situation of Jews, but he would covertly do all in his power to assist her.[8]

In light of this knowledge, Judy could not let the External Affairs' 1983 assessment of the state of Syrian Jewish affairs go unchallenged. A sometimes testy correspondence between her and External Affairs followed.[9] To keep one step ahead of her and her relentless crusade on behalf of Syrian Jews, Ottawa kept a closer watch on the issue of Syrian Jews than they might otherwise have done. But publicly the department promised little.[10]

Judy Feld Carr and her supporters wanted the government to openly affirm that Canada was willing to accept Syrian Jews as immigrants. She turned to the minister of Immigration, John Roberts, who, like his Conservative predecessor, Ron Atkey, represented a heavily Jewish riding in Toronto. In November, 1983, she told Roberts that the Canadian Jewish community would guarantee that any Jew admitted to Canada from Syria would not become a public charge. The minister's responded that "it has been a policy of long standing for Canada to assist oppressed minorities who manage to leave their own country and do not wish to return." Those with relatives in Canada, or for whom the Jewish community would provide settlement assistance, might well be admissible.

The minister had two "provisos." He cautioned that Canada was not a "transit country for the purposes of immigration elsewhere"—that is, Israel. Anyone approved for Canadian entry would have to "declare an intention to settle in Canada." Second, the minister asserted, "We cannot be a party to any processes related to clandestine departure from Syria or other forms of departure. Anyone who manages to leave, however, can be helped without regard to the manner of their departure." Expedited immigration processing for Canada could be handled either in Damascus by visiting Canadian diplomats or by Canadian officials at several points in Europe.[11] As of 1978, Canadian immigration policy had been changed to expand Canada's definition of legitimate refugees. Since Syrian Jews could claim a legitimate fear of persecution if they returned, they would be eligible for refugee status.[12]

Judy Feld Carr was delighted by the new co-operative spirit and met with Roberts. She asked that Syrian Jews be processed in Toronto, as had been done in the Dahab case. People who often had only twenty-four hours notice that they were being permitted to leave Syria might not be able to prearrange stopovers in Europe. Roberts said that he would "respond sympathetically on those occasions when a person has no other choice but to come directly to Canada without prior documentation." Since there was no direct air link between Syria and Canada, it might be possible to arrange for processing at the point of transfer. Canadian officials in Rome had processed Jews permitted to leave Ethiopia, and could do the same for Syrian Jews.[13] Roberts cautioned Judy that since Canada's ability to admit Syrian Jews rested on Syria's willingness to allow Jews to leave, publicizing Canada's readiness to work with the Jewish community in welcoming them could "have the potential of being counterproductive to the Syrian Jews we are trying to assist."[14]

In February 1984, Roberts delivered a talk on "Canadian Politics in the 21st Century" to the Men's Club at Beth Tzedec. Several questions from the audience pressed the minister on the issue of visas for Syrian Jews. Roberts repeatedly explained that Canada could not open Syria's doors—only Syria could do that—nor could he give any group blanket prior authorization to enter Canada. However, he confided that the government would not deny entry to any Syrian Jew who was in a position to come to Canada.[15]

On December 28, 1983, the Syrian Jewish community and its supporters were horrified by yet another brutal murder. Victor Abadi, a prominent Aleppo Jew, answered the phone in his office and heard a man's voice say, "Son of a bitch. Are you still in your office? Go home, see what happened to your wife and children." He rushed home to find his wife, Lillian, five months pregnant, and his two children, Joseph, seven, and Salica, three, dead on the living room floor. Lillian had been shot, her throat cut, and her breasts slashed. Her abdomen was slit open, exposing her fetus. On the floor beside her lay her two children, their lifeless bodies mutilated. As word of the brutal murders spread, fear gripped the Aleppo Jewish community. Several other prominent members of the Jewish community and a local Armenian merchant reported phone calls warning them, "You are next."[16]

Even by Syrian standards, the Aleppo murders were shocking. Israeli and international Jewish media gave the murders wide coverage. In Canada, an External Affairs official confided to Alan Rose of the Canadian Jewish Congress that:

> We have asked our Embassy in Beirut to provide us with further information about the circumstances of this crime. I am very anxious to learn whether this was essentially an isolated incident free of broad implications for the Jewish community, or something indicative of a change of atmosphere which could call for a re-evaluation of our assessment.[17]

American officials were concerned that the murders would unleash a Diaspora Jewish demand for the emigration of Jews from Syria.[18] George Gruen, director of Middle Eastern Affairs for the American Jewish Committee, wrote a long letter to the *Wall Street Journal* suggesting that these murders were an obvious next step in the wholesale abuse of Syrian Jews.

After the 1947 United Nations vote to partition Palestine and create the state of Israel, Arab rage was turned on the Syrian Jewish community of Aleppo. Jews were attacked and murdered, and their homes and businesses were looted and torched. The anti-Zionist rioters set fire to Aleppo's ancient synagogue and left it in ruins.

In 1971, Rubin and Judy Feld established a committee in support of Syrian Jews, the Canadian Committee for the Rescue of Jews in Arab Lands. Above is the group's first public demonstration, in Toronto City Hall Square in 1972.

The Feld's committee sent the first box of religious books and articles to Rabbi Ibrahim Hamra in Damascus in 1972. Judy Feld Carr continued to send these shipments over the next twenty years. Pictured here are Rubin Feld (left) and Rabbi Mitchell Serels with the first parcel.

Over the course her twenty-year campaign to free Syrian Jews, Judy Feld Carr used every available platform—from public demonstrations to the World Jewish Congress—to raise public awareness of their plight. (Above) Judy speaks out on behalf of Syrian Jews in North York, Ontario.

Simon Khabas was the first Syrian Jew that Judy Feld met. In 1974, after eight years of pleading, Syrian officials relented and allowed Simon, then seventeen, to seek medical treatment abroad for his congenital heart disease. Sick and missing his family, Simon (pictured right) met with Judy in Jerusalem. After Judy returned to Toronto, Simon underwent an operation in one last effort to save his life. He did not survive and died in Israel.

Syrian Jews did manage to secretly slip into Canada and visit Judy Feld Carr in Toronto. With the co-operation of Canadian officials, there was no record of these unauthorized side trips. Rabbi Hamra (pictured here with his wife and son, and Judy Feld Carr and Donald Carr) first came to Toronto in 1980 while on a trip to the Syrian community in New York.

PHOTO CREDIT: ORA BUCK

Rabbi Hamra left Syria at the end of 1993. He and his wife visited Judy Feld Carr and Donald Carr in Toronto, thirteen years after their first secret visit. When they left for Israel, Rabbi Hamra took with him the precious Damascus Keter, a fourteenth-century holy book that Judy helped to smuggle out of Syria. Rabbi Hamra, his wife, and the Damascus Keter now safely reside in Israel.

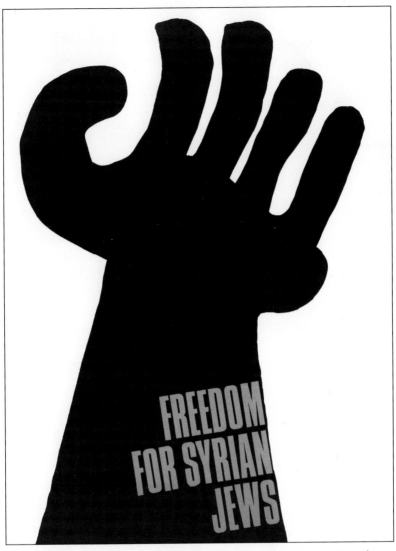

One of a series of posters produced by Israeli and American Jewish organizations in support of Syrian Jews.

Baksheesh—bribery—is rampant in Syria, and Jews were forced to pay for everything. Syrian officials were very creative in finding "special costs" involved in processing exit visas—even after the ban on foreign travel was lifted. Judy Feld Carr considered this money nothing short of ransom. Above is a receipt for money deposited in the Syrian central bank to cover some of these special costs.

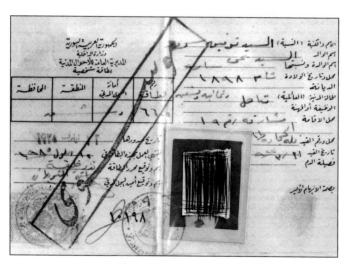

Syrian Jews were issued identity cards that bore a distinctive red stamp with the word *Mussawi* in Arabic. The term translates as "follower of Moses" and identifies the bearer as Jewish. The card pictured above shows the stamp, which is red on the original, enclosed in the rectangular box across the centre.

6

Selim and Elie Swed were imprisoned by the Muhabarat and suffered unspeakable treatment for almost five years. In a celebration of the family's survival and renewal, and of Judy Feld Carr's role in their survival, Judy and Selim are carried aloft on chairs in a dance at the wedding of Selim and Sarah Swed's daughter in Tel Aviv in June 1996.

When Jews arrived at the airport in New York, they often encountered a joyous melee as family, friends, and supporters gathered to welcome them. In the picture above, a relieved family celebrates the arrival of two children who had been forced to remain in Syria for four years after their parents had been allowed to leave.

Throughout most of her campaign to rescue the Jews of Syria, Judy
Feld Carr worked closely with the Israelis, particularly in her covert
work to ransom or smuggle Jews out. Although the relationship was
often difficult, the Israeli government itself sometimes turned to Judy
for help in getting Jews out of Syria, and Israel recognized Judy's
extraordinary contribution in the rescue of Syrian Jews. Here Judy is
greeted and congratulated by future Israeli Prime Minister Shimon
Peres in Jerusalem, April 1995.

Some suspect the members of Rifad Assad's [President Assad's brother's] defense companies carried out this atrocity as part of a plan to terrorize the Jewish community and enrich themselves. The special defense companies, whose ostensible mission is to protect President Assad, have in the past entered home and extorted money from wealthy Syrian families and engaged in numerous atrocities....

If the Syrian President truly wishes to show that he is responsive to humanitarian appeals, then let him once and for all stop holding the Jewish community hostage.[19]

However, a Canadian official in Damascus described as "ludicrous in the extreme" any notion that the government of Syria "condoned or tacitly inspired" the murders. He described Syrian authorities as "ultra-sensitive" to minority questions. A diplomatic dispatch out of Washington suggested that dissident elements might attack Jews as a way of undermining President Assad's credibility and proving to the world that minorities were unsafe in Syria. Foreign observers were convinced that the Syrians were making a genuine effort to solve the murders. The Syrians could just as easily have "fabricated evidence and executed [a] scapegoat," much as they had tried to do in the case of the four murdered Jewish women in 1975.[20] A Canadian dispatch described Victor Abadi as a prominent businessman subject to personal enmity. American, French, British, and Italian diplomats in Damascus were also inclined to dismiss the notion that the murders were part of a wholesale vendetta against Syrian Jews.[21]

Six months after the murders, a Canadian diplomat reported that, while the Abadi murders remained unsolved, the situation for Jews in Aleppo was very relaxed. Law and order in Aleppo had much improved, and the entire community wanted to put the matter behind them. According to the diplomat, the unanimous view of Western diplomatic community in Damascus was that Israel and the international Jewish community were exaggerating the whole issue to discredit Syria.[22]

In October 1984, an unverified report circulated that two Aleppo men had been found guilty and executed for committing a "long and lurid" list of crimes. In addition to murdering an Armenian priest, they had also confessed to the Abadi murders. Alan Rose relayed the same report, credited to a "usually reliable source in Europe," to a meeting of Canadian Jewish Congress officials. Judy thought that she would have heard if the report were true and double-checked with sources close to the Abadi family. Her sources confirmed that the report was a fabrication designed to take the heat off the Syrians.[23] A Canadian diplomat in Jordan further verified that the "story reported on execution of criminals involved in Aleppo murders is in all likelihood a government [of Syria] plant."[24] The murders remain unsolved.

In the Canadian House of Commons, an Opposition member asked why, in light of the Abadi murders, Canada was not making representations to Syria to allow the Jews to move to Israel, possibly to Canada, or the United States. The minister for External Affairs, obviously not briefed on the specifics of the murders, opted for vagueness:

> The Hon. Member knows that matters are within the internal management and prerogative of the government concerned, in this case the Government of Syria. It would be easy enough for us to make either public or private representations which might have a short-term effect in meeting the Hon. Member's request but not be very helpful in getting the job done in Syria. That is what we have to keep in mind.[25]

At the time of the murders, Edmond Antebi, brother of Lillian Abadi, was living in Brooklyn with his parents. They had come to the United States on short-term exit visas so that his ailing father could receive medical care. Once they were in the United States, they applied for political asylum. Their request was denied. Then Edmond heard the news about Lillian and her children. He was convinced that the murders were part of a government-sanctioned terror campaign against Syrian Jews. Edmond was frantic to avoid returning to Syria and desperate to get the rest of his family out. Reports that others in the Aleppo Jewish community had received threatening phone calls only increased Edmond's fears. Who would be next?

Edmond had not told his parents about the murders for fear that the shock would be too much for them. Where could he turn for help? In the midst of his despair he heard from Judy Feld Carr. When she heard about the murders from a contact in the New York Syrian community, Judy wrote to Edmond expressing her sympathies and offering him help. To reassure him that she was trustworthy, she suggested that he talk to her contact. "I am sure he will explain to you what I do."[26] Edmond called her. Would she bring the rest of his family out of Syria? Judy promised to help, and offered to see what she could be do about Edmond and his parents' status in the United States.

Judy had no direct connections with the American State Department, but she was the Canadian representative on the board of the New York-based Hebrew Immigrant Aid Service (HIAS). She asked HIAS to intercede with American authorities on Edmond's behalf. The director promised to do what he could. Less than four months later, the family was allowed to remain in the United States.[27]

Getting permission for Edmond and his parents to stay in the United States was one thing. Getting a family of five out of Syria was another. But by now, Judy was confident that it could be done—for the right price. She instructed Edmond to phone his family in Syria and coached him on exactly what to say. He told his family in Aleppo to go to the Muhabarat and apply for permission to visit the United States. They were not to worry about the cost.

Syrian authorities granted permission for the family to leave after only two months, and allowed them to leave as a complete unit. Why had the authorities agreed? One possibility is that they were glad to be rid of the family and, with them, some of the pressure to solve the Abadi murder case. The father's deteriorating health provided the Syrians with an excuse to grant them special permission to leave together. Assuming that Edmond's father knew about the death of his daughter and grandchildren, the Syrians were being asked to permit a heartbroken old man to see his remaining daughter and her family once again before he died.

In addition to the cost of round-trip airline tickets, the authorities demanded a payment of $5,000 for each adult and $2,000 for each child for passports and temporary exit visas. Judy promised money from the Feld Fund. She did not haggle. Never before had she had the opportunity to remove an entire family at one time, a family that had already suffered so much pain. This was not a time to negotiate. Judy told Edmond to notify his sister and her husband that the money coming, and sent Edmond two cheques.[28]

But the Feld Fund did not have nearly enough money to cover the airline tickets and the ransom. She had to find the money or the cheques would bounce. As luck would have it, the next Saturday was *Shabbat Zachor*. A number of Toronto synagogues would be making a special reference to the plight of Syrian Jews. For the first time, Judy decided to attach a direct fundraising plea to *Shabbat Zachor*.

With no time to lose, a few of Judy Feld Carr's supporters began phoning rabbis around Toronto. The rabbis were told only that the Feld Fund needed an immediate infusion of cash to rescue an endangered family. Could the rabbis dig into any discretionary funds they might have and make a contribution? Or would they make a direct appeal to their congregants for individual contributions? No donation was too small. Anyone wishing to make a personal contribution could deliver it to the Carr home.

A number of rabbis made the announcement, and the word spread. For the next three days, a parade of people arrived at Judy's door and pressed money into her hand. Sometimes people had to wait in line to have their donation accepted and recorded. Donations came by cheque and cash. Several large synagogues each contributed $1,000. Many individuals contributed $18 or multiples of eighteen, the numerical equivalent of *chai*, the Hebrew word for "life." But some people gave amounts as small as $2. Judy worried that some elderly pensioners might be taking food out of their own mouths in order to contribute, but out of respect for their dignity, no offering was refused. When the final tally was complete, the Feld Fund could more than cover the emergency.[29]

On April 2, 1984, only two weeks after Judy had sent Edmond the cheques, he called from New York in excitement. All five family members had just been issued Syrian passports and exit visas, and American visitors' visas. They were on their way.[30]

The family reunion in New York was bittersweet. Lillian's father and mother still didn't know that their daughter and grandchildren were dead. Every effort was made to keep the truth from them. The new arrivals brought gifts they said were from Lillian. The family even arranged for "letters from Lillian" to be mailed from Syria, and they made excuses to explain why they couldn't call Lillian in Aleppo. Everyone in the closely knit Syrian community of Brooklyn must have known of the murders, and it would have been hard to keep the truth from leaking out eventually. The secret was kept just long enough. In June, a little more than six months after one daughter and her children were murdered and a month after his other daughter and her family arrived from Syria, their father had a stroke. He died soon afterward.[31]

This was the first time Judy Feld Carr had brought a whole family out together. It was especially gratifying because hundreds of ordinary community members had responded with extraordinary generosity. A week after the family arrived in New York, Judy received a personal note of congratulation from Alan Rose for her part in the "rescue." "Indeed," he wrote, "it is *pituach nefesh* [affirming the primacy of human life] to rescue a Jewish family from Syria. Surely your endeavors must be unique and a source of enduring satisfaction!" She wished she could publicly share her satisfaction with all those who had reached into their pockets to make it happen. She couldn't. Not yet.[32]

Fundraising required constant effort, but getting the money into Syria could also be a problem. Sometimes a visitor to Syria or a Syrian returning home after a temporary visit abroad agreed to deliver American dollars. In the early 1980s, a Damascus Jew who was visiting New York on business phoned Judy. As much as he preferred not to go back, he told her, he could not abandon his family in Syria. He had heard talk that a woman in Canada had ways of getting people out of the country. Would she help the family escape?

Judy agreed to meet the businessman in New York. More often than not, Syrian Jewish men were unused to dealing with women as equals. It was difficult for them to accept advice, let alone orders, from a woman, even if it meant freedom for their families. This time, however, she had no sense that her advice was being discounted because she was a woman. He was eager to confide in her in a way she had rarely experienced with other Syrian men.

She took down all his information and carefully walked him through the Syrian exit system, advising him whom he would need to bribe, how best to do it, and what price would be fair. Money would not be a problem—he was a wealthy man. He had been secretly taking what money he could out of Syria as a protection against inflation in Syria and in the hope that he and his family would eventually be able to leave. He knew that everything left behind would be lost, and had opened an American-dollar account in a New York bank. Other wealthy Syrian Jews who had access to American dollars were doing the same thing.

There was an opportunity here. Judy asked if she could help him and others get their money out of Syria and, at the same time, reduce her problem of getting money in. The scheme was simple. If she needed $10,000, or the equivalent in Syrian lira, to be paid for a passport or exit visa, to post a bond, or for a "gift" to a Muhabarat agent, a wealthy Jewish businessman in Syria could put up the money. She would then deposit the equivalent amount of American dollars into his American bank account. The money would be available without worrying about getting it into Syria. The person who put up the money in Syria, as an apparent act of charity, would in reality have shifted $10,000 into an American bank account. As Judy and the businessman talked, the idea took shape. When they parted, she promised to work on getting his family out of Syria. She had the number of his New York bank account and a simple code that would enable her to signal him how much money she needed and whom to give it to. She had also acquired her first in a series of silent partners.[33]

The new plan hinged on Judy being able to communicate directly with people in Syria, preferably by telephone, even with the Muhabarat monitoring every long distance call. She found a solution with the help of Batya Barakat.

Batya was originally from Qamishli, a few miles from the Syrian border with Turkey. While she was still a girl, her family had moved to Aleppo so that she and her siblings could receive a Jewish education. Just after she turned eighteen, Batya married and she and her husband, Baruch Barakat, moved back to Qamishli. Shortly thereafter, the 1973 Israel-Arab War exploded. Batya remembers the war and the fear it created within the Jewish community. For six months the Jews of Qamishli were kept under virtual house arrest. No one was allowed in the street except small children who were granted a few hours outside to stock up on groceries. While the government claimed the restrictions were for the protection of the community, Jews regarded them as a punishment for the Israeli victory in the war and occupation of the Golan Heights. A sense of helplessness, fear, and anxiety gripped the small Jewish community.

The restrictions were eventually lifted, but for Batya, her husband, and their baby daughter, born in the shadow of the war, the experience was scarring. She and her husband had but one imperative—escape. Others in the community harboured the same dream, and in 1979, Batya, Baruch, and their now four children joined two other Jewish families—twenty-seven persons in all—in an escape attempt. Led by four well-paid and "honest" smugglers, the group drove to a spot an hour outside Qamishli, where they waited for nightfall and what they thought would be a six-hour overland trek through rugged terrain to the border. Just before they started out, all the children were given pills or wine to help them sleep or at least keep them quiet. Each adult carried a child.

About twenty minutes after the group started their night march toward the frontier and freedom, everything went wrong. A Muslim neighbour, who had pretended to help arrange the escape, is believed to have betrayed the group. The Muhabarat lay in wait. Headlights from trucks suddenly lit up the night, and without warning, the Muhabarat began shooting at the terrified band of Jews.[34]

> We fell to the ground and my four-year-old daughter started crying, stood up and started running, because she was frightened. All the children began to cry, and we were all calling out that they [the Muhabarat] should stop the shooting. But the shooting continued like rain over our heads. When my daughter was running, I got up from the ground to bring her back. The Muhabarat saw me by the lights of the cars and shot me.
>
> One shot hit my kidney and another hit my spine.

The instant I was shot, I could not move my legs and I was bleeding from my back. I fell on my daughter, and even the Muhabarat did not know who was hit—my daughter or I—because my daughter was covered with blood from my own bleeding.[35]

Batya was taken to a military hospital, where doctors gave her only few hours to live. When she did not die as expected, Batya—hooked up to intravenous tubes and given only minimal sedation to deal with her excruciating pain—was put in an ambulance and sent off on a long trip to hospital in Aleppo. From time to time during the nine-hour drive, the ambulance pulled into local hospitals for a change of intravenous. Otherwise, Batya remembers receiving no medical attention. She barely survived the trip, and Aleppo promised little relief. Doctors at the Aleppo hospital wanted no part of a Jewish woman who was shot trying to escape. Finally one doctor, a Jew, stepped forward to treat her.

Batya was released from hospital four weeks later. She suffered constant pain and could no longer move her lower body or control her bodily functions. A year later, on payment of a $10,000 deposit, she was granted permission to travel to Italy for medical treatment, accompanied by her elderly mother. In Rome, Batya contacted the Israeli embassy which helped her secretly go to Israel for sixteen months of further medical treatment, including three operations. For their own protection, not even her husband or family knew where she was.

The abortive escape meant prison for her husband and four small children. The children were released from prison only after the family obtained a court order. But the Muhabarat refused to release Baruch Barakat or the other adult men. They were held for a year in unspeakable conditions, repeatedly beaten and subjected to electric shocks. After his release, a desperate Baruch Barakat made yet another nighttime escape attempt. This time Batya's five brothers, her sister, and the sister's husband joined him and his four children. They again hiked overland toward the Turkish frontier under the cover of darkness. After they had travelled for five hours and were almost in sight of Turkey, the Syrian border police caught them. The Jews were forced to walk the five hours back. As they walked, the adults were beaten. The men, the youngest only thirteen, were imprisoned for another six months, first in Damascus and later in Aleppo, and tortured. Even the thirteen-year-old was not exempt. On several occasions, the boy was beaten until he passed out. A second brother was beaten so badly that his sight was permanently impaired.[36]

As soon as Israeli authorities learned that Baruch was back in prison, they whisked Batya out of Israel and into a hospital in New York. Baruch would pay the price if the Syrians were to learn Batya's whereabouts. Once she was out of Israel, Abe Dwek of the Committee for the Rescue of Syrian Jews, and the American Jewish Committee thought that publicizing Batya's plight might pressure the Syrian authorities to soften their treatment of Baruch. They told her story to the Jewish community and the American government. The U.S. State Department inquired about the condition of Batya's husband and children, so the Syrians would know that their actions were under scrutiny.[37]

Batya's private world was a difficult and lonely one. After yet another operation in New York, she went to hospital outpatient clinics several times a week for therapy. She was almost alone in a strange city, without friends, language skills, or resources. A Hassidic family took pity on the lonely wheelchair-bound woman they found crying in the hospital lobby on the Friday afternoon of her release and offered her the basement apartment in their house. What kept her going was the determination to be reunited with her husband and children.

When Baruch got out of prison, he applied for visas for himself and his four children to visit his wife in Brooklyn. After some negotiating, the Muhabarat agreed that if they paid $7,000, the family could leave. It was a king's ransom to a recently imprisoned man with no income.

Batya heard about Mrs. Judy from Abe Dwek and called her. Judy told her not to worry; whatever money was needed would be there. She arranged for an Aleppo businessman to deliver $7,000 to Baruch. At the last minute, however, the Muhabarat reneged on the deal and granted permission for Baruch to leave with only two of his four children. The oldest, seven, and the youngest, only three, would have to stay behind. The thought of leaving two children behind was devastating, but Baruch could not pass up a chance to take two children out of Syria. He agreed to the Muhabarat's terms. He placed one child in the care of Batya's sister in Aleppo and the other with her mother, now back in Qamishli, and then Baruch and his two middle children left for New York.[38]

Batya and Baruch had managed to get part of their family out of Syria, but their problems were far from over. Batya still lived with chronic pain. Doctors told her that additional surgery might ease her suffering, but it would not give her back control of her lower body.[39] Baruch was also a broken person; he had twice endured imprisonment and torture. They could never go back to Syria, but they would never give up hope of bringing out their remaining two children. Judy promised that she would not rest until the two children were reunited with their parents.

It was not clear who could negotiate on behalf of the children. The Muhabarat assured Batya's parents that, in principle, the children could leave. They identified problems to be resolved—signalling that there would be special costs. Before the children could travel abroad, their names had to be added to their parents' Syrian passports. Unfortunately, these passports had expired. Once the passports were renewed, the children could visit their mother. Batya and her husband sent the two expired Syrian passports to the Syrian embassy in Washington with appropriate documentation. Without explanation, the expired passports and accompanying documentation were returned unprocessed a few weeks later.[40] Judy thought she knew what had gone wrong. The Muhabarat would not approve the passport renewals for free. It was again time to begin the ritual dance of dollars.[41]

Batya thought that international expressions of concern might help her case and wrote to the secretary general of the United Nations, asking thim to intervene with the Syrians on her behalf. She received no reply. Her doctor wrote a letter to Syrian authorities explaining that Batya needed another life-threatening operation to ease her pain and that a reunion with her children "would be most advantageous in her endurance and healing." The Syrians remained unmoved.[42]

It would be ransom or nothing. Following Judy's instructions, Batya told her mother to go to Damascus once a week to plead with the Muhabarat for the release of the children. Batya's mother made the long bus trip to Damascus week after week. Each time she visited Muhabarat headquarters, gifts in hand, and each time pleaded that the children be allowed to visit their sick mother. At last, the Muhabarat set a price. The children could leave for $5,000 and their round-trip tickets. The grandmother could accompany the two grandchildren on their journey, but would have to leave her husband and children behind.

There were more complications. The American embassy in Damascus was hesitant to grant American visas to the children. HIAS stepped in to resolve the problem. The Muhabarat raised the agreed price by another $500. One of Judy's businessmen partners put up the money in return for an equal amount deposited in his New York account. The children and their grandmother were bumped from an Air France flight at the last minute, to a flight that transferred in Amman, Jordan. Would the Jordanians permit the transfer of an elderly Jewish woman and her two grandchildren?[43]

Everything went as planned. Batya's children and their grandmother flew out of Damascus on the appointed date, transferred without problem in Amman, and arrived in New York. Batya and Baruch were waiting at the airport as their children arrived. The six-year-old was shy; she had been only nine months old when Batya was shot. It would take her time to bond with a mother who had been never given up on reuniting her family.[44]

Judy Feld Carr usually kept at a distance from those she was trying to help. Rarely did anyone meet her, nor were they allowed to know anything more than was absolutely necessary about her or her work. Many did not even know her real name, referring to her as Mrs. Judy, and even addressing letters to her by that name.

But with Batya, Judy Feld Carr bent her rules. She allowed herself the luxury of getting to know Batya, and in truth she was in awe of her. Here was a woman who would never walk again, a woman battling chronic pain, who remained tenacious about getting her family out of Syria. During the time that it took to get them all out, Batya and Judy Feld Carr spoke often. In the process, Judy and Batya became close friends.

Would Batya do for others what she had done for her own family? A native Arabic speaker with a Syrian accent who spoke a more and more credible English as time passed, Batya gladly offered to assist Judy in any way possible. She soon became another of Judy's key informants. Calling herself Mrs. Gross, the name of a woman who lived in the apartment one flight above, Batya often phoned Syria, pretending to be a Syrian Jewish woman, now married to an American Jew, who was innocently calling home to family and friends. But each of her calls was in reality a carefully scripted conversation that passed on coded messages about when and how to negotiate a deal with the authorities, details of money transfers, and even plans for an overland escape. In addition to passing information to persons in Syria, "Mrs. Gross" gathered information, also in code, about what was happening in Syria. Sometimes Judy used Mrs. Gross to selectively feed the Muhabarat information or misinformation. Knowing that the Muhabarat were listening, Mrs. Gross learned to be just as measured in what she did not say as what she said.[45]

In the spring of 1984 Mrs. Gross learned about Ava Tzion Lalo. The Tzion Lalo family was originally from Qamishli. In the mid-1980s, they had moved to Aleppo, where their seven-year-old daughter Ava was diagnosed with a congenital heart disease requiring medical care that was not available there. The Muhabarat had told the family that Ava could go abroad for medical treatment, but the Tzion Lalos were never able to raise the amount of money they demanded. As the child's condition worsened, the family became more despondent.

Batya turned to Judy Feld Carr for help. Judy agreed to put up the ransom money, but Ava did not have much time. Judy moved the negotiations along as fast as she could, but despite the girl's worsening condition, the Syrians were in no hurry to deliver an exit visa. The authorities took almost a year before allowing Ava out.

This time Judy demanded a guarantee that the Syrians would issue two exit visas—an ill seven-year-old could not travel alone. For $4,000, the Syrians issued two passports—one for Ava and the second for Ava's unmarried twenty-year-old sister, Suad. Judy also asked that Ava and Suad be allowed to travel to Turkey overland by bus rather than by airplane.[46] In February 1985, Suad was called to the Muhabarat offices, where she picked up two passports stamped with appropriate exit visas. Without wasting another moment, the now desperately ill Ava and Suad were on a bus to Turkey.[47]

Why did Judy insist that they travel by bus? She was worried that an airline might not allow the sick child to board the airplane unaccompanied, and didn't trust the Syrian officials to honour Suad's passport. Bus transportation was a safer bet. Moreover, an overseas flight would require a stopover in Europe, and a lengthy flight would overtax Ava's heart. The bus trip was much shorter. Judy arranged for the two girls to be met on the Turkish side of the border, and transferred to a more comfortable inter-city taxi for the long ride to Istanbul. Once the girls were in Istanbul, Israeli officials took them to Israel for medical help and a new life.[48]

When Ava arrived in Israel, she was rushed to the Hadassah Hospital in Jerusalem and admitted under an assumed name. "Her skin was blue from the heart disease and the doctors determined there was no choice but to operate on her to save her life." It was too late. Ava's heart had been severely weakened by years of disease. She never recovered from open-heart surgery. Three days after surgery, she developed breathing difficulties and died as a medical team worked to save her.[49] For a second time, Judy Feld Carr felt as if she had lost a child.

> When I heard the news the other day, I cannot tell you how I felt. The doctors were sure this little girl had a chance, and it took me over a year to get her out either with her mother or older sister. The Syrians would not let the mother go, so for extra money I got instead her twenty-year-old sister. Now I am trying to get the terrible news to her parents in Syria so they can sit shiva. Unfortunately, I cannot call or put it in a letter because of where Ava died. I even bought dolls and all kinds of toys to bring her when I go to Israel.[50]

Shortly after Ava's death, Judy Feld Carr wrote to Rabbi Farhi in Aleppo. Without telling him where the child had died, Judy asked the rabbi to let Ava's parents know of her death so they could sit shiva for her. The only consolation she could offer the grieving parents was "that everything that anyone could do was tried in order to save her life."[51] Saddened as she was by Ava's death, Judy had the satisfaction of knowing that Suad had found a new life in Israel.

CHAPTER EIGHT

So They Can Marry

I N FEBRUARY 1985, Judy Feld Carr was invited to Ottawa by the Middle East Bureau of External Affairs. Department officials had dealt with Judy on the issues of Syrian Jewry for many years. Some viewed her as an insistent and outspoken propagandist for Israel, but she spoke with the authority of the Canadian Jewish Congress and she made it her business to know External Affairs' political masters. The department wanted to know what she was up to. If they met with her, officials would also be able to tell anyone who was concerned about Jews in Syria that they had conferred with Mrs. Carr on the issue.

When they invited her to Ottawa, Judy assumed that External Affairs officials wanted a briefing from her on Syrian Jews, a subject she believed they knew little about.[1] She was wrong. In preparation for her visit, officials in Ottawa had requested an updated report on the situation from the embassy in Amman, Jordan. (After the outbreak of the civil war in Lebanon and the 1982 Israeli invasion, the Canadian embassy in Beirut was closed and its duties, including responsibility for Canadian interests in Syria, were transferred to the Canadian embassy in Amman.)

An embassy dispatch to Ottawa restated External Affairs' standard line—conditions affecting Jews in Syria had "greatly eased over the past several years." But beneath the surface, this dispatch was more guarded about the status of Syrian Jews than earlier cables had been. The community was "hostage to continuing conflict between

Syria and Israel." Syrians still regarded Jews as a people apart, subject to restrictions, harassment, and controls, particularly on travel. "In effect, abuse of freedom to travel freely and emigrate overshadows many rights and privileges this community enjoys." The Canadian diplomat speculated that only half of all Syrian Jews would leave if the opportunity presented itself. And he accepted the version of their story that Rabbi Hamra and other Syrian Jews told to strangers, reporting that Jews were unlikely to go "to Israel of which they have generally poor opinion."

The Jews of Damascus, the dispatch continued, had two private Jewish schools funded largely by money from Jewish communities in France and the United States. Half the students in one of the schools were Palestinians, reflecting the influx of Palestinians into the Damascus Jewish quarters. What the report did not say was that placing Palestinian children into Jewish schools was both a way for Syrian authorities to dilute the Jewish content of school programs and a back-door tax on Jews abroad for the education of Palestinian children. Jews were free to cash foreign cheques "no questions asked while veritable inquisition usually attends attempts by Christians to do so." The diplomat offered no explanation for this Jewish privilege, although a community largely engaged in commerce would be expected to require the cashing of foreign cheques. Allowing Jews to cash cheques from family abroad brought foreign capital into Syria, and often this money flowed into the pockets of Syrian officials. And while others, including Christians in Syria, had to pay a "symbolic" exit fee, the few Jews allowed to travel abroad had to put up a large bond of about $4,000 "depending on perceived worth of applicant." Jews who applied to travel abroad had to deal with "military rather than civilian authorities" for passports and exit visas.

The Canadian official reported that the prohibition against emigration was most problematic for unmarried Jewish women. After the Syrian government had allowed the fourteen unmarried Jewish women to leave in 1977, ostensibly to proxy husbands awaiting them in the United States, they allowed a few additional single women out each year under similar terms. This did not solve the problem for the numerous unmarried Jewish women who wanted to emigrate to marry, there being a shortfall of young men (suggesting that larger [number of Syrian Jewish men] than we were aware of may be successful in fleeing the country or remaining abroad when on travel). However, we understand that 10 Jewish girls were recently refused permission to emigrate to France for this purpose, the Syrian authorities having decreed that girls must be at least 23 years old (and thus deemed to have exhausted their search for spouse locally) and have received a specific marriage proposal. Inter-marriage is socially unacceptable to the Syrian Jewish community, and need of Jewish spouses abroad is recognized by the regime.[2]

Judy Feld Carr painted a picture of Syrian Jewish life that was sharply at odds with the diplomatic assessment. She spoke of anti-semitism being endemic to Syria and "torture, degradation, humilia-tion," and "fear" being the lot of Syrian Jews. She characterized the refusal of Syria to permit Jewish emigration as no more a minor restriction than keeping people in chains is a minor inconvenience. Contradicting the Amman dispatch, she argued that almost every Jew would embrace the chance to leave Syria. Many, she insisted, would go to Israel. The most desperate, knowing full well the punishment for illegal escape, were already risking everything on such attempts.

Judy asked External Affairs officials to prevail on the Syrian government to allow approximately fifteen unmarried Syrian Jewish women humanitarian leave to come to Canada "so they can marry." The officials remained noncommittal, only agreeing to consider the plan and accept a list of Syrian Jewish women ready to come to Canada.[3]

A week later, Judy sent External Affairs a list of single Jewish women supplied by her Syrian Jewish contacts. She promised that "if these women are permitted to come to Canada, the Canadian Jewish Community will undertake as they have done in the past, that in no way would they be a public charge."[4] But for Canadian authorities, the issue was not whether Canada would accept the women as immigrants, but whether Syria would allow unmarried Jewish women to leave, and how Syria would respond to Canadian officials actively promoting this scheme.

A little over a month after Judy sent the list, an Israeli official cautioned a Canadian diplomat against moving ahead on any scheme regarding unmarried Syrian women. During a recent visit to Syria, French President François Mitterand had broached with President Assad the possible emigration of single Jewish women to France. Mitterand had given the Syrians a list of unmarried women for whom French Jewish husbands were waiting. Until the Syrians responded to the French initiative, Canada was warned, any approach on the same issue could be dangerous for the women. What if a woman turned out to be on both the French and Canadian lists? How could she have a fiancé in both Canada and France? Without clearing the names on the Canadian list with the French, any Canadian initiative was both premature and risky.

Unaware that External Affairs had been warned off by the Israeli, Judy remained optimistic. As soon as the Canadian government agreed to approach the Syrians, she would arrange for Rabbi Hamra to act as intermediary. He would distribute Canadian immigration forms to the women on the list, collect the completed forms, and return them to Canadian officials. Canada could then appeal to the Syrian government on behalf of those who had indicated they wished to immigrate and marry in Canada.[5]

But Canada wasn't prepared to approach Syria. External Affairs advised Judy of the warning from the Israeli without telling her what country had made the earlier proposal. Canada was not prepared to undermine the other initiative, she was told, so the plan was on hold. Judy was furious. Without consulting her, the Israelis had ruined everything. Whoever had advised the Canadians clearly didn't know what he was talking about. Judy complained to the Israelis that they had sabotaged her efforts and demanded that they clean up the mess. The Israelis protested that they had only cautioned Canada to co-ordinate the Canadian list with the French list so that representations were not made on behalf of the same women by two different countries. Nonetheless, Judy demanded that the Israelis give the Canadians some sort of "a green light immediately."[6]

Trying to undo the damage was like trying to unscramble an egg. Everybody was sorry, but nobody was prepared to take responsibility and intercede with the Canadian government. The Israeli Foreign

Office and the Israeli embassy were hesitant about encouraging Canada to bring Syrian Jewish women to Canada. Why would Canada want to be seen acting as an agent of Israel? Israel did not want to be held responsible for persuading Canadians to go ahead if the scheme backfired.[7]

Judy had no choice but to try to get the proposal back on the rails herself. She met with External Affairs and Immigration officials in Ottawa again at the end of April 1985, accompanied by the head of the Jewish Immigrant Aid Service in Canada. She tried to breathe new life into the project by arguing that it be regarded as a Canadian humanitarian effort. No country, she insisted, should have a veto power over Canada's foreign policy.

Canadian officials had always had reservations about her proposal; nothing they heard from Judy now changed their minds. External Affairs hinted that "other things are going on" with regard to unmarried Jewish women in Syria and that until the issue was clear, External Affairs would keep "it under review."[8] In any event, the Islamic observance of Ramadan was in the offing, and nothing would get underway during the holy month. Everything was on hold.[9]

Judy was determined to resuscitate her scheme. In the late spring of 1985, she tried to launch a letter-writing campaign by enlisting the support of Jewish campus organizations. But the end of the school year was not a good time to start a student-based campaign, so the initiative failed. Judy wrote personal letters to political leaders decrying Canada's failure to respond to a humanitarian need. But accusing Canadian politicians of being deaf to humanitarian appeals when the country had just absorbed an estimated 100,000 Vietnamese refugees was unreasonable. She received polite but noncommittal responses.[10]

When Judy visited Israel in July 1985, she approached key nongovernmental spokespersons for help, including the head of the Israeli Council for the Rescue of Jews in Arab Lands. He agreed to write to the Israeli Foreign Office on her behalf. She also spoke to influential officials in Israeli government ministries and the Jewish Agency. They recognized the importance of what she wanted to do, but they were not willing to approach Canadian officials and ask them to reconsider the scheme. Nobody wanted to take responsibility for the mess, and there was no way to correct the error without admitting that one had had been made.[11]

Judy still refused to concede defeat and continued to lobby Canadian officials. When a personnel shuffle in External Affairs brought new faces into the Middle East Bureau, she took this as another opportunity to impress on them the urgency of approaching the Syrians on behalf of the fifteen women. She had no luck. Although Judy didn't know it, Canada had learned in the meantime that the Syrians were refusing to act on the list of unmarried Jewish women that Mitterand had given Assad. There was no reason to believe a Canadian initiative would fare any better.[12]

As an alternative, External Affairs officials offered to present four or five cases from the list of fifteen girls to the Syrians as a routine immigration matter. All the women had to do was fill out Canadian immigration forms, and Canada would take their cases to the Syrians. This approach was especially promising because Canada was preparing to open an embassy in Damascus. As a gesture of good will to the new embassy, the Syrians might be willing to co-operate.

After several months, the newly appointed ambassador in Damascus still had not presented his credentials. Embassy staff assured Judy that they were ready to proceed "in a low-key, business-like manner" in the hope that "appropriate circumstances should soon exist for the sort of quiet approach which seems to offer the best chance of achieving something useful." However, the director general of External Affairs Middle East Bureau did not share that hope.

> All indications are that we should not count too much on favourable results, but if progress proves possible, we shall carry on accordingly. I fear that there will be no results to report in the immediate future, but if something is ultimately achieved, without complicating life for other members of the [Jewish] community in Syria, that will be a source of modest satisfaction.[13]

Judy remained convinced that with Rabbi Hamra's co-operation, her scheme to bring out all fifteen women at the same time would work. As the months dragged by, the department continued to express reservations about proceeding with her plan. They knew that Judy trusted Rabbi Hamra, but in the past the rabbi had repeatedly reassured diplomats that Syrian Jews did not face any persecution. Canadian officials had incorporated his reassurances in their dispatches to Ottawa. Why would they ask him to help the women leave Syria when he had told Canadian officials that there were no problems? The department thought that it made much more sense to bring the women to Canada through an open process. Why not "test the waters" with a few straightforward immigration cases? The paperwork could be handled by the new embassy in Damascus.[14]

An exasperated Judy Feld Carr fired off a letter to External Affairs.

> It is axiomatic that people living under oppression and in constant fear of their wellbeing will express different views from those who are free and beyond the reach of the notorious Syrian Police—the Muhabarat. These who are free will give you quite a different story from those evidently being listened to by your Department in Syria.
>
> And if there is any improvement in the lot of Syrian Jews, why do so many try to escape, and expose themselves to imprisonment and torture if caught?
>
> Putting it bluntly, neither I nor anyone conversant with members of the Syrian Jewish community accept what you put forward, either as statements of fact or of opinion, concerning the question of the effect of representations to the Syrian Government or the conditions in which people are living there.
>
> So, too, we do not accept as valid the fears expressed by you about what would happen to others in the Syrian Jewish community if the activities which we have been urging and which were originally accepted by your Department were to be undertaken. I am afraid that too often in the past have these "fears" been used by too many people as an excuse for not mounting appropriate efforts on humanitarian grounds to rescue other hapless individuals, in different countries and at different times. Tragically, hindsight has always proven these people to have been wrong.[15]

A sympathetic MP, Robert Kaplan, inquired about the government's efforts on behalf of the Syrian women. The embassy replied that they would help any of the women who wanted to come to Canada, but "to date, none of those concerned has been in contact, either directly or indirectly, with the Canadian embassy in Damascus to explore the possibility."[16]

Again Judy was outraged. External Affairs just didn't get it. How, she demanded, could the government give the impression that a Syrian Jewish woman could enter the Canadian embassy and apply to immigrate to Canada without putting herself at grave risk? If External Affairs truly believed that to be true, it was small wonder that nothing was happening. But as weeks turned into months, External Affairs remained determined to proceed at its own pace. The project was going nowhere.[17]

In March 1986, another turnover in External Affairs staff brought in a new director general of the Middle East Bureau, Percy Sherwood. He was no doubt aware of the often stormy relations between his predecessors and Judy Feld Carr, but Sherwood decided to work with Judy to breathe new life into her moribund proposal. Shortly after assuming his new duties, Sherwood called her from Ottawa and they talked about the problems of bringing the unmarried Jewish women to Canada. Judy proposed that they meet at his convenience to explore the matter further. Rather than summoning her to a formal meeting in Ottawa, Sherwood suggested that they talk over lunch when he came to Toronto. Judy invited him to her home.[18]

Ten days later, Judy Feld Carr, Percy Sherwood, and Herb Abrams, director of the Jewish Immigrant Aid Service, gathered over a light lunch in Judy's dining room. They chatted informally, and only at the end of the meal did they turn to the issue of Syrian Jews. Sherwood outlined efforts by the newly opened Canadian embassy in Damascus to make connections in the Jewish community. American embassy staff had been co-operative in sharing information and assisting the newly arrived Canadians to find and protect the confidentiality of Jewish contacts. He told Judy that there might be some movement on the immigration of the Syrian women. A Canadian diplomat had approached a Syrian Foreign Office official about granting the women leave to marry husbands abroad. The Canadian was reassured that there was no prohibition against such emigration, although each case would be reviewed on its merits. The Canadians were now considering how to proceed with the paperwork necessary to bring the women on Judy Feld Carr's list to Canada.

Judy could hardly believe her ears, but she still foresaw one big problem. If the women were seen entering the embassy offices, located in the Damascus Sheraton Hotel, there could be trouble. She again suggested asking Rabbi Hamra to act as an intermediary. Sherwood was interested in the idea. He hadn't known that Rabbi Hamra had passed along Canadian immigration materials on at least one previous occasion, in the case of Rabbi Dahab's daughter Olga. Sherwood promised to look into her plan and get back to her.

As the meeting drew to a close, Sherwood asked Judy a question she rarely asked herself. Why was she so involved with the cause of Syrian Jews? Judy fumbled for an answer. She had trouble articulating what was for her emotional—something less reasoned than understood. It had to do with history, she explained. Jews all over the world—including those in Syria—are bound by a common historical thread. To deny the plight of Syrian Jews would be to deny that bond, to deny her own past and her people's past. That is why she could not turn her back on the women on her list. Leaving Syria was their only chance for a full life. She wanted to give them that chance.[19]

Sherwood had promised to get the project moving, but every step took time. While Judy waited for a breakthrough in Ottawa, she succeeded in buying a number of the women out of Syria. None of them came to Canada. She was increasingly frustrated with a process that was expensive and cumbersome. The Canadian initiative to remove fifteen women at one time would set a precedent for a new, legal, and less expensive route to get Jews out. Hoping that External Affairs could still deliver, Judy occasionally updated the list, removing the names of those who were no longer in Syria and replacing them with others who were just as eager to leave for Canada.[20]

A plan to process the Canadian immigration applications slowly took shape. Ottawa agreed that Rabbi Hamra should act as the go-between. The embassy in Damascus would protect the rabbi by inviting Syrian religious leaders of all faiths—Muslim, Christian, and Jewish—to visit, a routine step for newly established diplomatic missions.[21]

The time between the distribution of the Canadian immigration applications to the fifteen women, the return of the papers to the embassy, and the appeal to Syrian authorities had to be kept as short as possible. All the players had to be in place at the same time. Throughout the summer of 1986, this proved no easy task. First, the Canadian ambassador was on vacation. Then Sherwood went on vacation. And Judy spent much of that autumn in Israel.[22]

In late September, Judy and Herb Abrams went to Ottawa at Sherwood's request. Twenty months after she had first been assured that the Canadian government was going to seriously consider her proposal, everyone was still arguing over process. She again explained step by step her plan to get the immigration applications filled out, return the papers to the embassy, and approach the Syrians on behalf of the women. She again explained why Rabbi Hamra, rather than a local Jewish businessman recommended by the American embassy, should be entrusted with contacting the women. The government officials questioned everything she said. She answered all their concerns but had to admit that there was no guarantee that the Syrians would let the women leave. Judy again reassured the officials that all the expenses for tickets, passports, and settling the women in Canada, as well as any "special costs," would be assumed by the Canadian Jewish community.

The officials were also concerned about security. As if Judy didn't already know it, they reminded her that the Syrians were watching the embassy. How could Rabbi Hamra's safety be assured? In Syria, Judy responded, nobody's safety could be assured. Rabbi Hamra knew what he was doing. The embassy was supplying him with a cover; as spokesperson for the Jewish community of Damascus, he was visiting the embassy with other religious leaders.

Sherwood asked for a photograph of Rabbi Hamra to give to the embassy. Judy had one with her, taken during his secret visit to her home several years earlier. So that the rabbi would not be further compromised if the photograph fell into the wrong hands, she carefully snipped herself and her husband out of the picture.

This would be the perfect time to invite the rabbi to the embassy and start the immigration process moving. It would soon be the Jewish High Holy Days, and the rabbi and the women would be in synagogue. Even though Muhabarat agents would also be in synagogue, the High Holy Days presented a golden opportunity for Rabbi Hamra to distribute and collect the applications. Embassy staff should act quickly if they wanted the rabbi to have the necessary documents for distribution.[24]

A week after the Ottawa meeting, Rabbi Hamra visited the Canadian embassy. There was, however, an unexpected communication problem. The rabbi spoke almost no English, and his French left much to be desired. The Canadians spoke little Arabic. The embassy hired Arabic speakers locally, and officials were concerned that if they relied on them, there might be a security problem. The only solution was to have the rabbi return to the embassy a few days later with his wife, who spoke French. They did so, and details for filling out the immigration papers and returning them to the embassy were carefully worked out.

Almost two years after Judy had first presented her plan to External Affairs, everything seemed to finally be falling into place. Rabbi Hamra arranged for the women on the list to fill out the necessary immigration papers. In anticipation of quick Syrian approval for their departure, Canadian Immigration authorities agreed to authorize "expeditious" entry of the women to Canada on temporary permits, pending a medical examination on arrival in Toronto. After passing the medical, the women would be granted final approval as immigrants to Canada.[24]

But two events, hard on the heels of each other, threw a monkey wrench into the works. One was a botched escape attempt in late September 1986. Judy was not involved in the attempt by two families from Aleppo, who were betrayed to Syrian authorities by their smuggler just as they were about to cross the border into Turkey. The Jews were found to be carrying a large quantity of cash equivalent to $12,000. Apprehended with so much money, the families were charged under a recent law dictating a fifteen-year prison sentence for those found guilty of smuggling illegal contraband, including cash, out of the country.

News of the failed escape alarmed the Syrian Jewish community. There was an "apparent toughening of the Syrian position against the departure of Syrian Jews," and the order of the day was to lie low. Rabbi Hamra, cautious about being seen dealing with the Canadians on anything that smacked of immigration, wisely kept his distance. He held on to the completed Canadian forms he had retrieved from the fifteen unmarried women and everything was again put on hold.[25]

The second event that damaged the immigration plan took place in London in late October 1986. A British court found a Jordanian, reportedly working for the Syrian secret service, guilty of attempting to smuggle a bomb on board an Israeli airliner at Heathrow Airport. The British broke off diplomatic relations with Syria. Canada quickly recalled its ambassador to Ottawa "for consultations." The Canadian Jewish Congress applauded the move as a signal that Canada would not sanction normal relations with any state that abetted the murder of innocents or sheltered terrorists. The United States also withdrew its ambassador, and several other Western states followed suit or sent diplomatic signals of displeasure to Damascus.[26]

Syrian Jews pushed further into the shadows, hoping to remain invisible until the crisis blew over. Whatever protection the presence of a Western foreign diplomatic corps in Damascus had afforded them had been weakened by the withdrawal of several Western ambassadors and the scaling-down of diplomatic contacts by others.[27]

Scrambling to safeguard her project, Judy suggested that Syria might approve such a high-profile humanitarian gesture in order to avoid diplomatic purgatory. The Canadian ambassador was gone, but couldn't someone among the remaining embassy staff broach this with the Syrians? External Affairs told her that the ambassador was the only Canadian diplomat with the connections and the diplomatic clout necessary to approach the Syrian Foreign Office on the immigration scheme. Judy was invited to talk to the recalled ambassador in Ottawa. He reaffirmed his commitment to the project and said that once he was back in Damascus, he expected Syrian officials to facilitate the women's departure.

Unknown to Judy or Canadian embassy staff, while the Canadian ambassador was in Ottawa, the Muhabarat questioned Rabbi Hamra about his relationship with "Mrs. Judy." Unsure how much they knew about his dealings with her and the Canadian embassy, he stuck to his previous line. He had no contact with Mrs. Judy other than to arrange for the parcels of religious items and money she sent to assist the community—all gifts that he duly reported to the Muhabarat. Was the interrogation a warning that they knew of his involvement with Mrs. Judy or Canadian officials? Rabbi Hamra was unsure, but the Muhabarat succeeded in shaking him up.[29]

Rabbi Hamra kept his distance from the embassy. In mid-December, while the ambassador was still in Ottawa, the embassy invited visitors, including the rabbi, for pre-Christmas festivities. Rabbi Hamra felt that under these conditions the coast was clear enough to deliver the documents. On December 18, 1986, External Affairs informed Judy that embassy staff now had the immigration applications and they were being processed. The embassy prepared to interview each applicant to verify that she was truly ready to leave for Canada if Syrian authorities gave their approval. To ensure the women's safety, embassy officials arranged to meet each of them discreetly, after regular business hours and not in the embassy's offices but elsewhere in the hotel where the embassy was located. There would be nothing unusual in finding Western diplomats gathering informally there in the evening. The presence of a well-dressed young woman with a companion, an older chaperone, would hardly be noticed amid all the comings and goings in a busy lobby. In this way, officials interviewed five or six of the women and determined that they should be granted Canadian entry.

The process ran into another snag. A Syrian Jewish family, including a woman on Judy's list, made an escape attempt. They were apprehended and imprisoned. The embassy was concerned that while she was under interrogation, the young woman might expose the secret Canadian immigration plan. They discontinued the interviews. The arrest did not end up implicating the other women on the list or compromising Canadian officials, but no one could any longer be certain what the Muhabarat knew.[29]

The women that Canada had secretly interviewed and approved for entry into Canada could not leave without Syrian approval, and only the Canadian ambassador could approach Syrian officials on the matter. The process could not move forward until his return. If Syria agreed to Canada's immigration requests on behalf of the women, those who had already been through the Canadian interview could apply to Syrian authorities for exit visas.[30]

Early in 1987, the Canadian ambassador returned to his post in Damascus, the first from the West to do so. In March, the ambassador was finally able to arrange a meeting with the Syrian vice-president and the foreign minister, during which he intended to raise the issue of the Jewish women. He knew the men well and was looking forward to the meetings as an opportunity to smooth over Canadian-Syrian relations. He met first with the vice-president and later with the foreign minister in their respective offices. The reception was cool. When he broached the topic of the unmarried Jewish women, the response was even cooler. The ambassador explained that there were men in Canada ready to marry the women. As a humanitarian gesture, would Syria consider allowing some Syrian Jewish women to marry Canadian men and move to Canada? Without hesitation, the answer was no. The Syrians not only turned down the ambassador's request, they dressed him down for even raising the issue. The Syrian officials suggested that if the Canadian fiancés were sincere, they could come to Syria, marry their brides, and live in Syria. As they had done with Mitterand's similar request almost two years earlier, the Syrians refused to entertain further reference to any issue they regarded as an internal Syrian matter. The Canadian ambassador had expected a courteous hearing and ready approval of his request. He left with neither.[31]

The scheme was dead. Judy Feld Carr attempted to revive it by suggesting that a personal appeal by the Canadian prime minister to President Assad might unlock the door, just as a personal appeal by the American president had done nearly ten years earlier. But the Syrians would have none of it. Canadian External Affairs and Immigration officials who had personally committed to making the immigration scheme happen were disappointed. The effort on behalf of these women had taught them about the oppression under which Jews lived in Syria, and they now understood that the removal of fifteen women to Canada would have been a victory against that oppression. All they could offer Judy Feld Carr and the women in Syria was that any of them who was courageous enough to apply to the Syrians on her own for an exit visa could be assured of a very sympathetic response from Canada. But the problem, as always, was getting Syrian permission to leave.[33]

Judy conceded defeat. She was not used to failure. Through this whole period, she had managed to successfully get hundreds of Jews out of Syria—some on purchased passports and exit visas, others through illegal escapes across Syria's borders. But her failure to bring the fifteen women to Canada remained a major disappointment.

CHAPTER NINE

Prisoners of Damascus

I N SEPTEMBER 1990, a week after the celebration of the Jewish New Year, four young Syrian Jews from Aleppo were apprehended as they tried to slip into Turkey. The four, a married couple, the wife's sister and her fiancé, were no more than a few feet from the border when Syrian police, firing at the ground in front of them, ended their dash to freedom. They were handcuffed, blindfolded, and bundled off to Damascus, the men to one prison, the women to another. The trial was only a formality. They had been caught red-handed trying to escape. As punishment, they were kept in prison and tortured.

For one of the arrested Jewish women, Garcia Jamil Guindi, the horror of torture went beyond any pain inflicted on her body. When arrested, Garcia was five months' pregnant. She and her husband had jumped at the chance to escape from Syria in the hope that their baby could be born in Israel. Instead, Garcia found herself in prison, her belly swollen and her husband's whereabouts unknown. She was not even allowed to know if he was still alive.

News of the four arrests shocked the small Syrian Jewish community. As word spread that Garcia was visibly pregnant, the concern became even more acute. Shortly after the arrests, Judy Feld Carr asked one of her informants in New York if there was anything she could do. Her informant told her that the families of those arrested were afraid that any inquiry from abroad would only exacerbate the situation and they hoped to successfully intercede with the authorities on their own.[1]

The families were permitted a visit with their children in prison, but their appeals for leniency and quick release went unheard. Not even the pregnant Garcia would be given any special consideration. The Israelis requested that the international community intervene. Perhaps international disapproval could provide the four Syrian Jews a measure of protection, lessen the torture, especially of the pregnant Garcia, and even reduce the term of their imprisonment.[2] American and French Jewish organizations approached their respective governments, and in November Judy wrote to the minister of External Affairs asking that Canada make representations on behalf of the four. They were not going to Israel, she suggested, "doubtlessly, they were hoping to get to the U.S. or Panama, where close relatives reside." Whatever their sin, their punishment offended any civilized standard of justice or protection of human rights.

> Information just received by us reveals that they are all undergoing the type of interrogation and torture by horrendous means for which the Syrian authorities are well-known to you and your Department.
>
> The young pregnant woman, who has previously suffered two miscarriages, has been told by her jailers that they could not care less whether or not she gives birth and that, if she does, she will do so on the stone floor of her cell.[3]

Garcia did give birth in prison. Several years later she recounted what happened.

> The (female) prison guards kept beating me and kicking me in the stomach. They used to tell me that I will rot in jail all my life. I was in jail with (female) criminals and I suffered from their abuse and beating as well, because I am a Jew. They accused me of spying and beat me until I went unconscious. There was no bed in the cell and I slept on a cold floor without blankets. We were only given bread and water. The whole time I was worried that something might happen to the fetus. When labour became intense the prison guards refused to open the door. I knocked on the door very hard and yelled until they opened it. They put me on a chair in a dirty room and delivered my baby. They kept threatening me that they will take my baby away

when it is born, so immediately after the birth I took the baby, got off the chair and ran to my cell. I wrapped her in a torn blanket and held her tight so they wouldn't take her away from me.[4]

Weeks later, before Judy heard back from External Affairs, Garcia and her sister were freed. The department eventually advised Judy of the women's release, the location of the prison in which the men were still being held, and the fact that the prisoners were allowed once-a-week visits by family. By this time, Judy already knew all of this from her own sources in Syria, but the fact that the Canadians had the information meant that Western diplomats were closely monitoring the situation. That was all that Judy asked of External Affairs, hoping that the Syrians would think twice about abusing prisoners who were the focus of international attention. She also brought the case of the four to the attention of Amnesty International, which ran a short piece on the arrest in its September 1991 *Bulletin*.[5]

What few people knew at the time was that Judy Feld Carr went well beyond public lobbying on behalf of the prisoners. She was instrumental in covertly supplying material for their physical needs, including those of the newborn baby. When she was advised that the imprisoned mother was not lactating, Judy sent bribe money to allow milk formula into the prison for the baby and oranges for the mother. But the prison had no facilities to store the formula, so Judy sent money to purchase a small refrigerator for the prison. She also sent extra money to be placed inside the refrigerator before it was delivered into the hands of prison officials.[6] There was no note or explanation. Within days of the refrigerator's delivery, prison officials released the two women and the newborn infant, almost dumping them out into the street in front of the prison on barely a moment's notice. The refrigerator and the money stayed behind.[7] The Syrians may have released the women and the baby because the international exposure had embarrassed them. Or maybe the bribe worked.[8]

The men were less fortunate. The court had sentenced them to several years in prison and the authorities were unlikely to entertain an appeal for an early release. The men were, however, transferred from a prison in Damascus to one in Aleppo, where it was easier for family to visit them. Otherwise, the conditions were harsh. The men were held in damp, windowless, interior cells where prisoners were beaten for even the slightest infraction of the rules. Judy sent more money to Rabbi Henri Farhi, one of her key Aleppo contacts, to ensure the two men received decent food, including kosher meat. She also sent money to support Garcia and her baby. Rabbi Farhi wrote to Judy thanking her for the money. In a simple code, referring to the prison as the "hospital" and the prisoners as the "sick," he made it clear that the money was well spent.

> I visited the sicks in hospital more than three times and I gave them in their hand every one 2000 Syrian pounds and every month 1000 Syria pounds [to the jailers] from your help and I buy every week chicken meat to eat in hospital, and this week I buy for them medicines for them, and milk for the baby and all are good. Pray with us to give them the health as soon as possible. Amen.[9]

The fate of the two men was ultimately determined by events taking place far beyond their prison walls—the collapse of the Soviet Union, which removed a key Syrian ally and source of weapons; the afterglow of Syrian support for the American-led assault on Iraq in the Gulf War; the opening of the Israeli-Palestinian talks; and the announcement of impending American-brokered bilateral Syrian-Israeli talks in Madrid, scheduled for October 1991. In the shifting *realpolitik*, the Syrians granted amnesty to the two men in Aleppo and, within hours, released another two Jewish men being held in a Damascus prison.[10]

Two prisoners who were not permitted to see the light of day, however, were the Swed brothers, Elie and Selim. Syrian authorities had approached Elie Swed at the Damascus airport in November 1987 as he waited for his luggage to come off his Alitalia flight from Rome. Would he come with them for five minutes, please? He accompanied the officials into an airport office, where he was promptly handcuffed, blindfolded, and hustled off to a Muhabarat prison. He was then twenty-eight years old. Those five minutes were to become almost five years.[11]

Elie Swed is still pained by memories of his Syrian incarceration. The day he arrived at the prison and endured his first full-body search, even the fillings in his teeth were removed, lest he might be concealing something in his mouth. He was put in an underground cell measuring barely one by one and a half metres, not even enough space for him to stretch out on the ground. He was forbidden to make any noise, even to talk to himself. Once, when he was overheard mumbling, he was hauled out of his cell and searched in case he had smuggled some kind of recording or communications device into his cell. Finding nothing, the guards beat him for good measure and tossed him back. He was fed once a day—a cup of water, a single pita bread, and some bean mash. There was no washing, no change of clothes, and only a single, filthy sheet to ward off the cold and dampness that nightly invaded his underground cell. The cell had no toilet facilities and Elie was only permitted to relieve himself once a day. Permission to go more often was at the discretion of the jailer, but whether the answer was yes or no, he was often beaten for asking. If he was denied permission and soiled his cell, he was beaten again.[12]

These beatings were minor compared with the horrors of interrogation and systematic torture. The nightmare began the second night of his incarceration and continued every night for the next month and a half. No atrocity seemed out of bounds—sleep deprivation, electric shocks to his genitals, submersion of his head under water, more severe beatings. Eventually, he told them what they wanted to know. He confessed that he had visited Israel. This confession did not end his ordeal, but only refocused the questions. His torturers accused him of spying for Israel and demanded to know what he had done there. Where had he been? Whom had he seen? Whom did he speak with? Elie explained he had gone to visit two sisters who had left Syria before his birth. How could he know anything that could compromise Syrian security? He was not a spy.

The youngest in his family, Elie had several siblings who left Syria before he was born in 1959. One ended up in Argentina, another two sisters went to Israel. Elie grew up hearing stories of this family abroad. Letters from Argentina, including coded information about the sisters in Israel, were important in holding the family together. After high school, Elie, a bright student, applied to university. For a year and a half he was denied entry—the Jewish quota was full. He persisted and was eventually admitted. After graduating, he began work in a pharmacy that he opened with his brother. Soon thereafter Elie applied for a passport and visa to visit his family in Argentina. He had long dreamed of travelling abroad. It took a year to complete the necessary paperwork, but in 1987 he was allowed permission to visit Argentina.[13]

From there he spoke to his sisters in Israel for the first time. He decided to visit them and flew to Rome, where he visited the Israeli embassy and arranged a flight to Israel. To ensure secrecy, Elie left his Syrian passport with the embassy and travelled to Israel on a *laissez-passer*. He spent a month in Israel. His brother Selim had secretly made this same trip, using a temporary exit visa to cover a side trip to visit friends and family. With the co-operation of Israeli authorities, there was no paper trail and no entry visa to give Syrian security officials reason to suspect a Syrian Jew of visiting Israel.

Selim had returned safely without the Syrian authorities learning about his trip. But in Elie's case, the authorities had somehow found out. Elie had no inkling of a problem during his stay in Israel and his family there had tried to persuade him not to go back to Syria. But he had feared the punishment that his father and other siblings would suffer if he did not return.

At the end of November 1987, Elie flew back to Rome, where he retrieved his Syrian passport at the Israeli embassy. He phoned his family in Damascus to tell them he was in transit from Argentina and that he would be arriving in Damascus the next day on an Alitalia flight. After a one-night layover, he boarded his flight from Rome to Damascus. In the Damascus airport, as he was picking up his luggage, Elie was taken into custody.[14]

Elie's family, waiting for him in the arrivals terminal, had no idea he had been taken away. When he did not appear, the family went to the Alitalia desk to inquire about him. They were told his name was not on the passenger list. Alitalia had no idea where he was. Presuming that he had been delayed and would come on a later flight from Rome, the family went home to await word. They heard nothing from Rome and nothing from the Syrian authorities. The family considered the possibility that he had decided to go to Israel. But he would have got word to them somehow. Elie's father, already a sick man, was ashen with worry. If Elie was in violation of the time limit of his exit visa, the family could be severely punished. One month after Elie disappeared without a trace, his father died.[15]

The family had barely finished with the shiva when six men grabbed Selim Swed, Elie's older brother, in broad daylight on a Damascus street while he was on his way to purchase candles for the first day of Chanukah, in December 1987. The forty-seven-year-old father of seven vividly remembers being hustled into a waiting Land Rover, and his head being covered and beaten during the short drive to the nearby Muhabarat prison. His head still covered and bleeding, he was shoved down a set of stairs and tossed into an underground cell.

When Selim did not return home as expected, with every passing hour his wife, Sara, became more and more uneasy. He would have phoned if he was delayed, particularly since Sara and the children were waiting to light the first Chanukah candle. Sara and another of Selim's brothers called local hospitals. No Selim. They notified the police, who claimed to know nothing. They approached the Muhabarat office in the Jewish quarter for information. The security police dismissed Sara's concern, saying that men had a way of going missing, and then showing up sheepishly the next day. She was told to go home, take an aspirin, and not to worry. But Selim did not return.

Sara went back to the Muhabarat the next day, and the day after that, and the day after that, for a week. Each time she was told that they knew nothing of her husband's whereabouts. After a week Sara threatened a hunger strike in the office of the local Muhabarat. Only then was she told her husband was in prison because of his association with his brother, Elie. Sara was confused. What did Elie have to do with Selim's disappearance? Elie wasn't even in Syria. She begged for an explanation, to see her husband, to know where he was being held. All her pleas were refused.

More than a year passed before word leaked out that Selim was still alive and that he and Elie were being held in prison. The family was still not allowed to visit. They were given no explanation of why the brothers were being held, no word on what prison they were in, and no information about their physical condition. They were not being held with the other Jewish prisoners. These Jews could be accounted for. Their families were allowed to visit and, with money, it was often possible to ensure they had proper food, clean clothes, and even a cell with a window. Only the Muhabarat knew where the Sweds were being held.[16] Sara sank into despair. What would become of her, her children, and most of all, what would become of her husband? She lived on rumours, rolling them over in her head every night. It was harder and harder to shelter her children from images that cursed her sleep.

Selim's ordeal was worse than she imagined. He still had no idea Elie was in Syria, let alone in prison. Each brother was unaware of the other's presence; they were held in tiny underground solitary-confinement cells only a few yards apart. Like Elie, Selim was subjected to a nightly ordeal of systematic torture. The torture was intended to force Selim to confess. The confession might not bear any relationship to to the truth, but until the Muhabarat got the confession they wanted, worded the way they wanted, the nightly orgy of pain would continue. And since the security police were already satisfied that Selim was guilty of the crime, the torture would also serve as punishment. If the torture continued long enough, Selim would eventually confess or die—apparently the Muhabarat didn't care which happened first.

In the end, Selim signed whatever document they put in front of him. He didn't even bother to read it. The regular torture ended, but the beatings and the inhuman conditions of incarceration continued. Selim was held in isolation without charges, without a trial, and with no hope of seeing his wife and children again. The guards enjoyed brutal jokes at his expense. Playing on his loneliness and growing desperation, they told Selim to prepare himself for release. As his hopes soared, they even gave him some Syrian money to get home from the prison. Then, amid gales of laughter, the guards told him it was all a joke. He would never leave prison alive.[17]

After eight months, Selim and Elie caught a glimpse of each other for the first time. Not one word or even a knowing nod passed between the two. Any sign of recognition was forbidden. The ravages of repeated beatings, the insufficient diet, isolation, dirt, cold, and loneliness took their toll on the health of the two men. Selim suffered chest pain and heart palpitations. When a doctor was finally summoned, Selim was found to have extremely high blood pressure and an erratic heart rate. He would have to be taken out of the isolation cell or, the doctor protested, he could not be responsible. Elie, meanwhile, was diagnosed with tuberculosis.[18]

In May 1989, Elie and Selim were removed from their cells and were transferred to another Muhabarat prison. For a time, the two Jewish brothers were thrown in among imprisoned members of the Muslim Brotherhood. Although the Sweds feared for their lives, the Muslim radicals generally let them be. Maybe they were simply prepared to let the system take care of the Jews. Folk wisdom among prisoners was that nobody ever left this prison alive—the only prisoners allowed out were those released for burial.

This new prison was unaffiliated with the previous one. Their new jailers didn't care that the two brothers had been moved because of their deteriorating health, or that they had already been questioned. As new prisoners the Sweds would have to undergo new interrogations. Torture began again and continued until the prescribed confessions were again exacted.[19]

After a month, in June 1989, the two brothers were moved into a tiny underground cell together. They were both sick, their strength was failing, and they were drained of any hope that they would ever be released. They prayed, sometimes for freedom, sometimes for death. When a jailer discovered the men praying, he beat them. In desperation, the two even contemplated starving themselves to death as a way to end their agony.

It had not taken the Israelis long to piece together enough information to satisfy themselves when and where Elie had been taken into custody by the Syrians. But then what? If he and his brother were locked up in the usual Muhabarat prison where Jews were held or put in the civil prison, word would have leaked out. If they were not already dead, they must be in a different facility. Why? And why the silence? On one occasion, Selim and Elie's mother went to see the head of the special division of the Muhabarat that handled "Jewish issues" to beg for information about her sons.

She went "down on her knees and kissed the man's feet begging to see her son[s]." The answer was no. The family had forfeited any right to know anything. Requests for information from Rabbi Hamra and other leaders of the Syrian Jewish community during 1988 and into the spring of 1989 went unanswered, and not even the promise of money could pry information out of usually compliant informants.[20]

The story of the Sweds' arrests and subsequent disappearance slowly filtered out of Syria. Jewish organizations in Israel and the Diaspora added Elie's and Selim's names to the list of Syrian Jews known to be held in Syrian prisons. But they could not monitor the Sweds' treatment or grease administrative palms to ensure more humane treatment. In the face of persistent silence, there were growing fears that the brothers might already be dead.

Western Jewish organizations undertook a series of initiatives to focus international attention on Jews in Syrian custody, especially the Sweds. In the United States, the influential Anti-Defamation League of B'nai Brith protested Syrian arrests without trial in its June 1989 *Bulletin* and repackaged the article, "Prisoners of Damascus," in a press release. Other leading American Jewish organizations, including the American Jewish Committee and the National Jewish Community Relations Advisory Council, joined in publicizing the Sweds' plight. Two sympathetic members of the House of Representatives' Foreign Relations Committee drafted a letter to President George Bush asking him to personally intervene on behalf of the imprisoned men. Copies of the letter were sent to all members of Congress, asking them to co-sign. Many did.

In Europe, the Paris-based and newly energized International Committee for the Liberation of Syrian Jews approached friendly governments on behalf of the imprisoned men and organized a number of protest meetings. Among the organization's most important successes was a personal endorsement of their campaign by the president of the European Parliament. He called on Syrian President Assad to use all his "power to ensure a speedy resolution of the plight of these detainees."[21]

Throughout 1988 and 1989, Judy Feld Carr tapped all her sources for reliable information on the Sweds. She approached

External Affairs for assistance and met with American consular officials. The Americans promised to pass on her inquiry about the Sweds' whereabouts to their embassy in Damascus. The American embassy, like other Western diplomatic missions in Syria, had been pressing for information on the Sweds to no avail, but it was important to keep up the pressure. Four months later, in the early spring of 1989, the American consulate in Toronto received a dispatch from the American embassy in Damascus. "Tell Mrs. Carr that there is NO, I repeat NO information about their whereabouts, and their status. They were arrested over a year ago and have not been seen since."[22]

Judy also approached the Canadian section of Amnesty International, hoping they would take up the Sweds' cause. At their request, the organization's International Secretariat in London added the Swed brothers to its list of prisoners of conscience and issued an urgent worldwide appeal for supporters to write Syrian officials protesting the detention of Jewish prisoners of conscience. An estimated five thousand letters from around the world were sent to Syria. Amnesty International was invited for the first time in ten years to a convention of Middle East lawyers held in Damascus in June 1989, and the human rights organization told the Syrian government publicly that its treatment of prisoners of conscience, especially the Sweds, was a major Amnesty International concern. Amnesty International also supported Judy when she asked the Geneva-based United Nations Centre for Human Rights to intercede with the Syrian government for information about the Sweds.[23]

For once, the Syrians bent under international pressure. In November 1989, two years after the Sweds were first apprehended, Syrian authorities officially informed the United Nations agency that they were holding the brothers in custody. But the Centre for Human Rights was simply advised that

Elie and Selim Swed are under arrest because both of them have broken the law; investigation is in progress according to the judicial procedures and trial will take place as soon as possible.

No mention was made of the fact that, for almost two years, the family had been denied access the prisoners, denied information on their location and condition, and denied even the knowledge that they were still alive. No mention was made of the fact that not even a representative of the Jewish community or a lawyer had been allowed to visit the two men in prison. The Syrians would only admit that the two men were under arrest and the state planned to put them on trial "as soon as possible"—which turned out to be another year and a half.[24]

The Syrian government was beginning to feel some heat. That same month, the *Jerusalem Post* revealed that Syrian officials in the United States had approached major American Jewish organizations to set up a meeting with the Syrian vice-president, who was about to visit New York to address the United Nations. According to a Syrian spokesperson, the meeting was to encourage "better relations with the American Jewish community." The organizations rejected the meeting, but the unprecedented move hinted that Syria was more vulnerable to international pressure than it ever had been before.[25]

Elie and Selim Swed knew nothing about any of this. After almost two horrific years in Muhabarat hands, the Sweds were moved for the third time in September 1989. They were transferred from the Muhabarat prison, where political prisoners and security risks were held in absolute secrecy, into Adra prison, the main police prison in Damascus. The Swed family was still not told of their whereabouts. The brothers were again locked in tiny cells in the underground section of the prison, but the worst of their physical torture and daily beatings was over.

Adra was not as closed off to the outside world as Muhabarat-run prisons, and word soon leaked out that the Sweds were there. The source of the news was another Jewish prisoner in Adra, Jack Lalo, who had been imprisoned in 1987 after his family's failed escape. Lalo and his wife had been allowed to visit New York on business, but to ensure their return, the Lalo children remained behind in Syria. While in New York, Jack contacted several people with links to smugglers who had previously secreted Jews across the frontier into Turkey. A Turkish smuggler would cross into Syria, contact Jack, and escort him and his family across the border. What guarantee would Jack have that the man was genuine and not a Muhabarat plant? Jack set up an elaborate identification code, giving his New York contacts one of a matched set of hand-crafted earrings. The smuggler would receive no names or home addresses, only the earring and a time and place for a meeting. If the smuggler made it to an appointed meeting place at a set time and had the earring, Jack would know he could trust him. The earring code also protected the smuggler, who would know he had met a Jewish family, not Muhabarat agents.

Unfortunately, the Turkish smuggler was caught soon after crossing the border, and the earring was confiscated. The smuggler confessed but had no idea which family he was to smuggle out. Jack Lalo and his family might have been safe were it not for a local Muhabarat officer who, independent of the Turk's arrest, had a run-in with Jack and ordered his gift store searched. The officer found an earring hidden in the store and matched it to the one confiscated from the Turkish smuggler. Jack spent the next four months in a Muhabarat prison, squeezed into an underground cell sixteen metres square with fifty or sixty other men. There was barely room to sit, let alone lie down and sleep. He was tortured and eventually confessed to his part in the escape attempt. There was no need for a trial; he would serve whatever time in prison the authorities thought appropriate.[26]

Even in a Muhabarat prison, enough money slipped into the right hands bought a prisoner family visits, better food, better accommodation and washing privileges, exercise time in the prison yard, and some protection from severe beatings. Jack's wife, Esther, knew where Jack was being held, and to buy life for her husband, she gradually bled the family store dry.[27]

After four months, Jack was also transferred to Adra prison. Adra was like a bazaar. Everything was for sale—every bite of kosher food, every stitch of clean clothes or linens, medications, and even the sunshine that flowed into Jack's above-ground cell were all paid for in cash. As the family's wealth drained away, Esther grew desperate and turned to Rabbi Hamra. He asked Judy Feld Carr for help. The money Judy sent from Feld Fund bought better care for Esther's husband and several other Jewish prisoners.[28]

In September 1989, the Adra prison rumour mill was abuzz with word that two new prisoners had been brought in. Nobody knew who they where. The word was that they were Jews but were they Syrians? Nobody seemed to know. They just disappeared into the prison underground.

Seven months after their arrival in Adra, the two men were removed from their confinement and taken through a central area of the prison. Under armed guard, the men passed near Jack Lalo with their backs to him. Jack feigned a cough. The two prisoners turned around for a second. Jack could not believe his eyes. The two were sickly, thin, dirty, stooped, and bearded, but he recognized them—Selim and Elie Swed. Jack gave a quick sign of recognition, then turned away. When his wife next visited, he told her what he had seen. She passed the information on to Sara Swed and Rabbi Hamra, who in turn informed Judy Feld Carr. Two and a half years after they had disappeared, the Sweds had been found. They were in a deplorable state, but at least they were alive.[29]

Sara went directly to Adra prison and pleaded with prison officials to allow her to see her husband and brother-in-law. After the necessary money was paid under the table, Sara was granted permission for one visit, accompanied by one of her daughters and two prison guards. When the two prisoners were brought forward, Sara could not believe that these men were truly Selim and Elie. She turned to the police and demanded that the two men be allowed to wash, to shave, and be given proper food and medication. The police ignored her. They were only there to monitor every word that passed between Sara, Selim, and Elie. The three said little. Rather than talk, they wept.

Selim Swed only wanted to know how his children were dealing with his absence. Was there money enough to put food on the table, to pay the bills? Sara consoled him. "Don't worry. The children have a second mother. There are angels walking on earth." [30]

Sara was speaking of Judy Feld Carr. Judy made it her business to comfort those most cruelly hurt by the disappearance of Elie and

Selim Swed—their family in Damascus. While the Sweds' where-abouts were still unknown, Judy had written to the Sweds' sister, Leah Hazan, living on a kibbutz in Israel, telling her that everything possible was being done to locate and secure the safety of her brothers. Leah wrote back, sharing her pain.

> All I want to know is if it is for sure they are alive, that they exist... [you] must know that I am worrying so much about them, about my whole family especially about my nephews and nieces with no father. I feel terrible that I can't do anything for them. I am sure Judith you understand me and thanks a lot for all what you do and you have done for that.[31]

A regular correspondence developed between the two women. Judy was able to assure Leah that her family in Damascus was being taken care of because she was the one supplying much of the care. She had learned through her contacts that Sara Swed and her children were financially strapped. Sara felt desperately alone. Friends and family kept their distance, afraid that associating with her might make them targets for the Muhabarat. The pharmacy that her husband had operated with Elie was closed. The assistance she received from family abroad or Rabbi Hamra was not enough to cover the day-to-day costs of supporting herself and her children. And only Rabbi Hamra dared maintain contact with Sara and her children.

Judy sent $1,000 to Rabbi Hamra for Sara Swed through a courier and then wrote to her directly, enclosing a bank draft for $300 to help defray the costs of the coming Passover.[32]

> You do not know me, but I have heard from my friends who live in New York that you have seven children and that you will need some financial help for you and your children for Pesach.
>
> I am sending you in this envelope a bank draft for Pesach so that you can buy what you need for you and the children for the holiday.
>
> I hope that you and your family are well. I hope you will find someone who can translate this letter for you into Arabic.
>
> Please answer me as soon as you receive this letter. You can write me in Arabic and I will have someone translate it for me.

Please write me what you need for you and the children, and I will send it to you as soon as I receive your letter.

I wish you and your whole family much luck and good wishes from the Jewish Community of Toronto for a healthy Pesach.[33]

Judy Feld Carr knew that the Muhabarat would intercept and read the letter, but would they allow it to be delivered and, if so, would the bank draft still be inside?

A few weeks later, Judy received a letter in Arabic addressed to the Honourable Mrs. Judy Feld.

I have received your very kind letter with it very humane sentiments and it reduced the anguish that I am living through with my children since more than $1^1/_2$ years.

Life is very tough here. With the children who are still going to school and your words emanate from your heart are lightening my burden and my days and I trust and pray that you will not delay in answering me, and that noble attention that was something I have not received from any person around here.

I extend to you my fondest wishes for a glorious Passover and that the duration of the holiday in its entirety will be a source of joy and happiness. May everything that is hateful be far away from you, and may God watch over you.[34]

Judy replied, enclosing another bank draft for Sara to buy her children summer clothing—"I know how quickly children grow out of their clothes." She also asked Sara for a photograph of herself and the children. She hoped Sara might also include photos of Selim and Elie, which could be used in the campaign on their behalf.[35] In her reply, Sara opened up to the woman she had never met. She wrote of her longing for her husband, who might be dead; of her efforts to shelter her children from the misery she endured; of her fear that the horror would never end.

Dear Judy, I wish I did not have to burden you with the disclosure and I am opening my heart to you and explaining everything to you and you have become one of my best friends. And perhaps one of these days we will be getting together and the words that emanate from the heart are the greatest testimony as to this friendship and I am most grateful to you for your kind sentiments and I pray that this friendship would last forever.[36]

Judy and Sara formed a strong bond. Judy felt like a sister to Sara Swed and a second mother to the Swed children. The letters from Toronto gave Sara reassurance that she was no longer alone. The two women invented a simple code that allowed them to make guarded reference to specific people, places, or issues without giving too much away to the Muhabarat. For example, writing of the weather being hot or cold was code for the state of Jews in Syria as good or bad. They used "hospital" instead of "prison," "gift" instead of "bribe," "family" instead of "Elie and Selim," "Montreal" instead of "Israel," and "first friend" instead of "Rabbi Hamra." In the months and years that followed, money sent to Sara from the Feld Fund repaired their winter-damaged roof, bought them clothes, put food on their table, and even paid the dowry and wedding costs for one of their daughters. However, more than six months after Sara Swed had bought her way into Adra prison for one visit with her husband and brother-in-law, the two things that money could not buy were family visits and better conditions for the two prisoners.

Western states continued to lobby the Syrian government for information on the Sweds. In addition to Amnesty International's requests, there were repeated inquiries from the Canadian, Australian, French, and American governments. A January 1990 letter from 101 American Congressmen called on President Bush to "make immediate, humanitarian appeal to President Assad to release" Jewish prisoners.

> We recognize that the United States-Syrian relationship is a strained one, and that the prospects for significant improvement in the near future are uncertain. Nevertheless, we feel it is important for the Syrians to know that how they treat their Jewish community, and more specifically, their position with respect to Jewish emigration, will be one of the factors that the Bush Administration will take into account in assessing its policy towards Syria.[37]

At a meeting with Assad, former president Carter raised the issue of Syrian Jewish prisoners. Senators Howard Metzenbaum and

Robert Dole also broached the Swed brothers case in a meeting with Assad in Syria. Canadian External Affairs Minister Joe Clark told Judy that during a meeting of the United Nations Commission on Human Rights "Canada raised the question of human rights in Syria and stressed once again the importance we attach to the observance of due judicial process in that country and the protection of the rights of the accused. Syria was called upon to ensure its full respect of these important principles."[38]

The Syrians realized that if they set up a show trial, they would have to produce the Sweds for the world to see. After years of torture and horrific incarceration, the brothers were in terrible condition, a living indictment of the Syrian prison system and proof positive that Amnesty International's accusations about Syrian abuse and torture of prisoners were true. In a hasty attempt to repair some of the damage, in March 1990 the Syrians moved the brothers to a hospital where they were carefully examined and treated. Elie Swed received treatment for his tuberculosis.[39]

The Sweds were transferred back to Adra after their hospital stay, but their conditions changed dramatically. They were placed above ground, in a light, airy cell, and allowed access to comforts that were available for purchase. Money, much of it from the Feld Fund, bought the Sweds kosher food, fresh fruit, medication, clean clothes and linens, and exercise periods in the prison yard—everything they had been denied for years. And Sara Swed was permitted to see the brothers twice a week.

Sara knew Judy Feld Carr had played an important part in procuring the improved conditions. Judy had stood by her in their time of need as nobody else had. And the opportunity to visit gave Sara new hope that her husband and brother-in-law would soon be released. She wrote to Judy in an upbeat mood.

> I wish to inform you that we have visited our family and they are, thank God, well and better than before. And they send you their best regards and that is why I am rushing to write to you so you will be the first one to be informed of the good things and I wish for all my heart that you would persist with your efforts for everything to turn out up to your expectations. Kindly share my deepest gratitude with all those

who may have contributed to this humane effort from me personally and I pray for its continuation.[40]

Still there were doubts. Were the Syrians just preparing for a show trial? There was no word on when the trial would be held. When the Syrians first notified the United Nations that the Sweds were in custody, and that they would be put on trial "as soon as possible," Judy Feld Carr had sent money to hire a lawyer, "fair legal counsel...one that does not work for the Muhabarat." The hired lawyer had tried to get the two released on bail pending trial. His request was denied. The Sweds would remain in jail until the trial, whenever that might be.

The group of American senators who met with President Assad in the spring of 1990 suggested that, in the name of better relations with the West, the Sweds be released without trial. The Syrian president rejected the idea. The Sweds had visited the enemy state of Israel. They would be tried like any other Syrians who had consorted with the enemy. Such treason could carry a death penalty, but the American ambassador to Syria assured the visiting senators that no one expected a death sentence.[41]

Western notions of judicial process do not apply in Syria. No independent judiciary or built-in notion of defendants' rights protects the accused. Priority is accorded to defence of the state, not to the individual. But once again money could make a difference. There were rumours that money could buy Syrian judges. For the right price, judgments could be bought like any other market commodity. Judy Feld Carr quietly let her contacts in Syria know that if someone was selling, she was willing to buy. It was to no avail.[42]

Court proceedings in Syria are not public. Not even the accused men knew that their trial was already under way. In November 1990, Syrian court authorities received a statement of defence from the Sweds' lawyer, even though he was never presented with a formal statement of the charges against his clients. He submitted a seven-page statement acknowledging that the two had visited Israel but only to see family. They did not have any information that could have compromised Syrian security. The court also received a statement of charges from the public prosecutor. The court met to consider the submissions behind closed doors, without the accused present.

In May 1991, three and a half years after the Sweds had first been arrested and more than a year after the Syrian government promised a hearing "as soon as possible," the brothers were brought before an in-camera court session. In a few short minutes, the court went through the state's written indictment accusing the Sweds of violating Syrian security laws by travelling to Israel and revealing information prejudicial to the security of the state. The proof of the accusations were the defendants' own confessions. Neither the Sweds nor their lawyer was permitted to challenge the state's claim of facts or ask questions. The written defence statement was duly noted and dismissed. The two were found guilty and sentenced to another six and a half years at hard labour. There was no appeal. Elie and Selim were sent back to prison pending written confirmation of the sentence by the Syrian Ministry of the Interior.[43]

Sara was crushed. The day after the verdict was made public, she wrote to Judy:

> I received your last letter before Shavuot by a few days, and I delayed my reply so that I can give you good news but God did not will it. Please excuse me because I am not able to write to you as usual because my nerves can no longer bear it, and I do not know what will happen. Surely you heard the very bad news, which we did not expect at all, and so I beg you to please be with us because in the last days we are not able to bear it at all, and the children are devastated and they are still at such an early age and before they can see or taste anything from life. I am unable to continue, and the road ahead of me is so long and I am unable to bear it. The relatives [the Swed brothers] are completely finished and probably the unthinkable will happen to them. Hashem [God] is not answering us, but maybe Hashem will respond to you. So, please, please, I beg you to be with us.[44]

According to an American State Department source, until the written confirmation of the sentence was issued, there was still a slight chance that President Assad might be prevailed on to pardon the Sweds or commute their sentence. Hoping to draw attention to their plight, the brothers began a hunger strike.

> I am in great worry because our relatives, for the past three days, have abstained from eating. They are insisting to refuse this oppression and injustice, and this destiny, and death is by far much easier for them.

Sara Swed and the leaders of the Damascus Jewish community wrote to the president of Syria pleading for clemency. Judy was still convinced that money could make a difference. She sent $29,000 that she hoped would find its way into the hands of Syrian officials who had the power to release the Sweds.[45]

Amnesty International issued yet another appeal to its members worldwide to write the Syrian government on behalf of the Sweds. Judy asked that the Canadian ambassador in Damascus request clemency. A Canadian approach was soon followed by a similar initiative by Australia. The American Congress relayed its concern for the Swed brothers through the Syrian ambassador in Washington. But President Assad offered no clemency. The Sweds' six-and-a-half-year sentence was confirmed.[46]

Life for Elie and Selim in Adra prison and for Sara and her children in Damascus took on its own horrible routine. Money from the Feld Fund bought Sara twice-a-week access to her husband and brother-in-law. Additional money from the fund paid for their meagre comforts. Money also bought food and clothing for Sara and her children. When Judy learned that the Sweds' daughter, Berta, wanted to marry but didn't have money for the customary dowry, she offered it to Sara.

> I also thought about the wedding of Berta. I have thought about it as if she were my daughter also. Since you ask me my advice about the wedding, I will give it to you.
>
> I hope that Berta loves this young man very much, and that he loves her with all his heart. If this is so, Berta should not wait for a better time to happen. She has to get married now. When someone is blessed such great love, you must have a *simcha* [party] to celebrate it. Life is too short to wait until everything is alright in your life. I am sure that [Selim and Elie], even if they are not able to be there, will be at the wedding with their hearts and their spirit. The wedding does not have to be extravagant...it just has to be in the synagogue with all of

your closest friends and the rest of the family there. Take a lot of pictures so everyone can remember it. I will be there in spirit also.

Because of this, I have told [Rabbi Hamra] that he is to give you, Sara, the necessary amount from me for the dowry, and you will give it to the young man when you accept him as your daughter's husband. I know that this is hard for you to do it alone, and that you wish with all your heart that your family would be with you, but I know that you will have the strength to do this for the sake of your daughter. Let us pray that life will be better soon for everyone but in the meantime, when there is a chance of a celebration, you must do it.

I want Berta to buy a beautiful wedding dress with the help I have told the friend to give you from me, and I want you to send me a picture of her in it.

My wedding present to Berta is the dowry so please use it in good health, and with all my love for you all.[47]

Before the wedding, Western diplomats in Damascus began picking up hints that the Sweds would soon be pardoned. Syria was seeking accommodation with the West after the collapse of its Soviet patron, and hoped to participate in discussions of a possible Middle East peace accord. The continued incarceration of the Sweds was a stumbling block in their relations with the West. During a visit to the United States in late March 1992, Rabbi Hamra made another secret side trip to Toronto. He told Judy that Assad had hinted to the French ambassador and several visiting French dignitaries that the Sweds' release was in the offing. Assad also assured American Secretary of State James Baker that an act of clemency was in the works. Hoping to encourage President Assad to move a little faster, Judy asked Prime Minister Brian Mulroney to make a direct appeal to President Assad.[48]

In mid-April, Rabbi Hamra and a delegation of Jews were granted a long-awaited audience with Assad. According to one of Judy Feld Carr's informants, it "was a very successful meeting" and the president promised the Sweds would be out in a matter of days. On April 19, 1992, the last day of Passover, the eight-day holiday celebrating the exodus of the Hebrews from their slavery in Egypt, Judy received a call from Denis Grégoire de Blois, who had the

Syrian desk at External Affairs. He just had a call from the Canadian ambassador in Damascus. It was over. The Sweds had been released that very hour.

The next call was from the French ambassador in Damascus. Rabbi Hamra had given him the telephone number in Toronto, but no name to go with it, and implored the ambassador to tell whoever answered the phone that the Sweds were on their way home from prison. The rabbi could not make the call himself because he would not use the telephone on the last day of Passover. But he insisted that the person at the Toronto phone number had to be among the first to know the good news.

Judy immediately called Leah Hazan in Israel to tell her that her brothers were free. She then called her Israeli connections and Jewish contact groups. She wrote to officials in External Affairs to express her gratitude for their help. She then wrote a joyful letter to Sara Swed.

At 7:00 p.m. Toronto time, 2:00 a.m. in Damascus, after the end of the Passover, Rabbi Hamra called Judy directly from Syria—an almost unheard-of event. She could hear a crowd and music in the background. The community was still celebrating the Sweds' release, and the rabbi wanted Judy Feld Carr to be part of the festivities, just as she had been part of the almost five years of anguish. The Swed brothers also got on the phone. Although the speakers had no common language, the meaning of their words was clear. It was a sweet moment.[49]

During the next few weeks, Judy received an endless stream of telephone calls and letters, including several from key informants who had provided her with details about the Sweds in prison, from the minister of External Affairs, who had ensured that Canadian concern for the Sweds was repeatedly put before the Syrian government, from her contacts in Tel Aviv, and in understandably guarded fashion, from Sara, Elie, and Selim Swed in Damascus. Perhaps none was more touching than a letter from Leah Hazan, who knew more than most about the role of the Feld Fund in paying for her brothers' health while they were in prison and supporting Sara and her children, and the role of Judy Feld Carr in building international pressure for the Sweds' release.

What a joy it is to know that you did it. Accomplished what I sometimes feared to be the impossible. Words cannot describe the feelings
of gratitude that I have for you. The words "thank you" seem inadequate. But, of course, I do thank you for your time and efforts and endless patience. Without you, no doubt, results would have been
different.

My heart is freed from fear of the unknown. My heart is now full of
hope for a future together with my family. Our journey is still incom-
plete, the next course is in our direction.[50]

CHAPTER TEN

Opening the Gates

T HE RELEASE OF ELIE AND SELIM SWED in April 1992 was cause for rejoicing. Until the eve of their release, few had dared believe that they would walk out of prison before their full sentences were served—if ever. When Syrian officials had first begun to hint that a deal for the Sweds might be possible, Judy Feld Carr knew that the Feld Fund would have to pay for some of the "special costs."[1]

What had made the Sweds a marketable commodity, however, was something that money could not buy—a change in the geopolitical reality of the Middle East in the early 1990s. For the Syrians, the shift dictated a dramatic rethinking of policy toward the West. This in turn had immediate implications for all the remaining Jews of Syria. They had long been held captive against the day when they would be useful as a bargaining chip in the ongoing Israel-Arab conflict. As the parameters of that conflict changed and Syria found it necessary to reposition itself in the Middle East, Syrian leaders prepared to play the Jewish chip.

Nothing symbolized the possibility of change as much as the unprecedented face-to-face meeting of the Israeli prime minister, Yitzhak Shamir, with the Syrian foreign minister, Fauq al-Shara'a, at the Madrid Peace Conference in October 1991, six months before the Sweds were released from prison. The American-brokered Madrid Peace Conference was the outgrowth of monumental upheaval on the international scene. The first shift was the distintegration of the Soviet Union, the second was the Gulf War, and the third was the resuscitation of the long-stalled Arab-Israeli peace process. The collapse of the Soviet Union was a serious blow to the Syrians. Although not a Soviet satellite, Syria traded extensively with the Soviet Union and other Eastern-bloc countries and had an intricate system of credits, loan guarantees, and bartering deals. The Syrian military was heavily supplied with and dependent on Soviet and Soviet-allied military hardware acquired as part of larger trade deals. And Syria counted on Soviet-bloc support in the cat-and-mouse game of Middle East politics.

Even before the final collapse of the Soviet Union, a new generation of Soviet leaders under Mikhail Gorbachev was urging an end to the Cold War, opening up to the West, and holding out the promise of free market and human rights reforms in the Soviet Union. Syria could no longer count on Soviet economic and military backing. And as the Soviet Union sought to improve its relations with the West, Syria could no longer even count on Soviet support with respect to Israel. Other Arab states were climbing onto the American-driven Middle East peace bandwagon and the Soviet Union was reassessing its position in the region. Assad realized that unless he acted quickly, his regime might be one of the final casualties of the Cold War.

At a state dinner in Assad's honour during a 1987 visit to Moscow, Gorbachev had told the Syrian president that Syria had no chance of ever defeating Israel militarily. While the Soviet leader publicly pledged to support Syria in the event of Israeli aggression, he privately made it clear that the Soviet Union wanted a negotiated settlement in which the Soviet Union would play a partnership role with the United States. Before it could be an active player in any Middle East peace moves, the Soviet Union would need to have bilateral relations with all states in the region, including Israel. Moscow served notice on Syria that the Soviet Union was looking forward to reopening diplomatic relations with Israel in the near future. The Soviet Union was permitting the emigration of hundreds of thousands of Soviet Jews, many of whom could be expected to settle in Israel. It was a whole new game.

When the Soviet Union disintegrated in 1991, Russia and the other successor states were no longer in a position to meet even the watered-down obligations they had with Syria. To avoid isolation, Syria would have to find a way back into the good graces of the West. But any shift in policy might alienate domestic anti-Western forces, leftists, and Muslim militants, arouse its more anti-Western neighbours, and compromise Syria's strategic position in the Middle East, particularly in Lebanon. The foxy Syrian president was not ready to loosen his control of the state, and he was not going to allow change to run away with itself as had happened in the Soviet Union. Assad had to move carefully.

In January 1991, Syria had joined the American-led Gulf War coalition against Syria's old rival, Iraq. While not a major military player, Syria sent a contingent of troops to the Gulf and allowed coalition flights over Syrian airspace. When the United States used the opening presented by the war alliance to push for a new round of Middle East peace talks in Madrid, the Syrians found themselves being courted to participate. Syrian involvement would mean unprecedented Syrian-Israeli diplomatic contacts; Assad would would not take such a step lightly. But the moment was auspicious for a bold move. The United States, Syria, and by extension Israel were tossed together as allies in the Gulf War. Revelations about secret talks in Norway between Israel and the PLO, and subsequent American-sponsored talks raised new hope that settlement of Gaza and the West Bank issues was within reach. As a reward for Syria joining the anti-Iraqi coalition and to encourage Syrian participation in future Israel-Arab negotiations, the United States dropped Syria's name from the list of states said to be supporting terrorism and lifted existing trade barriers. The Americans also acceded to Syrian military actions in Lebanon, further solidifying de facto Syrian control of Lebanese affairs.[2]

In October 1991, Israel and its Arab neighbours sat across from one another in Madrid. Syria's participation was decidedly cool, and Syrian and Israeli speakers often traded insults, but for the first time the two sides were seated at the same table. Both agreed to participate in subsequent exploratory talks, unprecedented bilateral meetings, scheduled for Washington in January 1992. While neither side held out hope for an instant breakthrough in the enormous divide that separated them, rumours persisted that both sides were prepared to be flexible.[3]

In the weeks leading up to the Washington talks, Israel and Syria looked for signs that the other was ready to open up a dialogue. The Syrians began to hint that they might be willing to resolve one long-standing sore point with Israel: the removal of barriers to Jewish departures from Syria. Israel had already released a large number of Palestinian prisoners from detention, alleged supporters of Hamas and other organizations regarded as terrorist by Israel. In December 1991, just a month before the Washington talks were to begin, President Assad told a group of visiting Lebanese legislators that "everyone in Syria, including Syrian Jews, enjoys the right to leave the country."[4]

When the Washington talks opened, the question of Jewish departures from Syria was still unresolved. The Israeli delegation put the matter squarely on the table, reminding the Syrians that travel abroad by Syrian Jews was both difficult and expensive to arrange, and travel in complete family units was almost never approved by the Muhabarat. In the past, Israel had maintained that Syria's refusal to allow Jews to leave was a human rights violation and separate from the Israel-Arab dispute. This was the same position taken by Syrian Jewish advocacy groups in Israel and the Diaspora.

Publicly, the Syrian delegation rejected the linkage. Syrian Jewish issues, including emigration, were a domestic matter and no business of Israel. Israel had put Syrian Jews on the table and had better take them off the table. Privately, however, the Syrian response was less rigid. Judging by Assad's statement in advance of the Washington meetings, the party line was beginning to change.

The first round of Syrian-Israeli talks in Washington brought no breakthrough, but both sides agreed to a further round of bilateral talks three months later, in late April 1992. In the intervening period, the Israeli media openly speculated that the possibility of a land-for-peace deal with Syria was in the offing. Two weeks before the second round of talks began, Assad met with leaders of the Syrian Jewish community and publicly promised that Syrian Jews would be accorded the same rights as other citizens. Jews would be able to buy and sell property—freedom to sell property being a pre-cursor to emigration—and Syrian Jews would be permitted to travel abroad on business and for pleasure on the same terms as other Syrians—that is, in complete family units and without hefty bonds put up against their return. Only a week before talks were to resume, President Assad pardoned the Swed brothers.[5]

Assad did not promise to allow emigration; emigration of its cit-izens was not part of the Syrian political lexicon. He only talked about Jews being able to visit abroad. But every Syrian Jew at the meeting understood that granting Syrian Jews the freedom to travel abroad in complete family units was administrative code for sanc-tioning emigration. Once Jewish families were out of Syria with money from the sale of property in hand, few would return.

Assad's pledge to allow Jews to travel abroad may have made strategic sense, but it caught many in the Syrian bureaucracy off guard. In the six months following Assad's April 1992 announce-ment, more than 2,800 of the approximately 4,000 Jews still in Syria applied for short-term exit visas. Most applied to leave in complete family units. But even with the Syrian president's pledge to permit Jewish families to travel abroad, Jews, unlike other Syrians, still needed clearance from the Muhabarat.[6] The authorities had no precedent for such an exodus. But this would be the last chance for Syrian agents to line their pockets with Jewish money before the Jews were gone forever.

Syrian authorities began processing passports and exit-visa applications with due reverence to the time-honoured traditions of baksheesh. Syrian Jews with resources paid to get the necessary pass-ports and exit visas. Those with limited funds turned to relatives abroad or to Judy Feld Carr. Cash was best, but gifts in kind were sel-dom refused. Muhabarat members were only too happy to take per-sonal property off their hands. What did a Jewish family going abroad need with a VCR or a family car? How could any one woman wear so much jewellery? Leave it with someone who could really use it. If in so doing one also managed to avoid problems in processing a passport application or an exit visa, so much the better.

In June 1992, Rabbi Hamra notified Judy of a long list of people whose applications for passports and exit visas had been rejected or delayed. Now, approval was no longer a problem—as long as money was available up front. Rabbi Hamra needed $100,000 to cover the necessary processing fees, round-trip airline tickets, and extras expected by Syrian officials, and he needed half of it quickly. Judy never dreamed that all the cases she had been working on would be approved at once. She did not have that kind of money and was not sure if she could raise it in the few days she had before she left for Israel for the summer. She and her key supporter, Helen Cooper, pulled out all the stops. The two women hit the phones, tramped door to door asking previous donors to reach into their pockets yet again, and implored local rabbis to appeal to their congregants for assistance. Judy lost her voice in the process. Her doctor ordered her to give her vocal cords a rest, but the women persisted. In four days they added over $62,000 to the Feld Fund. The first installment of the money was safely delivered to Rabbi Hamra with a promise for the rest. The exit visas and passports would be issued.[7]

Ezra Levi and his ten-year-old son, Naim, had been permitted to leave Syria in September 1988 so that Naim could receive long-term cancer treatment in New York. The cost of the medical care was being covered by a Syrian Jewish charity in New York, the Sephardi Bikur Holim.

Later in 1988, Judy Feld Carr was asked to help bring Ezra's wife Tova and her two other children out of Damascus. Syria's doors were still closed to travel abroad by complete Jewish family units, but Judy thought she might be able to buy permission for a mother to leave Syria with her children so they could be at the bedside of a sick child. To reinforce their case, Judy asked the American ambassador in Damascus to approach Syrian authorities on the family's behalf. Muhabarat officials indicated that they would not allow both children to leave with their mother. Tova was heartsick, torn between a sick child in New York needing his mother's love and two children who would be left behind in Damascus. She eventually accepted the Muhabarat's terms and joined her husband and sick child. The two other children, Shalom, eleven, and Tikvah, only five, stayed behind in Damascus.[8]

Judy soon became aware that Tova was unable to reconcile her desire to be in two places at once. Torn by guilt and self-doubt she asked herself how she could have left two children behind to tend a third? Tova did not speak English and was dependent on others to translate for her, to explain what her son's doctors were saying, and to take her anywhere outside the small Syrian Jewish neighbourhood of Brooklyn. As months became a year, and a year threatened to become two, Tova grew increasingly disconsolate. She wept at the thought that her older son in Damascus was being called to the Torah at his bar mitzvah without either of his parents present. If her two children in Syria could not join her in New York, she saw no choice but to go back to them.

Concerned for Tova's welfare, Judy sent the financially pressed family money to cover the costs of telephone calls to Damascus so Tova could at least hear her children's voices from time to time. But she knew the real solution was to get the two children out. Working with her Syrian connections, she first tried to build a humanitarian case.[9] A key element of the application was a series of letters collected from Naim's American doctors, outlining the boy's medical treatment, the course of medical care he could expect to undergo during the coming year or more, and most important for Judy's plan, a statement that his medical improvement was being threatened by Naim's continued separation from his siblings.

> [Naim] is very distraught and despondent about this separation from his brother and sister. His mental as well as his physical well being is the key to a proper recovery. This deprivation from his family can retard his present progress. It is of paramount importance to rehabilitate him in conjunction with his psychological and social as well as his medical needs.[10]

The humanitarian appeal went nowhere. Suggestions in the early autumn of 1990 that the Muhabarat might approve one or the other of the children to travel to New York would not solve the problem; the departure of one would still keep the family divided.[11]

Judy's contacts in Damascus tried to find an intermediary to intercede with the Muhabarat on behalf of the children. The attempts were time-consuming and ultimately failed.[12] In February

1992, more than three years after Tova joined her sick son in New York, and a month after President Assad's announcement that Syrian Jews could travel abroad, Judy received word that the Muhabarat were willing to make a deal for the two children. They wanted a written appeal from the parents sent to the Syrian ambassador in Washington and a letter from a senior American Jewish spokesperson petitioning for the family's reunification. The letter from the parents was quickly sent. Judy composed a letter to be sent to the Syrian ambassador over the signature of the head of the American Jewish Congress.[13]

Even before the American Jewish Congress could mail off its letter, a Syrian embassy official told the parents in New York that their request for family reunification had been approved. The embassy even suggested that someone should accompany the children on the long flight.

Judy shared the parents' joy, but she knew that until the children were on the airplane and the airplane was in the air, something could still go wrong. Accordingly, she sent several thousand dollars to her contacts in Damascus to dole out the usual "ransom money" required to buy Muhabarat co-operation. Not wanting to hand the Syrians even the smallest propaganda advantage, she also quickly cancelled the American Jewish Congress letter.[14]

All the right payments were made and all the right approvals collected. Exit visas for the two children were issued. On May 10, 1992, three weeks after the Swed brothers were released, and days after Assad told the Syrian Jewish delegation that Jews could travel as a family, the flight arrived at New York's Kennedy Airport reuniting the children with parents they had not seen in almost four years. In addition to Naim, whose cancer was in remission, the two children met Joseph, their new baby brother, born in New York a year earlier.[15]

Another Syrian Jew arrived on the same flight that brought Tova's two children to New York. Damascus-born Yom-Tov Hassan, a thirty-two-year-old designer and pattern maker of ceramic tiles, made his way through American Immigration and Customs to the waiting embrace of his mother, Leah, and his sister, Chana. Leah had been granted a short-term exit visa three years earlier so that she could receive special medical treatment for her asthma and eye problems. Judy had helped Chana leave Syria to care for her mother.

Yom-Tov Hassan left Syria in the period between Assad's hinting at permission for Jews to travel abroad and the wholesale issuing of exit visas. Yom-Tov, single and living alone, first applied to travel abroad in 1989, years before President Assad removed restrictions of Jewish travel. He was not a rich man, but he gave a Muhabarat agent all the money he could raise. It was not nearly enough for an application to receive serious attention, and his application never went forward.

In January 1992, Judy received a call from Chana requesting help in getting Yom-Tov out of Syria. Judy asked for any information that might further his case, and Chana explained that Yom-Tov's life was difficult. He lived in a dilapidated third-floor apartment above a bakery. Yom-Tov had been his mother's major source of support in Damascus. Now Leah worried for the health and safety of her only son. Chana told Judy that Yom-Tov suffered from high blood pressure and suspected kidney problems.[16]

When Chana contacted Judy, there were already rumours of a new Syrian openness to Jewish travel abroad. Judy was not about to ease up on her own rescue efforts in the hope that the Syrians would make them unnecessary. Accordingly, she advised Chana that the best way to get Yom-Tov out of Syria was to pull together a well-constructed story that would legitimize his request to depart. She suggested that Yom-Tov plead his desire to visit his ailing mother in New York. To make it appear that he was truly planning to return to Damascus, Judy advised Yom-Tov to have his apartment painted. A single man with no family to leave behind as hostage was unlikely to be allowed out. But his promise to return might ring truer if he invested money in his apartment in Damascus. Why would he do that if was not planning to return?[17]

Judy Feld Carr sent a check for $1,000 from the Feld Fund to Chana to be forwarded to Yom-Tov if "she is 100 per cent sure that he is going to use it to get out."

To prop up the other half of Yom-Tov's story, a son's concern to visit with a sick mother, Judy decided to get personally involved. She took the unusual step of writing directly to Yom-Tov in Damascus, supposedly at the request of his sister. She wanted the Muhabarat informed of his mother's precarious health and loneliness for her son. Judy began her letter by introducing herself as a friend of Syrian Jewry who knew of Yom-Tov through his sister. She also knew Yom-Tov lived alone in an apartment "which is not in good condition," and enclosed a check for $100, assuming that the authorities would conclude the money was for his minor improvements.

> Your mother is very sad and misses you very much. Do you think that it would be possible for you to come to visit her for a short vacation? She is not well, and has been in the hospital many times, and would really like to see you.
>
> Please write me immediately to tell me if this could be possible.[18]

Yom-Tov replied in Arabic. When Judy had the letter translated, she was pleased with Yom-Tov's smoothness. He was a quick study and put on paper exactly what she wanted the Muhabarat to see.

> Concerning my situation you already know, but I was happy to learn of your concern for my mother's health and taking care of her. As for me fate demanded that I remain lonely and far away from my sick mother and unable to reach her to visit her until now, even though I know how much she needs me during this difficult time of her illness and her constant going to the hospital, and our condition is not good, and this affects me greatly and on my work and my daily health because it causes me to a let down and depression and pain in my heart. The worry does not leave me. I am trying continuously to get permission to travel so that I can visit my sick mother, but I do not know if I will be able to visit her soon because I did to get any definite answer, and this is the truth, and I do not have much to say concerning this question, and this pains me since several years.
>
> I, therefore, hope that for my sake and my mother's sake you will be able to help travel, and I apologize for the long explanation about my situation, but your letter gave me great hope.[19]

Judy responded quickly, enclosing another cheque so that Yom-Tov might "continue the painting [of his apartment] and for other things" he might need, and careful to play on a clever opening Yom-Tov gave her. If the Muhabarat could be convinced that he needed his mother—that being denied the opportunity to visit his mother was the cause of his own declining physical and emotional health—then maybe a deal could be arranged. It was important to let Muhabarat agents know that it would be worth their while to issue a passport and exit visa. In her next letter to Yom-Tov, Judy purposefully let slip that money was available and that "your sister will send you whatever you need if you let her know."[20]

Through the early spring of 1992, Judy and Yom-Tov continued to correspond. She regarded every letter as an opportunity to reinforce his case for humanitarian leave. On April 29, 1992, two days after the American State Department issued a statement noting with approval that President Assad had authorized foreign travel of Syrian Jews on the same terms as other citizens, Judy wrote to Yom-Tov, advising him in no uncertain terms that he should grab the offer. If the Syrians were making ready to open the door to Jewish emigration, then as many Jews as possible should get out while they could. Yom-Tov should forget about special pleading. Judy instructed him to reapply for a passport as quickly as possible and not worry about money.

> Yom-Tov, please understand that whatever help you will need to come to see your mother, it is ready for you and you should not worry about it. Now that people can come to visit the U.S. you also must apply as soon as possible and come. All you have to do is tell your sister that you have your passport to travel, and it will be arranged for you to have your airline ticket.
>
> As soon as you receive this letter, I want you to answer me, and your sister if you want to come.
>
> I am not sending you a present in this envelope...but please remember that whatever you need for your visit will be sent to you.
>
> You do not ever think that you have to repay me. It is an honour to help you in whatever way is possible.[21]

Even before he received Judy's letter, Yom-Tov gathered up what remained of the money she had previously sent along with some additional money from a small pool Judy had forwarded to Rabbi

Hamra, and handed it all over to the Muhabarat. He offered no humanitarian window dressing. This was a new game—pay as you go. Money was now all that the authorities seemed to care about. Ready to pay whatever he could, he received a passport and exit visa to visit his mother in New York. Barely waiting for the ink to dry on his visa, Yom-Tov—with a new set of clothes and fresh luggage paid for by Judy Feld Carr—boarded the flight for New York. He was out at last.[22]

With the Syrian door finally ajar, other outside sources of money became available. Judy continued to pay for the tickets for the people she had already been helping. She did not have the resources necessary to cover the travel costs of all the needy Jews lining up to leave. The American Joint Distribution Committee, which had long been sending money into Syria to support Jewish institutions, especially Jewish schools, offered to reimburse the travel costs of financially strapped Syrian Jews who received permission to travel abroad, including the cost of the round-trip tickets. Other costs, including money or gifts extorted by the Muhabarat, or losses as a result of property left behind would have to be born by the individuals and families leaving Syria.[23]

If they had had a choice, some Jews leaving Syria might have gone straight to Israel. That was not possible, as Syria and Israel only began to move cautiously toward bilateral discussions in the spring of 1992. Canada approved any applications for tourist visas from Syrian Jews.[24] For the vast majority of Jews leaving Syria, however, the destination of choice was the United States. Many already had family in the New York area, especially in Brooklyn, on whom they could count for assistance. They also knew there was an infrastructure of Jewish social and welfare organizations in New York to help get them oriented. The Sephardi Bikur Holim was especially active in meeting Syrian Jewish resettlement needs. The American administration had long been vocal in its support of the right of Syrian Jews to travel and, in most cases, granted them American tourist visas right away.

The visas assured the Syrian Jews of entry to the United States, but they were not officially immigrants or refugees. American authorities proved unwilling to automatically flip tourist visas into American immigration visas—the coveted green cards—or to grant the Syrian Jews refugee status. The new arrivals were unable to work and were barred from publicly funded social assistance. The Syrian Jewish community and New York Jewish organizations struggled to meet the financial burdens and social problems suddenly thrust on them. Jewish organizations, led by the Hebrew Immigrant Aid Service, approached Washington in an effort to find a legal or political solution to the problem.[25]

All the while costs mounted. The financial resources available to Syrian Jews varied from person to person and family to family. Some of the wealthier Jews had been dreaming of the day they would depart Syria for good, and had been husbanding their resources in preparation. A few covertly moved out whatever money they could, sometimes into secret bank accounts or into the hands of trusted family members already abroad. Still other Syrian Jews who applied for permission to leave in the wake of Assad's pledge scrambled to dispose of whatever little property they could not take with them. But many suspected that the homes and shops they left closed and other property they left behind would eventually be gobbled up by the state or fall into the hands of Muhabarat agents. Fees for exit visas were just one of the countless ways in which Jews paid just to get by.[26] The only difference after Assad granted wholesale permission for Jews to travel was that the exit-visa payments would be the last. Even as Jewish organizations in the West were publicly jubilant at Assad's permission for Jews to leave Syria, Judy was still quietly paying off Syrian officials to ensure exit for those without independent means. Uneasy that Syria would again shut its doors, trapping any remaining Jews inside, she was now less interested in haggling over price than in paying and getting Jews out fast.[27]

In mid-October 1992, just six months after Assad approved the wholesale exit of Jews from Syria, authorities abruptly reduced approval of passport and exit-visa applications to only one or two a week. One long-time American observer of Syrian Jewish affairs suggested that application approvals were being held back pending the outcome of the American election, only a few weeks away. Bill

Clinton was being touted to defeat George Bush, and Assad was holding up the release of remaining Syrian Jews as a card to play with the next American administration. In addition, American-brokered Syrian-Israeli meetings had not been very productive, and rather than stand by Syria in a united front against Israel, other Arab interests—the PLO, the Jordanians, and the Egyptians, among others—were intent on separate dealings with Israel. Closing the door to Syrian Jewish departures was a way to signal Syria's displeasure with the Middle East peace process.[28]

There may have been other reasons for the reversal. Maintaining the fiction that Jews were only allowed out for temporary travel abroad had served Syrian domestic policy needs. There is little doubt that other Syrians would have been pleased to get out if they had the chance. When the international media and Jewish organizations in the West began to publicly herald the departure of Jews, the Syrians may have had second thoughts. They wanted the West to play along with the distinction between the appearance of short-term travel and the reality of permanent emigration. If the West would not play the game, the game was over.

And many Syrian Jews were ending up in Israel. The overwhelming majority who left in the six months that the door stood open entered the United States on tourist visas. As far as Syria was concerned, the Jews remained citizens of Syria and as such were forbidden to travel to Israel, let alone use the United States as a way station for *aliyah*, permanent settlement in Israel. No doubt the Syrians expected that some, even many, of the Jews who left after April 1992 would end up in Israel. But in the past Israel had given no publicity to Syrian Jewish arrivals lest publicity endanger Jews left behind. After April 1992, the arrival of Syrian Jews was no longer kept secret, and was reported in the local press. The Syrians may have considered this a violation of an unwritten agreement to treat the departure of Syrian Jews as just temporary travel abroad, not emigration and, certainly, not emigration to Israel.

As suddenly as the door opened in late April 1992, it slammed shut in October. Officials made no announcement of the change. Syrian authorities reimposed the rule of keeping one or more family members back. An estimated one thousand of Syria's approximately fifteen hundred remaining Jews who still wanted to leave felt trapped.

It took a little while to grasp the fact that travel restrictions had been reinstituted. American Jewish organizations turned to their government, which had been so instrumental in persuading Assad to loosen the grip on Jewish travel. President Clinton's new Secretary of State, Warren Christopher, visited Damascus in February 1993, shortly after Clinton's inauguration, and raised the issue of the ban on Jewish travel with Assad and his foreign minister. They told Christopher that the drop in the number of exit visas was merely a statistical glitch. An inquiry from the Canadian embassy received a similar answer. Unfortunately things were not ironed out that quickly. Even ten months later, Syria's unspecified administrative and bureaucratic problems still remained unresolved.[29]

In May 1993 a bipartisan group of seventy-one American senators signed a joint letter to Clinton calling on him to again intervene with the Syrians. The senators reminded Clinton that in the spring of 1992, Assad had pledged his word to the United States that he intended to allow Jews to travel abroad and, after keeping his word for six months, had reneged. The Syrians had also failed to live up to a subsequent promise to Warren Christopher that exit visas would again be forthcoming. "We know too well after years of fighting for freedom for Soviet Jews—that such an excuse is neither acceptable nor accurate. President Assad has, as Soviet leaders had, the power to open the gates."[30]

Secretary of State Christopher flew back to Damascus for talks with President Assad and his foreign minister in the first week of December. Before he left Washington, he received a letter signed by fifty-eight members of the House of Representatives demanding that he "urge Syria to honour its pledge to permit Jews the freedom to travel." At the United Nations the Canadian ambassador, speaking before the General Assembly on human rights questions around the world, called on Syria to "honour recent laudable plans to eliminate barriers to travel abroad by Syrian Jews." The Canadian ambassador in Damascus repeatedly expressed the concern of the Canadian government about the withholding of exit visas from Jews, as did his colleagues from other Western embassies.[31] Christopher again raised the issue of Jewish exit visas during talks with the Syrian president and his foreign minister. They promised him that Jews wishing exit visas would be granted them by the end of December 1993.[32]

The Syrian promise of a deadline for issuing exit visas to Syrian Jews, and their willingness to reduce other outstanding irritants with both the United States and Israel, preceded an announced meeting in Geneva between Presidents Assad and Clinton in late January or early February 1994. Some American Jewish leaders were not pleased with the prospect of the meeting, arguing that it would confer international respectability on the Syrian leader and his regime when that country had yet to earn that respectability. There was no guarantee that the Syrians would live up to a new undertaking on Jewish departures any more than they had the last. To the surprise of almost no one, the Syrians failed to meet their December 31, 1993, deadline. In early January 1994, at a rally outside the United Nations building in New York, Jews demanded that Syria resume issuing exit visas.[33]

By mid-February, Judy Feld Carr was able to confirm that exit visas were finally being issued in Damascus. In Aleppo there were still problems getting administrative co-operation and, in some cases, officials resumed their former practice of only issuing exit visas to some family members, and denying them to others.[34] This on-again off-again issuing of exit visas was nerve-racking. There was also concern that, depending on the outcome of the Clinton-Assad summit scheduled for mid-January 1994, the one thousand or so remaining Jews, including children long denied permission to join family already abroad, might again be trapped in Syria.[35] Jews who were once hostage to the Arab-Israel conflict could now end up hostage to American-Syrian relations.

With all the agenda items for the scheduled summit in Geneva between Clinton and Assad, Judy was concerned that Syrian Jews would get short shrift. She was not alone in this concern. American Jewish leaders were pulling out all the stops in lobbying Clinton and his staff. But feeling that the Clinton-Assad talks might be the last chance Syrian Jewry had to reverse the insidious Syrian practice of holding back family members, Judy hit on an idea of putting the case of Syrian Jews before Clinton one last time before his meeting with Assad.[36]

One of Don Carr's friends and business associates was George Cohon, then CEO of McDonald's Canada, which operated the restaurant's outlet in Moscow. During the Soviet era, Cohon had used his personal entree with Soviet leaders to press them on the cause of Soviet Jewry. Judy learned that he would be in Moscow at the same time as Clinton was scheduled to make a state visit there, before his meeting with the Syrian leader in Geneva. Clinton. Moscow. Big Mac. Photo op. Cohon. Syrian Jews. Why not? If Clinton were to visit the Golden Arches in Moscow for a burger and fries, as he had done in the past, Cohon might be able to lobby him on behalf of Syrian Jews. Rather than phone Cohon, on New Year's Day 1994, Judy wrote him an impassioned letter requesting his assistance.

> I understand from Don [Carr] that you will be going to Moscow and that there is a good chance that you will spend some time with President Clinton.
>
> Just as you were so influential with Ambassador Yakovlev for Soviet Jewry, there is one major initiative which could be undertaken by you on behalf of Syrian Jewry—and it is a simple thing.
>
> President Assad of Syria promised Warren Christopher that the Syrians would give their Jews travel permits by the end of December. In fact, some have started to receive them.
>
> However, in typical cruel Syrian style, they are giving some families the exit permits for everyone, except one family member—usually a child. Thus, some families are not leaving, because they will not leave one child behind.
>
> It is important for President Clinton to know this before he meets Assad in Geneva. He will, no doubt, be told by Assad that the permits are being issued, as promised, but, of course, he will not refer to this ... process [of withholding permits from children].
>
> Anything you can do would be a mitzvah for our People...In the name of those left behind in Syria, I thank you.[37]

George Cohon phoned Judy as soon as he received her letter. He did not know if Clinton would be visiting the McDonald's in Moscow.

He offered to present a letter from Judy to the president if there was an opportunity. As an alternative, Cohon offered to pass the letter on to a key member of his McDonald's management team in Moscow, Marc Weiner, who was a longtime friend of Clinton's and who might be willing to give the letter to the president.[38]

Ten days later, Judy received a telephone call from Moscow. Clinton had not come to the restaurant, but Marc Weiner and his wife had been invited to visit the Clintons in their hotel suite following an official reception at the American embassy in Moscow. During the course of conversation, the discussion had touched on the president's coming talks with President Assad, Syria, Israel, and the peace process. Weiner had felt it appropriate to ask about the separation of Syrian Jewish families. Clinton was well informed about and sympathetic to the Syrian Jewish problem and hoped to discuss the issue of exit visas with Assad.

When Judy got the call from Moscow, she could hardly believe it. Being able to leap over all the briefings Clinton would have in preparation for his meeting with Assad and remind the American president that the Jewish exit-visa problem was an important human rights issue just two days before the Geneva meetings was remarkable. For Judy, the moment was full of historical significance. She was convinced that fifty years earlier, Jews in the safety of the West did too little, or even worse, cared too little to save Jews who would be murdered at the hands of the Nazis. She praised Marc Weiner and George Cohon for doing what she believes an earlier generation of Jews had not done—intervening at the highest level on behalf of threatened Jews elsewhere.[39]

Presidents Clinton and Assad met in Geneva on January 15, 1994. In a briefing for American Jewish leaders about two weeks after the meeting, Warren Christopher reported that President Clinton had raised the issue of Jewish departures from Syria. The United States was reassured that Syria would allow remaining Jews who wished to leave to do so. Reports from Syria confirmed that exit visas were being routinely issued again to almost all Jews who applied.

However some Jews were still encountering harassment from Syrian authorities. Jews who were eager to get out paid up, lest some last-minute problem in one family member's application prevent or delay a departure. Those who were in the bad books of local Muhabarat agents, Jews who had previously attempted to escape, who had balked at paying bribes, or who did not show proper deference to the authorities, were especially tormented. The Swed brothers, for example, were refused permission to leave Syria more than a year after their release from prison and more than a year after permission for Jewish travel abroad in family units had been approved.

In a few cases, the delays were self-imposed. Some individual Jews or families, secure with passports and exit permits in hand, held off leaving as they tried to dispose of property or clear up this or that personal matter. For others, there may also have been a sense of inertia, a reluctance to leave behind the only world they knew—no matter how bad it was—for a strange world beyond Syria's borders. Gradually, as family and neighbours departed, as Jewish institutions closed, even the most reluctant had to concede that it was time to go.

By the end of 1993, Rabbi Hamra knew it was also time for him to go. He had accomplished all he could to shelter his community from harm. On an almost daily basis, he had dealt with the Muhabarat, with those in charge of Syria's prisons and sometimes with those at the highest levels of government. Walking a fine line with the regime, he had been granted official, if limited, licence to deal with the diplomatic community. Although the Syrians had kept him on a short leash, Rabbi Hamra had still been able to use what little leverage he had to quietly negotiate with the Muhabarat the price of Jewish departures. He often participated in delicate dealings with the Muhabarat over the "special payments" required before passports and exit permits were issued. Rabbi Hamra was the one who handled the distribution of money from abroad. He helped manage an annual grant from the American Joint Distribution Committee earmarked for teachers' salaries and the repair and upkeep of Jewish schools in Damascus. He oversaw money sent from the Feld Fund to assist with the departure of Jews from Syria, to sustain those without resources until they too were able to leave, and to provide for those in prison. Rabbi Hamra had kept a log of all his financial dealings on behalf of the Feld Fund, and he sent Judy Feld Carr an exact accounting of every penny he spent. With Jewish life in Syria winding down, Rabbi Hamra finally applied for an exit visa, ostensibly to visit family in New York.[40] Also among the last granted permission to leave were Selim and Elie Swed and their family. After a discreet pause in New York, they moved on to Israel.[41]

The roots of Syrian Jews in Damascus, Aleppo, and Qamishli were as deep as their history was rich. Syria had been home to generations of Jews. Some families can trace their Syrian lineage back thousands of years. The stones in the graveyards reflect the depth of Jewish historical presence in Syria that was now being scattered. Syrian Jews were grateful to at last be able to leave Syria, but they still experienced a sense of loss—loss of the familiar, of community closeness, and of the unique symbols of Syrian Jewish identity.

Like Jews who had earlier left countries of oppression, many Syrian Jews brought out with them their most important symbols of family and individual identity. Praying that the Muhabarat did not confiscate personal heirlooms during baggage inspections at the airport, families packed their Sabbath candlesticks, the family *chanukia*, the *mezuzah* from the doorpost, precious documents and photographs, handed-down toys or baby clothing, or a cherished wedding gown.

What of communal property, those sacred objects that gave collective expression to Jewish life in Syria—Torahs, holy books well worn from study, synagogue art, the documentary written record of a thousand-year legacy of religious and community life? Synagogues and Jewish schools, some rich in art and architecture, would be left standing empty. With no Jewish presence, weeds would soon grow between the graves in Jewish cemeteries, or the land would be desecrated and turned to other uses.

Syrian authorities who adhered to the fiction that Jews were only travelling abroad temporarily were not willing to allow Jews to take the community's Torahs, holy books, and other precious items with them. If objects, even religious objects, had any real historic, artistic, cultural, or monetary value, Syrian authorities were also inclined to regard them as part of the Syrian cultural legacy, the historical property of the state to be included in the inventory of Syrian national treasures. The removal of such items from Syria might be regarded as illegal and grounds for punishment. An elder of the Damascus Jewish community lamented how much Syrian Jews were leaving behind.

> "There is the cemetery," he said, with thousands of graves from centuries of living here. "And there are the Torahs," the sacred Jewish Biblical scrolls that represent the word of God. "We are forbidden to take them out of the country. How can we leave them?"[42]

They didn't. Selected artifacts of the community's material heritage, including Torahs, were secretly removed from Syria as the community left. Some items were hidden in the baggage of a departing family. Some things were tucked away in commercial shipments. Others were carried out by business travellers and other visitors to Syria, ostensibly as gifts from Syrian Jews to family abroad. Some of these couriers may have known or suspected the nature and spiritual value of the items they were carrying. Others did not. Some objects fell into private hands, and others made their way into the care of existing Syrian Jewish synagogues in the New York area or in Israel, where congregations were only too pleased to reclaim parts of their historical legacy. Still other items were donated to museums and scholarly research centres where they will be protected and studied by generations of future scholars.

Some community treasures passed through Judy Feld Carr's hands. In the spring of 1990, several years before the final exodus of Syrian Jews began, a cardboard box wrapped in white gauze and mailed in Aleppo, was delivered to her home. It was addressed to "Mrs. Judy." The box, about the size of a carton that might contain a dozen large apple juice cans, had cleared Canada Customs unopened. Judy had no idea what was in the box or who had mailed it to her. Frightened, she asked the mail carrier to leave the box sitting on her front porch. She called the Israeli consulate and members of the consular security staff soon arrived at her door. They scanned the box with a metal detector. Nothing was found. They then gingerly carried it into her backyard. Keeping Judy at a distance, security personnel carefully opened it. Inside were cookies, three layers of chocolate wafers. Underneath the wafers were old Jewish religious texts, some dating back to the fifteenth century.

Several weeks later, a letter arrived from an elderly man in Aleppo inquiring whether Mrs. Judy had received the "six copies of our Bible" and asking that she acknowledge "receipt of them in order to tranquillise me." After checking with her Aleppo informants to make sure that the writer was not a Muhabarat plant, she responded that she had received the Bibles and sent further thanks for the cookies. Several more boxes soon arrived through the mail. This time, each box was opened by Canada Customs before being delivered to her. The first contained more cookies, and underneath them, more old books. Two more boxes followed, containing religious books concealed in rolled-up sheets of pressed apricot candy commonly referred to as shoe leather.

The old man in Aleppo asked Judy for the address of others in Toronto who might also appreciate this type of candy. Before long, Canada Post delivered boxes to two of her friends. Gradually, a collection of more than ninety books piled up on the floor in the Carrs' den. Judy sent money from the Feld Fund to reimburse the sender for his considerable postal costs, and until he left Aleppo, the man became another in her chain of informants, feeding her reliable information about goings-on in Aleppo and especially about any difficulties faced by individuals and families then in the process of applying for exit visas.[43]

After the sender had left Syria as part of the 1992 exodus and the shipments stopped, Israeli consular officials packed up the books at Judy's request, and shipped them to the Jewish National Library in Jerusalem. They were checked against existing library holdings and catalogued so that they would be accessible to scholars. The library already had copies of some of the books, but the ones from Aleppo were often in better shape. Duplicate books were earmarked for distribution to Syrian Jewish synagogues in Israel.[44]

Several of the books from Aleppo held importance to scholars beyond the printed page. Since they were not printed in Syria but in Holland, Poland, Istanbul, or elsewhere in the Jewish world, their presence in Aleppo offered scholars clues about the nature and extent of Jewish commerce from the late fifteenth through the early nineteenth centuries. Handwritten notes in some of the volumes provided information about the internal workings of the early Aleppo Jewish community. In one, blank pages were used to record synagogue accounts and a list of those who had paid their annual synagogue fees and those in arrears.[45]

Other holy items also came Judy Feld Carr's way, including a Torah from Aleppo. Among those grateful to be leaving Syria was a family of four from Qamishli. The husband had spent time in prison, and while he was there, Judy had sent money from the Feld Fund to care for him and his family and, eventually, to pay the "fees" negotiated for his release. In late 1993, she paid to bring him, his wife, and his two children out of Syria.

The departing Jew, with exit visas and passports for his family in hand, covertly made his way to his dark and empty Aleppo synagogue. He carefully took the Torah case from the ark and removed the Torah scroll from its protective decorative case. He placed the empty case back in the ark, hoping that if the authorities opened the ark they would assume the Torah was still rolled up inside it's case. He then carefully carried the Torah scroll home. The Torah was wrapped in a clean cloth and hidden inside one of the family's suitcases. At the airport, although authorities routinely searched all the luggage of departing Jews, the suitcase containing the Torah was slipped through. The family and all their luggage were waved on. The family boarded their flight and took off for New York.

When Judy next visited New York, the family found out that she was in the city and left messages that the husband had to meet with her. He did not say why. With rare exceptions, Judy shied away from meeting those she had helped get out of Syria. There were by now several thousand Syrian Jews who were grateful for her assistance, so many, in fact, that she had trouble remembering all their names. While she knew many felt a deep gratitude to her for all she had done, Judy didn't want to encourage any dependency on her or the now-depleted Feld Fund. She also wanted to protect her privacy and the security of the few outstanding Syrian files.

Judy knew the man had been in prison and had been a stalwart in both the Qamishli and Aleppo communities. She agreed to meet him at the home of one of her Syrian contacts in Brooklyn. It was an emotional meeting for both. He saw her as a miracle worker. She had twice saved him and his family. To express his gratitude, he insisted she accept the Aleppo Torah. He handed her the Torah scroll still wrapped in the cloth. The scroll, at least two hundred years old, was magnificent. Instead of the usual white parchment, the Torah from Aleppo was written on a soft, supple tan leather, probably deer skin. The hand-inscribed and classic Sephardi Hebrew lettering was deeply black and clear, as if the scribe had just finished his work.

There was an inscription in Hebrew at the end of the scrolls, likely written there by the person who first bought the Torah and placed it in the Aleppo synagogue. The inscription, dated the Jewish year 5574, corresponding to the secular year 1814, reads, "I have acquired this Torah for the worship of my creator. He is my glory and my beauty. May this be God's will. Amen." Judy arranged for the Torah scroll to be temporarily put on display in her own synagogue, Beth Tzedec, home of the Feld Fund and the first synagogue to commemorate *Shabbat Zachor* for Syrian Jews. The Torah was then sent to Jerusalem, where it was deposited for safekeeping with the National Library. Judy hoped that it would would eventually find its way to a synagogue whose congregants were from Aleppo "so that the tradition of hundreds of years would not be broken and those originally from Aleppo would be able to continue their glorification of God through the same medium that they and their forebears have done in years gone by."[46]

By the end of 1994, the final chapter in the history of Syrian Jews was almost complete. Today barely seventy or so Jews remain in Syria. The once-proud Jewish community in Syria is no more. Synagogues that once echoed to the sound of prayer stand silent and empty. In Aleppo and Qamishli, it is no longer possible to guarantee the requisite *minyan*, the traditional ten adult males assembled as one, for prayer and ritual reading of the Torah. Torahs, holy books, and other precious items of the millennia-old Jewish presence in Syria have either been taken secretly out of Syria or abandoned for all time by Jews who will rebuild Jewish life afresh elsewhere.

In one case, Judy Feld Carr actively sought out a very special book, a Damascus Keter. A Keter is a handwritten and often decoratively designed micrography of the twenty-four books of the Hebrew Bible accompanied by commentaries. Judy first learned of the possible existence of the Damascus Keter when she and her husband, Don, were in Israel in the summer of 1993. They visited the Israel Museum in Jerusalem where they were shown several items of Syrian Jewish origin in the collection. Among the items was a restoration of the original tenth-century Aleppo Keter, the earliest-known manuscript comprising the full text of the Bible. For generations, the Aleppo Keter had been cherished and zealously guarded by the Jewish community there. It was regarded as a symbol of community stability and dedication to God. Local tradition held that the community would be destroyed if the Keter ever left Aleppo. Even today the volume is regarded as of prime importance by biblical scholars.

In 1947, following the United Nations approval of the partition of Palestine, anti-Zionist rioters set fire to Aleppo's ancient synagogue. The Aleppo Keter was rescued from the flames, but it suffered severe fire damage. Many of the pages were scorched but salvaged intact. The text was so precious that every piece of burned parchment was carefully sifted from the fire's ashes. Tiny pieces were enclosed in lockets that are still worn as talismans around the necks of many Aleppo Jews. The intact pages of the Keter were divided into separate piles and hidden in different secure places, where they remained for ten years. After much detective work by Israeli agents, Keter pages were collected from their hiding places. The document was smuggled into Turkey and, eventually, into Israel "under still mysterious circumstances in the 1950s." In Israel, the Keter was painstakingly reassembled. It now contains 295 of the original 487 pages. Scholars still hope that more pages will eventually turn up.[47]

The curator of the museum's Middle East collection mused that there were also rumours of a Keter in Damascus. If there was a Damascus Keter, it was not widely known in the Damascus Jewish community. Perhaps the rabbis hid their Keter long ago, lest it suffer the same fate as the Aleppo Keter. If it did exist, it would be an invaluable treasure of Jewish heritage.[48]

Intrigued, Judy Feld Carr checked with contacts in Israeli intelligence. She was told there could well be a Keter, and if so, it was a manuscript of such rarity and intrinsic historic worth that it should not be left behind. But any Syrian Jew caught trying to smuggle out the Keter would suffer a severe punishment. Judy could not let the matter pass. She made guarded inquiries of her Damascus informants. If it existed, where was it and in whose care? No reply. When she attended a Syrian wedding in New York, a trusted confidant told Judy that a Keter had been tucked away in a Damascus synagogue for centuries, unknown to all but a few community leaders. Rabbi Hamra, then still in Damascus, would know about it.[49]

In communications with Rabbi Hamra that she knew to be secure from the Muhabarat, Judy still did not dare use the term "Keter." Searching for a code phrase that someone who knew about the volume would understand, she asked about a "book that is better than any of the others." When she was satisfied that Rabbi Hamra understood, Judy altered her code to talk about meat and chickens or simply "the product." Rabbi Hamra told her that "the product" was still in the basement of a Damascus synagogue. He also told her that Syrian authorities knew about its existence. They had made an inventory of communally held books and artifacts, and the Damascus Keter was discovered and added to the inventory, though it is doubtful that they understood its historical and religious significance.[50]

Concerned that this particular Jewish treasure not be left behind as booty for the Syrians, Judy asked Rabbi Hamra to help her get the Keter out of Syria. Rabbi Hamra was sympathetic but uneasy—removing the Damascus Keter from Syria would be dangerous. However, the rabbi agreed to work with Judy if she could come up with a foolproof plan.[51]

Judy approached an Arabic-speaking Westerner who had acted as a courier for her in the past. He would soon be making another business trip to Damascus. Would he do her a personal favour? She explained that the rabbi insisted on sending her a gift from Damascus. Nothing much—she understood it was some kind of small prayer book. She joked that she would rather have a gold necklace, but from a rabbi you get books. The rabbi did not trust the post office. Would the visitor mind picking up the gift from him at his home? There should be no problem. The Muhabarat was used to Rabbi Hamra, as chief rabbi and spokesperson for the Jewish community of Syria, meeting with diplomats and other Westerners. The handover of a harmless gift would still need to be done discreetly, so the visitor was to just accept it quietly.[52]

The Westerner agreed, sensing that there was more to this gift story than Judy was letting on. He had enough experience with her to realize that she would not go to all this trouble over a gift that was of little importance to her. At some personal risk to himself, he was ready to help.

It was arranged for the Westerner to visit Rabbi Hamra at his home. The rabbi went to the synagogue, and when he left he had the Keter with him. He took it home, although he was not comfortable having the Keter in his possession.

In the course of the visit, Rabbi Hamra handed a small, leather-bound book in a multi-coloured cardboard sleeve to the Westerner, who put the book into an innocuous black plastic shopping bag. When he left the rabbi's house a few minutes later, he slipped the bag under his shirt and put on a light raincoat he had brought with him. Still talking casually, the rabbi walked his visitor out to a main street. The Westerner flagged down a taxi. The two men shook hands and parted company.

The Westerner assumed that the taxi driver reported to the security police on foreigners he picked up. But with a close-cut beard and no tie, the Arabic-speaking Westerner knew he could easily be mistaken for an Iranian. He asked the driver to take him to the Iranian embassy. When the taxi pulled up across from the embassy, he paid the fare and got out. He waited to cross the street as the taxi drove out of sight. He then turned and walked across town to his true destination, the book still hidden under his shirt. When he left Syria several days later, the gift for Judy Feld Carr was hidden among his business documents. Shortly thereafter, Rabbi Hamra also left Syria for good.[53]

Within days, Judy had the Keter. It was exquisitely preserved, showing hardly any wear in spite of its age—it was probably completed in the fourteenth century, but determining the date when a scribe meticulously and beautifully copied the full biblical text onto the bound pages of the Keter would have to await expert examination. The book contained two handwritten and witnessed contracts of sale inscribed on the inside back cover, one in Judeo-Arabic and the other in Rashi script. The first details the purchase of the Keter in Castile during the reign of King Enrique IV (1454–1474), before the expulsion of the Jews from Spain in 1492. The second records the sale of the document in Constantinople in 1515. These contracts suggest the Keter was among the treasured effects of a wealthy Jew escaping the Inquisition. It may then have made its way from Constantinople to Damascus, with Jewish merchants expanding eastward during the post-Spanish-expulsion era. In Damascus they built a synagogue where the Keter would have been given an honoured place.[54]

Before his departure for Israel, Rabbi Hamra visited Judy in Toronto. He asked her permission to take the Keter, so important to the Jews of Damascus, with him to Israel. The Keter is now stored in the National Library in Jerusalem. At this writing, plans are in progress for a symbolic presentation of the Keter to the president of Israel as a gift from the Syrian Jewish community to the entire Jewish people.[55]

EPILOGUE

Survival and Renewal

O N A WARM TEL AVIV EVENING in June 1996, five hundred guests, most of them recent arrivals from Damascus, joined in celebrating a wedding. Anyone who has attended a Syrian Jewish wedding knows they are loud, exuberant, rambunctious affairs. Food and drink are plentiful. Dancing and laughter continue well into the night. This was no exception, but to many who were there, this was more than a wedding. It was also a celebration of survival and renewal. The bride was a daughter of Selim Swed. Like many of their guests, she and her family had only been in Israel just under two years. For Selim and his brother Elie, memories of years in Syrian prisons are still with them. But there was joy on that spring evening as the bride, her groom, his family and hers, stood together under the *chupa*, the wedding canopy, which signifies the creation of a new Jewish home, and Rabbi Hamra recited the marriage blessings.

As the last act of the Jewish wedding ceremony, the groom smashes a glass underfoot. Some people interpret the breaking of the glass as a positive statement. In the act of marriage the bride and groom are symbolically breaking with their separate pasts to forge a new union as husband and wife.

The more traditional interpretation is that the breaking of the glass recalls the destruction of the Second Temple in Jerusalem. It is meant to remind the assembly that moments of joy are tinged with sadness and that for Jews no life event, not even an intensely personal moment such as a wedding, can exist in isolation from the larger historical drama of the Jewish people.

In their own way, most of the wedding guests had each shattered a personal glass. Sad as it was to leave the place that had been their home for generations, they embraced new beginnings, carving out a new life in a new home. If any of them needed to be reminded of the gulf that separated their new lives as citizens of Israel from their former lives as Jews in Syria, they only had to look at Selim Swed, a free man, celebrating his daughter's marriage. Whatever wounds of body and mind still remained to heal, Selim, his family, and his guests knew there were no Muhabarat informers keeping watch on the proceedings. There were no insults and there was no harassment awaiting them in the streets outside the reception hall. They were safe. They all had reason to rejoice.

At Syrian Jewish wedding receptions there is no reserved seating, just a bewildering free-for-all as guests good-naturedly organize themselves into tables of family and close friends. Eventually, everyone finds a place and a natural order emerges out of the tumult. At this wedding there was an exception to the rule—one table was set aside for several special guests.

In keeping with custom, when the dancing began, the bride and groom were lifted into the air on chairs and carried around the crowded dance floor as the assembled guests danced in circles below them. When the bride and groom were lowered back to the floor, their parents were similarly honoured. While Selim Swed was still held high, a woman from the special table was lifted on a chair to dance in the air with Selim. There was a sudden buzz. Who was this woman? Why was she singled out for such an honour? Word quickly spread around the room. The woman was Mrs. Judy.

When Judy was lowered down, a man she didn't recognize grabbed her hand. Trying to be heard above the music and dancing, he told her his name, explaining partly in Hebrew and partly in Arabic, that, like Selim Swed, she had rescued him and his family, from Syria. They embraced.

By the time Mrs. Judy made her way back to her table, a line had formed. With the help of a translator, many others whom she had helped to bring out of Syria introduced themselves and thanked her.

Judy remembered some by name, others not. But every one of them knew her and what she had done for them. As they introduced themselves, some wept with joy. A few were so moved at meeting Mrs. Judy that they could hardly speak. Some kissed her hand and blessed her and her family for all she had done. Many brought their children with them to her table so they too might know the woman who had ransomed them out of Syria.[1]

During Judy Feld Carr's more than twenty-five years of involvement with the cause of Syrian Jewry, she participated in the removal of about three thousand Syrian Jews. Publicly, she was their outspoken advocate, welcoming any opportunity to further their cause. With the help of a core group of Canadian supporters, such as her close friend Helen Cooper in Toronto, and the tireless assistance from supporters in Canada and the United States, Judy Feld Carr was also an active fundraiser on behalf of Syrian Jewry. She pieced together an extensive network of contacts in the Diaspora Syrian Jewish community and in Syria itself. As a result, she gathered valuable information on the inner workings of both the Syrian Jewish community and the Syrian regime.

Judy Feld Carr and her small group of supporters, however, were never as alone as they supposed. Well before Judy and Rubin Feld made Syrian Jewry their cause, financial support from various sources was funnelled into the Syrian Jewish community through the American Joint Distribution Committee. This money was critical in sustaining what limited Jewish institutional life the Syrian regime permitted, particularly Jewish schools. The World Jewish Congress had also earmarked the cause of Syrian Jews for political action. In many cases, Jewish organizations lobbied their respective governments and international agencies to lend their voices to a chorus of protest against the abuse of Jewish human rights in Syria. In different countries, Jewish organizations also set up Committees of Concern for the Jews of Syria. In the United States in particular, organizations such as the Conference of Presidents, the American Jewish Committee, the American Jewish Congress, the Anti-Defamation League, the B'nai Brith, the National Jewish

Community Relations Advisory Committee, and after 1989, a New York–based Council for the Rescue of Syrian Jews kept the cause of Syrian Jews before the American Congress and the president.[2]

Over the twenty-five years that Judy Feld Carr campaigned for Syrian Jews, sympathetic international agencies and governments like Canada also played a role in monitoring the situation. While the Syrian government was often effective in obscuring the truth, much important information on the state of Syrian Jewish affairs leaked out to the West and into the international media through the efforts of friendly diplomats and international agency representatives in Syria.[3]

The role of Israel in the rescue of Syrian Jews was crucial. Committed to being a home to world Jewry, the Israelis knew that the Jews of Syria were suffering in part because of their identification with Israel. But hanging over any Israeli initiative was the threat that it could validate Syria's accusations of Jewish disloyalty to the Syrian state and legitimize, in the regime's eyes, state oppression of the Jewish population. As a result, Israel often worked behind the scenes, enlisting friendly governments to ensure that Syria's oppression of its Jews would not go unreported or unpublicized. Similarly, Israel supported Jewish organizations around the world in their efforts to promote the cause of Syrian Jewry. Inside Israel, private individuals and voluntary organizations, such as the World Organization of Jews from Arab Countries, arranged conferences and published materials on the plight of Syrian Jews. Most important, Israel secretly facilitated their escape. Israeli intelligence agents were critical in planning underground escape routes through Lebanon and Turkey, often passing Jews from safe house to safe house, until arrangements could be made to transfer them to Israel. Judy Feld Carr successfully plugged in to those escape routes and, with Israeli co-operation, organized numerous escapes from Syria.[4]

Over time, she quietly developed a working relationship with Israeli intelligence officials that solidified as she gained their grudging respect and, to some degree, their trust. Israeli operatives eventually began to share information with her on individuals, escape routes, and even weather forecasts that were essential to the rescues and other covert activities that she was involved in. But the Israelis, understandably, are not forthcoming about their relationship with Judy Feld Carr. For her part, ready as she now is to describe most of her Syrian activities, she remains silent about her involvement with the Israelis. The most that can be said at this time is that a relationship existed. It grew close and it was mutually beneficial.

What can be said about Syria's attitude to the international campaign on behalf of Syrian Jews and to Judy Feld Carr's role in that campaign? There are only bits and pieces of evidence. No doubt the Muhabarat kept extensive files on Judy Feld Carr. Its agents had doubtless done their homework, both in Syria and Canada. On the occasions when Rabbi Hamra was interrogated by Muhabarat officials about his relationship with Mrs. Judy, they proved exceptionally well informed about her. And, of course, there were agents who had information that would never be found in police files. They were the ones on the take, pocketing the ransom money that Judy Feld Carr paid for their co-operation. But how much the Muhabarat knew of her secret activities—her dealings with smugglers and the details of payments made to officials—and what the Muhabarat did with that information remain unknown.

If the Muhabarat knew more about Judy Feld Carr's activities than she might have thought, the question persists—why didn't they stop her activities? That would have been in keeping with the Syrian regime's rejection of what it saw as foreign interference in its domestic affairs, and would have served notice on Syrian Jews that the regime would not tolerate unauthorized international contact, let alone forgive cross-border escape attempts.

But Judy Feld Carr was not closed down. Were Syrian authorities willing to tolerate her activities because she was a Canadian or, more correctly, because she was not an American? There can be no denying the enmity between the United States and Syria and between the United States and Syria's most important patron, the Soviet Union, during much of the twenty-five-year period of the Syrian Jewish rescue. The United States regarded Syria as a client state of the Soviet Union, condemning Syria as a supporter of international terrorism and a stumbling block to progress on Middle East peace and security. Syria condemned the United States as Israel's chief backer, a force determined to undermine Syrian military, commercial, and political stability and a barrier to Syria's expansionist aspirations in neighbouring Lebanon. With this level of mutual hostility, what room was there for American Jewish organizations or individuals to do what Judy Feld Carr did on behalf of Syrian Jews?

Several Americans did have a high-profile role in advocating on behalf of Syrian Jews, even within Syria—witness the important work by Congressman Stephen Solarz and businessman Stephen Shalom. Despite their efforts, they did not and maybe never could do what Judy Feld Carr was able to do.

Syrian administrative officials may have had their own reasons for allowing Judy Feld Carr to carry on her activities. For some, the best reason not to stop Judy Feld Carr was that they didn't want to stop the flow of cash. Many Syrian public officials regarded "gifts" that came their way not as graft but as an accepted perk of office.

President Assad by all accounts was personally above the money-grubbing that appeared to be so much a part of the Syrian administration. But when he first opened the door to Jews travelling abroad and allowed his officials to determine humanitarian need, the door also opened to graft. In the early 1990s, when Assad agreed to a wholesale exodus of Jews, officials saw no reason to deny themselves the lucrative rewards that might flow from the commerce of emigration. Thus, while the Muhabarat repeatedly warned Rabbi Hamra about fostering too close a relationship with the Canadian activist—a warning he took very seriously—as long as he and those like him were circumspect and the money continued to flow, officials were prepared to allow Judy Feld Carr's activities to continue.

The Jews of Syria themselves deserve the largest credit for the community's survival. Were it not for leaders like Rabbi Hamra in Damascus and Rabbis Sasson and Farhi in Aleppo, all the efforts by Judy Feld Carr, the Israelis, and others would have been in vain. These people, under the most trying circumstances and at great personal risk to themselves and their families, continued to work steadfastly on behalf of their community. The same must be said for the bravery of those who risked Syrian imprisonment or worse, by making the plight of their people known to the outside world, who supplied Judy Feld Carr with essential information, and who acted as her couriers. Without their courage, the network of contacts on which her efforts were so dependent would never have developed. And most of all, it is important to acknowledge the endurance of ordinary Syrian Jews in the face of state-endorsed oppression. With the doors of the Jewish quarter shut tightly around them, their lives circumscribed by repressive regulations, and treated with contempt as unwelcome aliens, they still managed to sustain their pride in Jewish life. Their determination to remain Jews stands out as the ultimate act of defiance against their oppressors and makes the success of their eventual exodus all the sweeter.

Today the Syrian Jewish community is putting down new roots—mostly in New York and Israel. In June 1993, some of those who will never forget Judy Feld Carr's efforts on their behalf gathered in New York to celebrate the final exodus of Jews from Syria. She could not attend, but in her absence the crowd applauded as the citation on an engraved plaque awarded to her by the Sephardi Bikur Holim was read aloud.

> Presented to Judy Feld Carr who arose while it was "still night" and woke up the world to the plight of our brethren in Syria.
>
> Through her efforts lives have been saved, families sustained and loved ones re-united.
>
> She has saved entire worlds and will be blessed by generations to come.

ENDNOTES

Note: Some spelling inconsistencies appear on personal file names.
The following abbreviations have been used throughout the notes:

EA   Department of Foreign Affairs and International Trade,
Ottawa

CJC   Canadian Jewish Congress National Archives, Montreal

JFC   Judy Feld Carr Papers, Toronto

JTA   Jewish Telegraphic Agency

RF   Ronald Feld Papers, Toronto

PROLOGUE:
The Determination to Survive

1 Nehemiah Robinson, *The Arab Counties in the Near East and Their Jewish Communities* (New York: Institute of Jewish Affairs, 1951), 77–78; Joseph B. Schechtman, *On Wings of Eagles: The Plight, Exodus, and Homecoming of Oriental Jewry* (New York: T. Yoseloff, 1961), 150–54.

2 Yehuda Dominitz, *Immigration and Absorption of Jews from Arab Countries, Israel's Experience 1948– 1986 [A Summary]* (New York: AJC, 1986), 6.

3 For a study of the trials of Syrian Jews since the Second World War, see Saul S. Friedman, *Without Future: The Plight of Syrian Jewry* (New York: Praeger, 1989).

4 Department of State, *Country Reports on Human Rights Practices for 1992 [Syria]* (Washington: Department of State, 1993).

5 Interview with Murad Guindi, August 3, 1996, Toronto.

6 Interview with Carol Robertson, November 5, 1997, Toronto.

7 JFC Papers. Correspondence Files. Letter from Prime Minister Rabin to JFC 1995 File. Yizhak Rabin to Judy Feld Carr, February 20, 1995.

CHAPTER ONE:
Half a World Away

1 Interview with Judy Feld Carr, Toronto, August 17, 1993.

2 For a discussion of Canadian refugee policy in the post-war period, see Irving Abella and Harold Troper, *None Is Too Many: Canada and the Jews of Europe, 1933–1945* (Toronto: Lester & Orpen Dennys,1982).

In the unprecedented national economic expansion that followed the second World war, labour-intensive Canadian industry faced severe shortages of workers. Domestic supplies proved inadequate to meet growing demand, and business leaders were soon clamouring for Ottawa to open immigration to the large labour pool available in the Displaced Persons camps of post-war Europe. Working in co-operation with employers, the government approved specific immigrant-recruitment schemes designed to import labour to capital.

[3] Interview with Judy Feld Carr, August 17, 1993, Toronto.

[4] Interview with Judy Feld Carr, August 24, 1993, Toronto.

[5] Bernard Malamud, *The Fixer* (New York: Farrar, Straus and Giroux, 1966), 314.

[6] For a useful outline of events in and around the Six-Day War as they relate to Syria, see Moshe Ma'oz, *Syria and Israel: From War to Peacemaking* (Oxford: Clarendon Press, 1995), 88–104.

[7] For a discussion of the impact of the Six-Day War on American Jews, see Charles E. Silberman, *A Certain People: American Jews and Their Lives Today* (New York: Summit Books, 1985), 181–203.

[8] Doubts about the viability of the survival of unassimilated Jewry and the Jewish tradition in Canada have emerged as a major subject of debate in the Canadian Jewish community in recent years. See *Task Force on Jewish Continuity, Assimilation and Intermarriage* (Toronto: Jewish Federation of Greater Toronto, 1994).

[9] For a review of the evolution of Jewish community institutional life in Canada, see Harold Troper and Morton Weinfeld, "Canadian Jews and Canadian Multiculturalism," in Howard Adelman and John H. Simpson (eds.), *Multiculturalism, Jews, and Identities in Canada* (Jerusalem. Magnes Press, 1996), 11–36.

[10] This was true for even the most militant of Jewish communal responses to the threat of antisemitism, N-3. In 1965 this group coalesced, as if out of nowhere, to do battle with a band of neo-Nazis then threatening to preach its antisemitic message in a Toronto park. In both Toronto and Montreal, N-3, named for Newton's Third Law—for every action there is an equal and opposite reaction—remained for a time outside Congress and was often critical of Congress and other mainstream Jewish organizations for being too soft on antisemitism and antisemites. But as N-3 formalized its structure, began self-defence training, and was more and more called on to informally assist police with security at Jewish events, it formed links with the mainstream Jewish community. It was not long until leaders of N-3 were absorbed into Congress, where they tended to support a more confrontational response to any and all manifestations of antisemitism. Harold Troper and Morton Weinfeld, *Old Wounds: Jews, Ukrainians and the Hunt for Nazi War Criminals in Canada* (Toronto: Penguin, 1988), 387–88; Frank Bialystok, "Delayed Impact: The Holocaust and the Canadian Jewish Community 1945–1985, unpublished doctoral dissertation, York University, 1997, 153–89.

[11] Yair Kotler, *Heil Kahane* (New York: Adama Books, 1986), 37.

[12] Interview with Judy Feld Carr, August 24, 1993, Toronto. For a comprehensive historical analysis of the Soviet Jewry campaign in Toronto see Mindy B. Avrich-Skapinker, "Canadian Jewish Involvement with Soviet Jewry, 1970–1990: The Toronto Case Study," Unpublished doctoral dissertation, University of Toronto, 1993.

[13] Interview with Judy Feld Carr, August 24, 1993, Toronto.

CHAPTER TWO:
The Jews of Despair

1 Elie Wiesel, *The Jews of Silence: A Personal Report on Soviet Jewry* (New York: Holt, Rinehart and Winston, 1966).

2 Interview with Judy Feld Carr, August 24, 1993.

3 Interview with Judy Feld Carr, August 24, 1993, Toronto. It has been argued that the wind went out of the JDL's sails in the United States in the aftermath of the bombing of the offices of Sol Hurok, the Jewish impresario who brought Soviet performers to North America. A twenty-seven-year-old secretary died as a result of the bombing, for which JDL members were indicted. Robert I. Friedman, *The False Prophet: Rabbi Meir Kahane—From FBI Informant to Knesset Member* (London: Faber and Faber, 1990), 142–45.

4 "Report from the Dark Ages," Near East Report, February 4, 1969, 10, as quoted in Lorenzo Kent Kimball, *The Changing Pattern of Political Power in Iraq, 1958 to 1971* (New York: Robert Speller, 1972),148.

5 Shlomo Hillel, *Operation Babylon* (New York: Doubleday, 1987), 292-295; Mitchell Knesbacher "The Jews of Iraq and the International Protection of Rights of Minorities," in David Sidorsky (ed.), *Essays on Human Rights: Contemporary Issues and Jewish Perspectives* (Philadelphia: JPS, 1979), 170–76.

6 *Debates of the House of Commons* 1968–69, Vol. 5, 5045, 5319.

7 EA, 45-ME-13-3, Vol. 2, Memorandum from G. G. Riddell to Consular Division, February 5, 1969, re Possible Immigration of Jews from the Middle East; Cable from Mitchell Sharp to Tel Aviv/Tehran/ Beirut/Cairo, February 6, 1969; *Globe and Mail*, February 10, 1969; *Globe and Mail*, February 14, 1969.

8 EA, 45-ME-13-3, Vol.2, Memorandum to R. E. Collins from G. G. Riddell, re Jewish/Muslim Emigration from Iraq, February 20, 1969; Memorandum to Minister from M. Cadieux, re Jewish and Non-Jewish Emigration from Iraq, February 25, 1969; Letter to A. J. MacEachen from Mitchell Sharp, February 26, 1969.

9 EA, 45-ME-13-3, Vol.2, Memorandum to the minister from M. Cadieux, re Jewish and Non-Jewish emigration from Iraq, February 28, 1969; Memorandum to file form E. J. Bergbusch, re Emigration of Iraqi Jews, March 5, 1969.

10 EA, 45-ME-13-3, Vol. 3, Draft Memorandum to the Cabinet, March 10, 1969.

11 EA, 45-ME-13-3, Vol. 3, DM, Manpower and Immigration to M. Cadieux, March 14, 1969.

12 EA, 45-ME-13-3, Vol. 3, Allan MacEachen to Mitchell Sharp, May 29, 1969; Cabinet committee on External Policy and Defence, Meeting of June 24, 1969, re Jews in Iraq.

13 Rahael Patai as quoted in Danielle Pletka, "Past Glories Shape Destiny of Arabs," *Insight*, March 4, 1991.

14 Resolution as quoted in Maurice M. Roumani, *The Case of the Jews from Arab Countries: A Neglected Issue* (Tel Aviv: WOJAC, 1983), 33.

15 Interview with N.M., January 27, 1997, Tel Aviv (anonymity requested).

16 Interview with Yehuda Dominitz, January 29, 1997, Jerusalem.

[17] See, for example, Yehuda Dominitz, *Immigration and Absorption of Jews from Arab Lands* (Tel Aviv: WOJAC, n.d.); *Jews in Arab Counties: Jewish and Arab Refugees and Refugee Movements—Some Facts and Statistics* (Tel Aviv: WOJAC, 1993); *Who Is a Refugee in the Middle East* (Tel Aviv: WOJAC, n.d.); Maurice M. Roumani, *The Case of the Jews from Arab Countries: A Neglected Issue*, fourth printing (Tel Aviv: WOJAC, 1983); *The Fourth National Convention: WOJAC and the Peace Process* (Tel Aviv: WOJAC, 1993).

[18] CJC, DA12, Box 13, File 8, Memorandum to All Affiliates of the World Jewish Congress from Armand Kaplan, re Tragic situation of the Jews in Syria and request for immediate action by all our affiliates.

[19] Interview with George Gruen, March 16, 1995, New York.

[20] Leonard Dinnerstein, *America and the Survivors of the Holocaust* (New York: Columbia University Press, 1982), 53–57, 246.

[21] Interview with Philip Katz, May 29, 1995, Montreal.

[22] Interview with George Gruen, March 16, 1995, New York.

[23] CJC, DA 12, Box 13, File 2, Telegram of Alan Rose to Armand Kaplan, September 15, 1971: Telegram of Alan Rose to Saltzman, September 22, 1971; Armand Kaplan to Alan Rose, September 23, 1971; CJC, DA 12, Box 13, file 8, Aide Memoire: Meeting of CJC Delegation with Mitchell Sharp, Ottawa, September 17, 1971.

[24] CJC, DA 12, Box 13, File 2, Alan Rose to Armand Kaplan, October 6, 1971; CJC, DA 12, Box 13, File 8, Memorandum to Members of the Governing Council from Armand Kaplan, November 2, 1971; Alan Rose to Max Malamet, October 13, 1971; CJC, DA 12, Box 13, File 7, Memorandum to National Officers from Alan Rose, January 21, 1972.

[25] CJC, DA 12, Box 13, File 2, Armand Kaplan to Alan Rose, September 27, 1971; Armand Kaplan to Alan Rose, January 13, 1992; Alan Rose to Armand Kaplan, January 20, 1972; Gabriella Tawfik to Kurt Waldheim, February 14, 1972. According to Yehuda Dominitz, some years later rabbinic authorities in Israel were satisfied that Elia's body had been handed over to Israeli authorities as part of a prisoner exchange and declared Elia dead and his wife a widow. Interview with Yehuda Dominitz, January 29, 1997, Jerusalem.

[26] CJC, DA 12, Box 13, File 8, Saul Hayes to John G. Diefenbaker, April 20, 1971; CJC, DA 12, Box 13, File 9, Emanuel Shimoni to Saul Hayes, November 17, 1969; Emanuel Shimoni to Saul Hayes, February 18, 1990; Memorandum to All Affiliates of the World Jewish Congress from Armand Kaplan, re Tragic situation of the Jews in Syria and request for immediate action by all our affiliates, October 28, 1971.

[27] Interview with David Satok, December 20, 1994, Toronto.

[28] *Canadian Jewish News*, November 26, 1971; CJC, DA 12, Box 13, File 7, Gunther Plaut to Alan Rose, December 16, 1971.

[29] CJC, DA 12, Box 13, File 7, Alan Rose to Gunther Plaut, December 20, 1971; Memorandum of Mayer Levy to Mayer Sharzer and all regional CJC offices re Jews in Syria, December 28, 1971.

[30] CJC, DA 12, Box 13, File 7, Rabbi M. Halpern to Rabbis, January 13, 1972.

31 CJC, DA 12, Box 13, File 7, Committee of Concern (New York), Statement on Jews in Syria, October 7, 1971; Memorandum to Regional Offices (ADL) from Abe Foxman, re Treatment of Jews in Syria, November 11, 1971; *La Monde*, November 8, 1971; *Christian Science Monitor*, November 24, 1971; *Jerusalem Post*, November 9, 1971; *Jerusalem Post*, November 16, 1971; *Jewish Chronicle*, November 12, 1971; JFC Papers, Case files, Published Information on Syrian Jews, Statement by Ambassador Joel Barrami in the Third Committee of the 26th Session of the General Assembly, November 29, 1971; Jewish Telegraphic Agency (JTA), November 30, 1971.

32 *New York Times*, January 28, 1972.

33 CJC, DA 12, Box 13, File 7, Memorandum from Ralph Lallouz to Alan Rose, re Conference Internationale pour la Délivrance des Juifs au Moyen-Orient, January 31, 1972; *New York Times*, January 28, 1972; RF Papers, Clippings and Reports on Jews in Arab Lands, Record of Evidence of the Hearings of Two Syrian Witnesses before an Independent Commission of Enquiry Taken in Paris, October 22, 1971; RF Papers. Sephardic Jews 1972–74, Minutes of the Proceedings of the Commission of Inquiry, Paris, October 30, 1971.

34 RF Papers, Clippings and Reports on Jews in Arab Lands, Shlomo Hillel, "Jews in Arab Lands—A persecuted Remnant," n.d.; CJC, DA 12, Box 15, File 16, Memorandum to Members associated in the World Conference of Jewish Organizations (COJO) from Yehudah Hellman, re Syrian Jewry, January 28, 1972.

35 CJC, DA 12, Box 13, File 7, Alan Rose to Donny Goody, January 7, 1972; Memorandum to National Officers from Alan Rose, January 21, 1972; EA, 45-ME-13-3, Vol. 5, Alan Rose to Robert Elliott, February 10, 1972; Proposed CJC Public Statement Concerning Conditions of Jews in Syria, n.d.; CJC, DA 12, Box 13, File 5, Canadian Jewish Congress: Jews in Syria, February 25, 1972.

36 EA, 45-ME-13-3, Vol.5, Memorandum for the Minister from A. E. Ritchie, re Syrian Jews, February 16, 1992.

CHAPTER THREE:
The Task At Hand

1 *Jewish Press*, January 21, 1972.

2 *Canadian Jewish News*, November 26, 1971; CJC, DA 12, Box 13, File 7, Gunther Plaut to Alan Rose, December 16, 1971: Alan Rose to Gunther Plaut, December 20, 1971.

3 Interview with Judy Feld Carr, September 2, 1993, Toronto.

4 Interview with Judy Feld Carr, September 2, 1993, Toronto.

5 *Canadian Jewish News*, January 14, 1972.

6 RF Papers, Correspondence 1971–73, Ronald Feld to Ambassador Joel Barromi, January 11, 1972; Joel Barromi to Ronald Feld, February 2, 1972.

7 RF Papers, Correspondence 1971-73, Ronald Feld to Lucius Clay, March 6, 1972; Ronald Feld to George Gruen, March 6, 1972; Ronald Feld to Abraham Dwek, March 9, 1972; Ronald Feld to Edward Sift, March 9, 1972; Lucius Clay

to Ronald Feld, March 20,1972; RF Papers, Clippings—Articles on Soviet Jewry, Arabs, Lucius Clay to Ronald Feld, April 17, 1972.

[8] RF Papers, Clippings and Reports re Syrian Jewry, Protest advertisement, "An appeal to the Conscience of Mankind on Behalf of Syrian Jews," *Jewish News*, n.d. (November 4, 1971?); Protest advertisement, "Freedom Not Tears" (January 23, 1972), *Jewish News* January 21, 1972; Protest advertisement, "Protest the Oppression of Our Brothers in Syria" (December 7, 1972), *Jewish Press*, December 1, 1972, and December 8, 1972; Committee for the Rescue of Syrian Jewry, December 7, 1972; RF Papers, Syrian Jewry Support in Toronto, Ronald Feld to Alain Poher, January 4, 1972; RF Papers, Correspondence 1971–72, Ronald Feld to Jamil Stanbouli, December 14, 1971; Abraham Dwek to Ronald Feld, January 24, 1972; RF Papers, Poher (French Syrian Committee 1971–72), Abel Cohen to George Bush, October 21, 1971; RF Papers, Clippings (UN 1972), Rabbi Leon Masliton *et al* to Richard M. Nixon, October 17, 1972.

[9] Interview with George Gruen, March 16, 1995, New York; RF Papers, correspondence 1971–73, Ronald Feld to George Gruen, March 6, 1972.

[10] Interview with Judy Feld Carr, September 2, 1993, Toronto.

[11] RF Papers, Clippings re Israel, Syrian Jewry, "Fact Sheet: Condition of the Jews in Syria" n.d.; addressed postcards, n.d.

[12] RF Papers, Materials Related to Teach-in February 20, 1972, Teach-in introductions, "Will You Abandon Them—Will You Abandon Them," n.d.

[13] Interview with Judy Feld Carr, September 2, 1993, Toronto.

[14] *Toronto Star* February 21, 1972; RF Papers, File 9. Ronald Feld to the Editor, *Toronto Star*, February 22, 1972.

[15] RF Papers. Rube's Early Articles/Syrian Jews, Omnibus letter of Ronald Feld. February 28, 1972; RF Papers, Letters from MPs re Invitation to Teach-in Feb. 20, 1972, Yael Bernstein and Debbie Siegal to CCRJAL, March 8, 1972.

[16] *Toronto Star*, March 11, 1972: Interview with Judy Feld Carr, September 21, 1993, Toronto.

[17] Mindy B. Avrich-Skapinker, "Canadian Jewish Involvement with Soviet Jewry, 1970–1990: The Toronto Case Study," Unpublished Ph.D. thesis, University of Toronto, 1993, 72–92.

[18] Interview with Rabbi Mitchell Serels, March 13, 1995, New York. The events surrounding this telephone call are remembered clearly by Rabbi Serels, Judy Feld Carr, and Rabbi Hamra. The details of the call as laid out here are pieced together from three separate interviews with the participants.

[19] Interview with Judy Feld Carr, September 2, 1993, Toronto; the Committee later arranged to get a Damascus telephone directory. RF Papers, Correspondence, 1971–73, Telegram to Phil Chasin for Rayes, December 11, 1972.

[20] Interview with Rabbi Ibrahim Hamra, October 1, 1994, Toronto; Interview with Rabbi Mitchell Serels, March 13, 1995, New York; Interview with Judy Feld Carr, September 9, 1993, Toronto.

[21] Later Judy Feld Carr found a supplier of religious items in New York who specialized in meeting the needs of anti-Zionist Hassidic sects. There were no symbols or other references to the modern State of Israel in his materials.

[22] Interview with Rabbi Ibrahim Hamra, October 1, 1994, Toronto.

[23] JFC Papers, Subject files, Original Cables to Syria 1972–1975. Telegram, Rabbi Ibrahim Hamra to Ronald Feld, n.d.; notes on telegrams to Rabbi Hamra, n.d. and June 6, 1972; File 96: text of note to Rabbi Ibrahim Hamra from Ronald Feld, March 19, 1973; March 20, 1973. All biblical references in this book are taken from *Tanakh, A New Translation of the Holy Scriptures According to the Traditional Hebrew Text*, (Philadelphia: Jewish Publication Society, 1985).

[24] *House of Commons Debates*, March 13, 1972, 756; External Affairs officials in the Middle East were concerned that any public statements by the Canadian government on behalf of Syrian Jews, even if only "tied to domestic politics," would compromise the ability of External Affairs to deal with the Syrians over the Jewish situation. EA, 45-ME-13-3, Vol. 5, telegram from Canadian Embassy, Beirut, to External Affairs, March 16, 1972; Memorandum of A. E. Ritchie to the Minister re: Syrian Jews, March 24, 1972; RF Papers, Letters Received After February 20, 1972 Teach-in, Minutes of the Canadian Jewish Congress Executive (Central Region), March 15, 1972. The confidential minutes of the meeting were sent to Rubin Feld by Ben Nobleman, a municipal politician and member of the executive.

[25] Interview with Judy Feld Carr, September 2, 1993, Toronto; RF Papers, Correspondence 1970–71, Harry Steiner to Friend, April 28, 1972; RF Papers, Clippings and Reports on Jews in Arab Lands, Handwritten notes of meeting of CJC Foreign Affairs Committee, May 8, 1972.

[26] RF Papers, Correspondence 1971–73.; Judith Feld to Ashen Wolfish, November 15, 1972; Judith Feld to Mordecai Ben-Porat, November 15, 1972; Mordecai Ben-Porat to Judith Feld, December 25, 1972; *Jerusalem Post*, November 7, 1972, 8.

[27] RF Papers, Speeches, Ronald Feld, "Syrian Jewry—The Jews of Despair," n.d. (1972?); Correspondence 1971–3, Rabbi Jordan Pearlson to Friends, May 16, 1972; Judy Feld to Albert Gellman, November 20, 1972; Rabbi Herbert Feder to Reg Gilbert, May 16, 1972; Judy Feld to Norma Altman, February 6, 1973; Model Letter, Ronald Feld to Pierre Trudeau, n.d., 1972; N. B. Rasky to Pierre Elliot Trudeau, February 16, 1993; Telegram N. B. Rasky to Hafez al-Assad, n.d., 1993; Henry Lawless to N. B. Rasky, February 27, 1973; N. B. Rasky to James Gillies, February 27, 1993; Ron Atkey to N. B. Rasky, February 28, 1973; Barney Danson to N. B. Rasky, February 22, 1973; Mitchell Sharp, March 20, 1973; Judy Feld to Maury Wasserman, March 1, 1973; Judy Feld to David Tennenhouse, February 18, 1972; RF Papers, File 2. "Syrian Jews—Beth Tikvah Synagogue," June 16, 1972.

[28] EA, 45-ME-13-3 Vol. 5, "The Plight of Jews in Syria," n.d.; "Petition to his Excellency Ambassador Tomeh on the Status of Jews in Syria," n.d.; Request for Action, J. Church to Minister, n.d.

[29] EA, 45-ME-13-3, Vol. 5, I. G. Mundell to Canadian embassy, Beirut, April 26, 1972; Telegram, Canadian Embassy, Beirut, to GAM, External Affairs, May 16, 1972. A handwritten note on the telegram commented, "This is interesting. Could it be shown in confidence to President Canadian Jewish Congress?" This

was not the first time that Feld's description of the position of Syrian Jews was disputed by External Affairs. In March 1972, Feld wrote to Sharp demanding that in view of the deteriorating situation of Syrian Jewry, External Affairs abandon quiet diplomacy in favour of a more high-profile intervention. The minister was advised that the Canadian ambassador in Beirut had not come upon any evidence to corroborate Dr. Feld's assertion that the situation of Jews in Syrian has deteriorated. The Ambassador believed that if there has been any change at all, there may have been a slight improvement. EA, 45-ME-13-3, Vol. 5, Memorandum of A. E. Ritchie to the Minister re Syrian Jews, March 30, 1972.

30 EA, 45-ME-13-3, Vol. 5, "Situation of Syrian Jews," May 23, 1972; Memorandum to the Minister through Mr. Church from Robert Elliot re. Syrian Jews, May 24, 1972.

31 EA, 45-ME-13-3, Vol. 6, Agenda, June 5, 1972; Memorandum, R. V. Gorham to GAM, re Syrian Jews—Call on the Minister by Canadian Jewish Delegation, June 7, 1972; CJC, DA 12, Box 13, File 5, Submission by Mitchell Sharp by Saul Hayes, June 5, 1972. Memorandum to Chairmen and Regional Offices from Ella Cohen, re Syrian Jewry, June 8, 1972; Canadian Jewish News, June 16, 1972.

In the few months before the meeting with Mitchell Sharp, several Canadians made application to sponsor the immigration to Canada of family in Syria. The applications won easy approval from Canadian Immigration officials but were not successful in reuniting the families. In one case, something of a Canadian test case for emigration from Syria and a case in which Rubin Feld took a particular interest, a Toronto man applied to bring his sister and her husband from Aleppo to Canada. Several problems quickly emerged. The initial application stated that the purpose of the sponsorship was to allow the Syrians to eventually resettle in Israel. This statement of intent was a difficulty for Canada. In the past, all Canadian dealings with Arab states on issues of Jewish immigration, like those with Iraq, were predicated on an understanding that Canada was not knowingly acting for "Zionist" interests. The Canadian ambassador to Syria was concerned that this application, if examined by Syrian authorities, would compromise Canada in Syria and the larger Arab world by making it appear that Canada was acting as an agent for Israel (something the Syrians already felt was more or less true of most Western countries). The Syrians never saw the application. Because of other problems, the process did not get that far. Under Syrian regulations, anyone wishing to apply for an exit permit had to have a visa in hand, in this case a Canadian visa. Normally this required the emigrant to visit the Canadian embassy and fill out the necessary forms. The Canadian embassy covering Syria was in Beirut, Lebanon. There was no way that Syrian authorities were going to permit Jews to go to Lebanon. As their sponsors and Rubin Feld in Toronto lobbied Ottawa for action, the Canadian embassy in Beirut first tried to communicate with the Aleppo family by mail. Its mail did not get through. In the end, the ambassador was authorized to make a discreetly humanitarian appeal to ranking Syrian authorities. He, in turn, wanted assurances that the family in Syria was indeed going to Canada to settle, not using Canada as a way station en route to Israel. His point was well taken by Ottawa, but they asked the ambassador to proceed when he felt the moment was politically opportune. Before anything concrete came of the plan for a humanitarian appeal, the Yom Kippur War in the fall of 1973 threw Syria and the whole Middle East into turmoil. The family was never reunited in Canada. RF Papers, Correspondence 1971–73, Ronald Feld to Maurice Edelman, August 24, 1972; Mrs. H. Strom to James Walker, February 15, 1973; EA, 45-ME-13-3, Vol. 6, Telegram, Gignac to GAM, re Syrian Jews, April 17, 1973; Telegram, External Affairs to Beirut, April 26, 1973; Memorandum for the Minister by A. E. Riddle, re Syrian Jews, May 7, 1973; Memorandum Director Home Services Branch to Director General, Foreign Services, re Sabbagh, May 8, 1973; For the Feld correspondence to and from the applicants, other supporters and those lobbied on behalf of the application, see RF Papers, Dr. Feld—Beth Tzedec Correspondence.

[32] CJC, ZA 1972, Box 2, File 15, Saul Hayes to George Tomeh, April 19, 1972; George J. Tomeh to Saul Hayes, May 25, 1972; *La Tribune des Nations,* May 7, 1971 (English translation); *Christian Science Monitor,* November 27, 1971; *La Libre Belgique,* December 27, 1971 (English translation); *New York Times,* February 4, 1972.

[33] CJC. ZA 1972, Box 2, File 15, Canadian Jewish Congress Delegation Meeting with the Representative of the Permanent Mission of the Syrian Arab Republic to the United Nations, June 9, 1972. Minutes of the meeting with Tomeh were sent by Congress to External Affairs. EA. 45-ME-13-3. Minutes of Meeting of the CJC Delegation with Dr. George Tomeh, June 9, 1972.

[34] *IOI* no. 655, April 28, 1972; CJC, DA 12, Box 14, File 1, "Task Force on Syrian Jewry," n.d. CJC, DA 12, Box 15, File 16, Press Release, Syrian Jewry Suffers Discrimination, Torture: Manifesto Issued to Canada, May 11, 1972; *Ottawa Journal,* May 15, 1972; *Ottawa Citizen,* May 15, 1972; *La Presse,* May 16, 1972; *Le Droit,* May 15, 1972; CJC, DA 12, Box 14, File 3, Sol Kanee to Jean Gascon, March 14, 1972.

[35] *Suburban,* June 21, 1972; *Gazette,* June 28, 1972; *Montreal Star,* June 28, 1972; *Le Devoir,* June 28, 1972; *IOI* no. 588, June 30, 1972; CJC, DA 5, Box 36, File 3.

[36] RF Papers, Correspondence 1971-73, All Jewish Affairs Representatives from Estelle Eisenberg (NCJW Foreign Jewry Coordinator), January 1973; RF Papers, Clippings re Israel, Syrian Jewry, "Resolution of Support and for Action Concerning Syrian Jewry" (ZOA) n.d.; CJC, DA 12, Box 13, File 5, Memorandum to Syrian Jewry Committee from Mrs. Chas. Balinsky (Hadassah-Wizo), May 17, 1972.

[37] CJC, DA 12, Box 13, File 7, Memorandum to Members of the Governing Council from A. Kaplan, re Jews in Syria, January 14, 1972.

[38] EA, 45-ME-13-3, Vol. 6, Memorandum to File from E. Way, re Syrian Jews, July 21, 1972.

[39] *Canadian Jewish News,* December 29, 1972; RF Papers, Rubes Early Articles/Syrian Jews, Ronald Feld *et al.* to Editor, *Canadian Jewish News,* January 12, 1993.

[40] *Canadian Jewish News,* February 2, 1973.

[41] Interview with Judy Feld Carr, September 21, 1993, Toronto; RF Papers,

Correspondence 1971–73, Handwritten notes, "Israeli Foreign Ministry," n.d.; RF Papers, Clippings and Reports on Jews in Arab Lands, "Yihudim ha'atzurim b'Suria" (transliteration), n.d.

42 Interview with Judy Feld Carr, September 9, 1993, Toronto; Interview with Judy Feld Carr, September 21, 1993, Toronto; Interview with Rabbi Ibrahim Hamra, October 1, 1994, Toronto.

43 Jeremiah 31:2–20 as quoted in English translation in Rabbi Sidney Greenberg and Rabbi Jonathan D. Levine, *The New Mahzor for Rosh Hashana and Yom Kippur* (Bridgeport, Conn.: Prayer Book Press, 1978), 228–29.

CHAPTER FOUR:
Be Strong and of Good Courage

1 Interview with Judy Feld Carr, September 9, 1993, Toronto; Interview with Rabbi Mitchell Serels, March 13, 1995, New York.

2 RF Papers, File 16. Judy Feld to Barnett Danson, June 21, 1973; Judy Feld to Mitchell Sharp, June 21, 1973; Judy Feld to Ron Atkey, June 21, 1973.

3 Interview with Judy Feld Carr, September 21, 1993, Toronto.

4 JFC Papers, Subject files, Haim Cohen 1973–74, Haim Cohen to Judy Feld, September 3, 1973.

5 Interview with Judy Feld Carr, September 9, 1973, Toronto; RF Papers, Sabbagh Family and Other Business after Feld's Death, Mrs. Norman Glick to Albert Gellman, July 16, 1973.

6 *links* (flier announcing the Dr. Ronald Feld Fund for Jews in Arab Lands), n.d. (August 1973?).

7 *Canadian Jewish News,* November 29, 1974; JFC Papers, Subject files, Beth Tzedec Jews in Foreign Countries, Judy Feld to Ralph Hyman, November 29, 1974.

8 Interview with David Satok, December 20, 1994, Toronto.

9 Interview with Judy Feld Carr, October 15, 1993, Toronto; interview with Judy Feld Carr, April 16, 1995, Toronto; interview with Helen Cooper, December 16, 1997, Toronto.

10 Interview with Judy Feld Carr, November 23, 1993, Toronto.

11 EA, 45-ME-13-3-ME, Vol. 6, Memorandum for the Minister from A.E.R., July 17, 1973.

12 The text of the telegram to Syria is quoted in *Beth Tzedec Bulletin,* October, 17, 1973: Telegram of Rabbi Ibrahim Hamra to Ronald Feld, October 5, 1973, reprinted in *Beth Tzedec Bulletin,* November 7, 1973.

13 Haim Cohen to Judy Feld, November 27, 1973, as quoted in *Beth Tzedec Bulletin,* November 27, 1973.

14 JFC Papers, Subject files, Correspondence with MPs 1973–73. Telegram to Mitchell Sharp from Mrs. Ronald Feld, October 7, 1973; Telegram to Kurt Waldheim, October 7, 1973; Lincoln Alexander to Mrs. Ronald Feld, November 5, 1973; Ron Atkey to Mitchell Sharp, October 22, 1973; John Diefenbaker to Judy Feld, October 10, 1973; David Lewis to Judy Feld, November 26, 1973.

15 JFC Papers, Mitchell Sharp to Ronald Feld, November 15, 1973.

16 JFC Papers, Subject files, Correspondence with MPs 1973–74, A. S. McGill to Mrs. Ronald Feld, December 31, 1973.

17 JFC Papers, Subject files, Rabbi Hamra telegrams, Telegram to Ronald Feld from Rabbi Ibrahim Hamra, March 3, 1974.

18 RF Papers, Clippings and Reports re Syrian Jewry, Flyer, "A Demonstration of Support for Syrian Jews," April 19, 1973. RF Papers, Correspondence 1971–73, Ronald Feld to City Editor, *Globe and Mail*, April 10, 1973; Press Release, n.d. (April, 1973?); Judy Feld to Abe Dwek, April 22, 1973.

19 JFC Papers, Subject files, Original Cables to Syria 1972–1975, Handwritten note, June 6, 1972; Prepaid cable, January 9, 1973.

20 JFC Papers, Subject files, Simon Khabas 1974–75, Judy Feld notes on conversation with Simon Khabas, Bat Yam, Israel, n.d., 1974.

21 EA, 45-ME-13-3, Vol.6, David Rubinstein to Mitchell Sharp, n.d. (February, 1973?); Mitchell Sharp to David Rubinstein, March 9, 1973; Howard Turk to Jim Walker, March 5, 1973; Jim Walker to Mitchell Sharp, March 9, 1973; J.P. Schoiler to Canadian embassy, Beirut, March 12, 1973; RF Papers, Correspondence 1971–73, Mitchell Sharp to Jim Walker, March 20, 1973; Judy Rubin to Abe Dwek, April 22, 1973.

22 *Beth Tzedec Bulletin*, July 3, 1974. RF Papers, Correspondence 1971–73, Judy Feld to Mordachai Ben-Porat, March 23, 1973; Judy Feld to Haim Cohen, March 25, 1973; Judy Feld to Fawzia Shalom, August 6, 1973.

23 *Beth Tzedec Bulletin*, September 4, 1974; JFC Papers, Subject files, Simon Khabas 1974–75, Judy Feld notes on conversation with Simon Khabas, Bat Yam, Israel, n.d., 1974.

24 JFC Papers, Subject files, Simon Khabas 1974–75, Mordechai Ben-Porat to Judy Feld, March 31, 1974.

25 JFC Papers, Subject files, Simon Khabas 1974–75, Hand written note of Bernard Goldman on copy of Dr. A. Khazzam to Dr. Bernard Goldman, July 17, 1974.

26 JFC Papers, Subject files, Simon Khabas 1974–75, Daniel A. Goor to Dr. A. Khazzam, February 13, 1975.

27 Interview with Judy Feld Carr, October 15, 1993, Toronto; *Beth Tzedec Bulletin*, March 23, 1975.

28 *New York Times*, April 14, 1974.

29 *New York Times*, April 14, 1974; CJC, DA 12, Box 13, File 6, Memorandum to all the affiliated Communities of the World Jewish Congress from A. Kaplan, March 13, 1974; JFC Papers, Subject files, Assorted Materials 1971–74–*Shabbat Zachor*, Memorandum of George E. Gruen, re Death of Four Syrian Jewish Women, March 14, 1974.

30 JFC Papers, Subject files, Assorted Materials 1971–71—*Shabbat Zachor*, Rabbi Joseph Harari to the *New York Times*, March 18, 1974; Committee of Concern, Statement on the Murder of Four Jewish Women in Syria, March 25, 1974; EA, 45-ME-13-3, Vol. 6. telegram to EA, Ottawa, from Canadian embassy, Tel Aviv, March 21, 1974; CJC, DA 12, Box 13, file 6. Memorandum to All the Affiliated Communities and Organizations of the World Jewish Congress from A. Kaplan

re Syria, March 27, 1974.

31 EA, 45-ME-13-3, Vol. 6, Confidential Memorandum to file of A. S. McGill, March 22, 1974; telegram to embassies Beirut/Tel Aviv/Washington/London from EA Ottawa, April 22, 1974; telegram to EA Ottawa from Beirut, April 23, 1974; telegram to EA Ottawa from London, April 24, 1974. Livio Caputo, "'We spoke with the Jews who live in Syria': Drama in the Ghetto of Damascus," *Epoca*, April 28, 1974.

32 Interview with Rabbi Ibrahim Hamra, October 1, 1994, Toronto.

33 Interview with Shlomo Kaski, January 28, 1997, Yaffa.

34 JFC Papers, Subject files, Beth Tzedec Jews in Foreign Countries 1974, hand-written notes on meeting with Mitchell Sharp, n.d. (April 21, 1974?).

35 EA 45-ME-13-3, Vol.6, telegram to embassies Beirut/Tel Aviv/Washington/London from EA Ottawa, April 22, 1974; telegram to EA Ottawa from Beirut, April 23, 1974; telegram to EA Ottawa from London, April 24, 1974.

36 JFC Papers, Subject files, Israeli Council for Jews in Arab Lands, telegram to Judy Feld from Mitchell Sharp, April 27, 1974.

37 JFC Papers, Subject files, Israeli Council for Jews in Arab Lands, Michal and Haim Cohen to Judy Feld, June 24, 1974.

38 JFC Papers, Subject files, Israeli Council for Jews in Arab Lands, Saul Friedman to Judy Feld, June 12, 1974.

39 JFC Papers, Subject files, Beth Tzedec Jews in Foreign Countries 1974, Saul Friedman to Judy Feld, June 12, 1974; interview with Judy Feld Carr, October 15, 1993, Toronto.

40 Robert Azzi, "Damascus, Syria's Uneasy Eden," *National Geographic*, April 1974: 520.

41 CJC, DA 12, Box 13, File 6, Memorandum from Phil Baum to Chapter and Division Presidents et al., June 27, 1974; Phil Baum and Mark A. Bruzonsky, "The National Geographic Portrayal of Syrian Jewry," American Jewish Congress, June 1974.

42 *National Geographic*, November 1974: 587.

43 JFC Papers, Subject files, Mike Wallace 60 *Minutes*, Memorandum of Isaiah M. Minkoff to NJCRAC and CJFWF Member Agencies re TV Program on Syrian Jewry—"60 *Minutes*," February 24, 1975; Isaiah M. Minkoff to Richard Salant, February 21, 1975; Judy Feld to Mike Wallace, February 24, 1995; *On Syrian Jews* (Washington: NAAA, 1976).

44 JTA, June 12, 1975, 4; *Detroit Jewish News*, June 13, 1975.

45 "60 *Minutes*, Volume VIII, Number 14 as broadcast over the CBS Television Network Sunday, March 21, 1976 7:00–8:00, EST" (New York. CBS, 1976) 1–8; CJC, DA 12, Box 14, File 2, memorandum to Area Directors and Executive Assistants from George E. Gruen, re CBS 60 *Minutes* Update on Syria, March 21, 1976; *New York Times*, March 24, 1976.

46 CJC, ZA 1974, Box 5, File 32, "Task Force on Syrian Jewry," n.d.; CJC, DA 12, Fox 14, file 1. Task Force on Syrian Jewry, Planning Meeting, July 30, 1975; meeting with Judy Feld, July 31, 1975; CJC, ZA 1975, Box 4, File 35, Stanley

Urman to Judy Feld, August 4, 1975; Stanley Urman to Abraham Dwek, August 4, 1975; Stanley Urman to Rabbi N. Gaon, August 4, 1975; Stanley Urman to Prof. S. Friedman, August 4, 1975; CJC, ZA 1976, Box 13, 38, Task Force on Syrian Jewry Meeting, Minutes, August 19, 1975; Planning Committee for Syrian Jewry, Minutes, January 13, 1976.

47 CJC, DA 12, Box 14, File 1, Syrian Jewry Meeting, Minutes, March 3, 1976.

48 JFC Papers, Subject files, 2nd Congress—Jews from North Africa, Canadian Jewish Congress (Ontario Region) News Release, October 22, 1975; Judy Feld, personal diary, October 26 - November 5, 1975; Programme, 2ème Congress mondial des originaires d'Afrique du Nord, Israel, October 26–November 2, 1975; Judy Feld, handwritten introduction to Congress address, n.d.; Shaul Ben Simhon to Judy Feld, December 28, 1975.

CHAPTER FIVE:
Carrying Their Fears with Them

1 EA, 45-ME-13-3, Vol. 7, Memorandum of H. B. R. for the Minister, Purpose: To outline the situation of Syrian Jews, as requested by you in your Memorandum to the under-secretary of January 29, 1975, February 5, 1975. For an example of the kind of explanation of its actions that the government of Canada was giving to those who inquired about Canadian policy regarding Syrian Jews, see JFC Papers, Subject files, Correspondence with MPs 1973–74, Allan J. MacEachen to Bob Kaplan, January 1975.

2 CJC, DA5; Box 36, File 4, A. Kaplan to N. Goldmann *et al*, June 19, 1975.

3 Interview with George Gruen, March 16, 1995; JFC Papers, Subject files, Members of Parliament 1975–76, Judy Feld to Allan J. MacEachen, May 20, 1975; JFC Papers, Subject files, Correspondence with MPs 1973–4, Allan J. MacEachen to Judy Feld, June 17, 1975; *Canadian Jewish News*, January 9, 1976. JFC Papers, Subject files, Letters to MPs from Synagogue Groups, Sisterhood Members, Beth Tikvah Synagogue to Pierre Trudeau, March 8, 1976; Clanton Park Sisterhood to Pierre Elliott Trudeau, March 31, 1976.

4 Interview with Judy Feld Carr, October 28, 1993, Toronto; interview with Don Carr, April 7, 1996, Toronto.

5 Interview with Alan Feld, February 1, 1997, Tel Aviv; interview with Don Carr, April 7, 1996, Toronto.

6 Interview with Alan Feld, February 1, 1997, Tel Aviv.

7 Interview with Judy Feld Carr, October 28, 1993, Toronto; interview with Don Carr, April 7, 1996, Toronto.

8 Interview with Alan Feld, February 1, 1997, Tel Aviv; interview with Helen Cooper, December 16, 1997, Toronto.

9 Interview with Judy Feld Carr, November 23, 1993, Toronto; JFC Papers, Subject files, CJC Committee Minutes and Agendas, Judy Feld, handwritten notes (June 22, 1976?), 4; interview with David Satok, April 21, 1995, Toronto; interview with Alan Rose, May 31, 1995, Montreal.

10 JFC Papers. Subject files, Meeting with MacEachen, April 26, 1976, Judy Feld

Carr, handwritten notes, April 26, 1976; EA, 45-ME-13-3, Vol. 6. Memorandum to File from GAM, re Meeting of SSEA with Canadian Jewish Congress Representatives, April 26, 1976—Jews of Syria, May 4, 1976; *Canadian Jewish News*, May 7, 1976; CJC, DA 12, Box 14, File 1. Minutes of Meeting, Committee of Jews in Arab Lands, Toronto, June 22, 1976.

[11] JFC Papers, Subject files, Memorandum to All Members from Judy Feld, re The Release of a Jewish Hostage from Syria, November 12, 1976; Original handwritten draft, "The Release of a Jewish Hostage from Syria, nd (1976?); Notes on interview, n.d. (1976?); Photocopy of Syrian Identity Card; *Canadian Jewish News*, November 19, 1976; *Bulletin, Jews in Arab Lands* (CJC), December 1976.

[12] Interview with Judy Feld Carr, October 21, 1993, Toronto; Judy Feld to Shmuel Ovnat, (*Confidential*—Not for Publication), May 26, 1976; Postcard, H. G. to Dr. Ronald Feld, May 17, 1976; Judy Feld Carr held another meeting with another businessman from Aleppo and his wife a little more than a year later. Her first visitors directed them to Judy Feld Carr as someone they could trust. Nevertheless, very much the same conditions of secrecy were requested before they agreed to visit Toronto. They updated her on conditions in Syria. Again, she was implored to do all she could to open Syria's doors to Jewish emigration. Judy Feld Carr, Report of a Meeting in Toronto with a Jew from Syria (*Confidential*—Not for Publication), September 30, 1977.

[13] Many restrictions were officially lifted in February 1977. JFC Papers, Press Clippings, File 1977–78, Memorandum from General Command of the Army and the Armed Forces Bureau of Intelligence—Al-Qamishli Branch, re President Decree [translation], February 11, 1977.

[14] JFC Papers, Subject files, Published Information on Syrian Jews, George E. Gruen, "The Present Status of Syrian Jewry," American Jewish Committee, May 3, 1976, 4.

[15] JTA, January 6, 1977.

[16] *Jerusalem Post*, May 3, 1977.

[17] Judy Feld Carr, Subject files, Syrian Change of Law—May 1977, General Command of the Army and the Armed Forces, Bureau of Intelligence—Al-Qamishli Branch, No. 245/3, January 25, 1977 ([translated into English by the U.S. Department of State, Division of Language Services —LSNO.61414 ZA/JRP Arabic).

[18] EA, 45-Me-13-3, Vol. 8. Syrian Jews, February 15, 1977.

[19] *Canadian Jewish News*, February 11, 1977, 4; JFC Papers, Subject files, Committee Correspondence 1974–79, Judy Feld Carr to Editor, February 13, 1977.

[20] Interview with Lulu Sasson, November 16, 1966, New York.

[21] *Jerusalem Post*, July 26, 1977; *Globe and Mail*, July 30, 1977; *Jerusalem Post*, July 31, 1977; *Jerusalem Post*, August 3, 1977; *Jerusalem Post*, August 9, 1977; JTA, August 12, 1977; JTA, August 15, 1977; *Canadian Jewish News*, August 26, 1977; *San Diego Jewish News*, August 12, 1977; *Los Angeles Times*, July 30, 1977; *New York Times*, July 31, 1977.

[22] JFC Papers, Subject files, Haim Cohen 1973–74, Council for the Rescue of

Syrian Jews to Stephen J. Solarz, May 9, 1991; interview with Lulu Sasson, November 16, 1996, New York.

23 JFC Papers, Subject files, National Council of Jewish Women Telegrams 1979, Marjorie Blankstein and Sarah Glatt to Syrian Ambassador to Canada, October 3, 1977; JTA, July 18, 1978; "Trapped in Syria: A Prayer for 'Next Year... '" *Philadelphia Inquirer*, April 30, 1978; interview with Rabbi Ibrahim Hamra, January 26, 1997, Hulon, Israel.

24 Interview with Judy Feld Carr, October 21, 1993, Toronto.

25 For the story of Eli Cohen, see Samuel Segev, *Alone in Damascus: The Life and Death of Eli Cohen* (Jerusalem: Keter, 1986); Don Reviv and Yossi Melon, *Every Spy a Prince: The Complete History of Israel's Intelligence Community* (Boston: Houghton Mifflin, 1990), 143–46.

26 Interview with Hannah Cohen, July 17, 1995, Toronto; JFC Papers, Subject files, Trip to Israel Meeting with Syrian Jews July 1977, Notes on interview of Judy Feld Carr with Hannah Cohen, n.p., n.d. (1977?); Subject files, CJC Committee Minutes and Agendas, Notes on interview with "Moshe Dahab—an Escapee from Syria—aged 16^1/$_2$," May 1978.

27 Interview with Judy Feld Carr, October 21, 1993, Toronto: JFC Papers, Subject files, Letters from Aleppo 1976–79, Rabbi Jacques Moise Sasson to the Jewish Community of Canada, June 10, 1977; CJC, Papers, DA 5/12/4. Judy Feld Carr form letter, n.d. (1977?).

28 JFC Papers, Subject files, Letters from Aleppo 1976–79, Rabbi Eliahou Dahab *et al* to Judy Feld, October 29, 1977; Judy Feld to Rabbi Jacques Sasson and Rabbi Eliahou Dahab, November 9, 1977; *Canadian Jewish News*, September 23, 1977.

29 *Toronto Star*, April 11, 1977; Minutes of the Meeting of the CJC Regional Executive, April 15, 1977, Toronto; *Jerusalem Post*, April 12, 1977; JFC Papers, Subject files, Barney Danson, Judy Feld Carr to Barnett J. Danson, April 19, 1977.

30 JFC Papers, Subject files, Committee Correspondence, Barney Danson to Judy Feld Carr, May 6, 1977.

31 JFC Papers, Subject files, Committee Correspondence, Judy Feld Carr to Barnett J. Danson, May 10, 1977; Judy Feld Carr to Barnett J. Danson, May 26, 1977; Subject files, Plenary Session CJC May 14/77 Montreal, Alan Rose to Judith Carr, June 3, 1977.

32 EA, 45-ME-13-3, Vol. 8. H.B. Singleton to Michael Shenstone, April 24, 1977; Michael Shenstone to Barney Danson, May 6, 1977; Michael Shenstone to Barney Danson, July 15, 1977.

33 JFC Papers, Subject files, Immigration of Dahab Family from Aleppo 1978–9, Nachman Shemen to Minister of Immigration, October 6, 1977.

34 CJC, DA5, box 12, file 4, Minutes of the National Committee for Jews in Arab Lands, January 10, 1978, Toronto.

35 EA, 45-ME-13-3, Vol. 9, J.C. Best to Judy Feld Carr, September 19, 1978.

36 JFC Papers, Subject files, Immigration of Dahab Family from Aleppo 1978–9, Judy Feld Carr to Richard Tait, March 29, 1978.

37 EA, 45-ME-13-3, Vol. 9, Judy Feld Carr to Richard Tait, August 10, 1978; J. C.

Best to Judy Feld Carr, September 19, 1978.

38 JFC Papers, Subject files, Immigration of Dahab Family from Aleppo 1978-9, Jacques Sasson to Hannah Cohen, September 29, 1978.

39 EA, 45-ME-13-3, Vol, 9, V. A. Sims to Judy Feld Carr, December 12, 1978.

40 JFC Papers. Subject files, Letters to and from Syria 1979, Faraj Sasson to Judy Feld Carr, October 20, 1978.

41 JFC Papers, Subject files, Committee Correspondence 1974–1979, Alan Rose to Judy Carr, May 8, 1978; Alan Rose to Judith Feld Carr, July 12, 1978; Judy Feld Carr to Alan Rose, August 10, 1978; Judy Feld Carr to Seymore Shatz, November 22, 1978; Rabbi Jacques Sasson to Judy Feld, 12 May, 1978; Subject files, Letters from CCAR Goldrick, Rabbi Norman D. Hirsh to Judy Feld, August 22, 1978; Rabbi Jacques Moise Sasson to Judy Feld, September 10, 1978; Rabbi Stephen S. Goldrich to Judy Carr, October 31, 1978; Subject files, Letters from Aleppo 1976–79, Jacques Moise Sasson, August 10, 1978; Subject files, CJC Committee Minutes and Agendas, Minutes of the National Committee of Jews in Arab Lands, Toronto, December 7, 1978; *Shaarei Shomayim Bulletin* 31, no.1 (October 1978), 7.

42 CJC, DA5, Box 12, File 4, Jacques Moise Sasson to Judy Feld, May 8, 1978.

CHAPTER SIX:
Deliver Them Out of Syria

1 JFC Papers, Subject files, Speakers Info, Alain Poher to Kurt Waldheim, December 12, 1978.

2 Interview with Judy Feld Carr, August 4, 1995, Toronto.

3 Interview with Jehudi Kinar, October 2, 1996, Toronto; interview with David Sultan, January 20, 1997, Toronto; interview with David Ariel, January 30, 1997, Jerusalem; interview with Benny Avileah, January 30, 1997, Jerusalem.

4 Interview with Judy Feld Carr, August 4, 1995, Toronto; JFC Papers, Subject files, Trip to Israel and England Report 1979, Meeting—Foreign Ministry of Israel, Diaspora Division, Judy 15, 1979.

5 JFC Papers, Subject files, Syrian Change of Law—May 1977, General Command of the Army and the Armed Forces, Bureau of Intelligence—Al-Qamishli Branch, No. 245/3, January 25, 1977 (translated into English by the U.S. Department of State, Division of Language Services—LSNO.61414 ZA/JRP Arabic).

6 *Beth Tzedec Bulletin* 28 (no. 9) June 3, 1997, 11.

7 JFC Papers, Subject files, Immigration of Dahab Family from Aleppo 1978–79, To whom it may concern, February 4, 1979; Rabbi Jacques Sasson to Judy Feld, April 1, 1979.

8 JFC Papers, Subject files, Immigration of Dahab Family from Aleppo 1978–79, Rabbi J. Benjamin Friedberg to Judy Feld Carr, March 13, 1979.

9 JFC Papers, Subject files, Immigration of Dahab Family from Aleppo 1978–79, Alvin B. Rosenberg to Judy Carr, March 27, 1979; Alvin B. Rosenberg to Miss Kakis, March 27, 1979; Judy Feld Carr to M. Jaworsky, March 28, 1979; notes

(n.d.), handwritten copy of telegram Judy Feld to Henri Farhi, March 27, 1979.

10 JFC Papers, Subject files, Letters from Aleppo 1976–79, Judy Feld Carr to Rabbi Sasson, March 7, 1978; Rabbi Sasson to Judy Feld Carr, February 25, 1979.

11 Interview with Judy Feld Carr, October 21, 1993, Toronto.

12 JFC Papers, Subject files, Committee Correspondence 1974–79, Judy Feld Carr to Nina Haviv, April 16, 1979.

13 JFC Papers, Subject files, Immigration of Dahab Family from Aleppo 1978–79, Patient Clinical Report, Final Summary, Rabbi Eliahou Dahab, April 16, 1979.

14 Interview with Jacques Sasson, January 26, 1997, Tel Aviv.

15 JFC Papers, Subject files, Immigration of Dahab Family from Aleppo 1978–79, Judy Feld to Henri Farhi, June 14, 1979; Meeting in New York, June 24, 1979; Enclosures: for renewal of the passport of Eliahou Dahab, Aleppo, June 25, 1979; Judy Feld Carr to Victor Guindi, September 4, 1979; File 35, Judy Feld to Jacques Sasson, May 17, 1979; subject files, Committee Correspondence 1974–79, Judy Feld Carr to Alan Rose, June 12, 1979; Subject files, Trip to Israel and England Report 1979, Notes on conversation with Yom Tov Dahab in Jerusalem, August 16 (1979?); Subject files, Letters to and from Syria 1979, Judy Feld to Ibrahim Hamra, September 6, 1979.

16 Interview with David Zifkin, July 19, 1995 (telephone).

17 EA, 45-ME-13-3, vol. 10, Memorandum of M. A. J. Lafontaine to the Minister, re Jews in Syria—Dahab, Farhi and Sabbagh Families, September 5, 1979.

18 JFC Papers, Subject files, Immigration of Dahab Family from Aleppo 1978–79, J. C. Best to Judy Feld Carr, September 15, 1979.

19 JFC Papers, Subject files, Immigration of Dahab Family from Aleppo 1978–79, Judy Feld to Ibrahim Hamra, November 8, 1979; Jacques Sasson to Judy Feld, December 28, 1979; Subject files, Letters to and from Syria 1979, Judy Feld to Jacques Sasson, November 8, 1979; Subject files, Immigration of Olga Dahab 1978-79, Judy Feld to Jacques Sasson, December 21, 1979; Judy Feld to Ibrahim Hamra, December 21, 1979; Judy Feld to Henri Farhi, December 21, 1979; J. H. Drapeau to Judy Feld Carr, January 3, 1980.

20 JFC Papers, Subject files, Immigration of Olga Dahab 1978–79, Henri Farhi to Judy Feld, January 20, 1980.

21 JFC Papers, Subject files, Immigration of Olga Dahab 1978-79, Ron Atkey to Judy Feld Carr, January 31, 1980; Interview with Rabbi Ibrahim Hamra, January 26, 1997, Hulon.

22 Interview with Judy Feld Carr, November 11, 1993, Toronto; JFC Papers, Subject files, Immigration of Olga Dahab, 1978–79, Henri Farhi to Judy Feld, March 1, 1980; Judy Feld to Henri Farhi, March 15, 1980; Henri Farhi to Judy Feld, April 8, 1980; Henri Farhi to Judy Feld, May 16, 1980; Ibrahim Hamra to Judy Feld, June 2, 1980; Much of the detail of Olga's departure from Syria was verified in an interview with Olga Koski, January 28, 1997, Yaffa.

23 JFC Papers, Subject files, Rabbi Henri Farhi, 1982–83, Judy Feld Carr to Rabbi Henri Farhi, June 17, 1981.

24 JFC Papers, Subject files, Rabbi Henri Farhi 1982-83, Henri Farhi to Judy Feld Carr, February 6, 1981.

25 JFC Papers, Subject files, Rabbi Henri Farhi, 1982–83, Henri Farhi to Judy Feld Carr, October 24, 1981.

26 JFC Papers, Subject files, Rabbi Henri Farhi 1982-83, Judy Feld Carr to Henri Farhi, November 20, 1981; Tomy Malic to Judy Feld Carr, January 23, 1982; Judy Feld Carr to Henri Farhi, September 13, 1982; Henri Farhi to Judy Feld Carr, January 6, 1983; telegram, Farhi to Judy Feld, January 23, 1983.

27 Interview with Judy Feld Carr, November 23, 1993, Toronto.

28 Interview with Judy Feld Carr, November 23, 1993, Toronto.

29 JFC Papers, Subject files, Rabbi Henri Farhi, 1982–83, Judy Feld Carr to Henri Farhi, April 6, 1983.

30 JFC Papers, Subject files, Rabbi Henri Farhi, 1982-83, "Information from Ava Dahab," January 30, 1983; Judy Feld Carr to Henri Farhi, May 1983; Judy Feld Carr to Henri Farhi, June 24, 1983; Judy Feld Carr to Henri Farhi, August 16, 1983; copies of Ketuba; interview with Olga Kaski, January 28, 1997, Yaffa.

31 Interview with Helen Cooper, December 16, 1997, Toronto.

32 Interview with Judy Feld Carr, May 15, 1997, Toronto.

33 JFC Papers, Subject files, Australian Correspondence 1980–81, Henry Pearl to Judith Feld Carr, November 11, 1980; Judy Feld Carr to Henry Pearl, November 24, 1980.

34 JFC Papers, Subject files, "Mr. Albert" Feb 25/79, Executive Committee Minutes, CJC Central Region, February 21, 1979, 3; "Mr. Albert—The story of an Escapee from Syria," n.d. (1979?); notes on Mr. Albert speech at home of Judy Feld Carr, February 25, 1979; New York Times, February 23, 1979; Jerusalem Post International Edition, February 25, 1979; Kitchener-Waterloo Record, February 23, 1979; JTA, February 23, 1989; Toronto Sun, February 26, 1979; Canadian Jewish News, March 15, 1979; Beth Tzedec Bulletin 28 (no. 7), April 8, 1979.

35 Interview with Judy Feld Carr, August 4, 1995, Toronto.

36 JFC Papers, Subject files, Letters from Aleppo 1976–79, Jacques Sasson to Judy Feld, January 6, 1979.

37 JFC Papers, Subject files, Rabbi Jacques Sasson's Arrival in Israel 1980, Jacques Sasson to Judy Feld, February 29, 1979; Interview with Jacques Sasson, January 26, 1997, Tel Aviv.

38 George E. Gruen, "Situation: Precarious," Keeping Posted (January 1977): 20.

39 Syria Amnesty International Briefing Book No. 16, 1979, 3.

40 George E. Gruen, "The Current Plight of Syrian Jewry," Israel Horizons 27 (no. 10), December 1979: 26–27.

41 "The Current Plight of Syrian Jewry": 11.

42 "The Current Plight of Syrian Jewry": 12.

43 JFC Papers, Case files, Aleppo, Mordechai Ben-Porat to Judy Feld Carr, December 17, 1979.

44 JFC Papers, Case files, Aleppo, Judy Feld Carr to Mordechai Ben Porat, January 2, 1980.

45 JFC Papers, Case files, Aleppo, Notes on telephone call, January 4, 1981.

46 JFC Papers. Case files, Aleppo, February 8, 1981.

47 JFC Papers, Case files, Aleppo, Ruth Shaul to Malka Shulevitz, March 10, 1981;

Malka Shulevitz to Judy Feld Carr, March 26, 1981; Judy Feld Carr to Ruth Shaul, April 20, 1981; Ruth Shaul to Judy Feld Carr, May 8, 1981; interview with Judy Feld Carr, Toronto, July 31, 1995.

48 JFC Papers, Case files, Aleppo, Judy Feld Carr notes of telephone conversation, n.d. (May 13, 1982?).

49 JFC Papers, Case files,Aleppo, May 18, 1982. In his rough English, Naim's brother, Victor, who had escaped from Syria more than ten years earlier, offered Judy a complete accounting of the costs of buying his father and brother out of Syria, which he calculated at $16,771. "No one would like to spend that money. My freedom it cost me to run away only $5 it's the cost to go to Lebanon by bus. It seems to me if we going to continue to buy freedom in this prices very difficult to get and sometimes it impossible if we can get money for every Jew in Syria does not mean the goverment they will give them the freedom because they hold them hostages and if we want make American goverment ask the Syrian to give them the right to go only God who save Israel from Egypt will save them from the hand of the Syrians." Letter to Judy Feld Carr, June 3, 1982.

50 JFC Papers, Case files, Aleppo.

51 Moshe Ma'oz, Asad; The Sphinx of Damascus (New York: Weidenfeld and Nicolson, 1988), 149–63; Asahi Evening News, December 9, 1982; Neue Zurchur Zeitung, March 1992; Milton Wiorst, "The Shadow of Saladin, "The NewYorker, January 8, 1990: 52–53.

52 Jewish Week—American Examiner, September 24, 1982.

53 JFC Papers, Case files, Aleppo, Notes on telephone conversation, December 23, 1982.

54 JFC Papers, Case files, Aleppo, Judy Feld Carr to Murray Koffler, April 18, 1983; interview with Judy Feld Carr, July 31, 1995.

55 JFC Papers, Case files, Aleppo, April 18, 1983.

56 Interviews with Judy Feld Carr, July 31, 1995, Toronto; August 4, 1995, Toronto.

CHAPTER SEVEN:
Ransoming the Captives

1 Interview with David Satok, December 20, 1994, Toronto.

2 JFC Papers, Subject files, Speeches on Syrian Jews 1983, "Syrian Jews," Speech to the Canadian Jewish Congress Plenary Session, Montreal, May 1983.

3 JFC Papers, Government files, 1983 Meetings and Correspondence, Canadian Jewish Congress Plenary, Resolutions—Syrian Jewry, May 1983.

4 House of Commons Debates, May 18, 1983, 25531.

5 For examples of letters to ministers, see JFC Papers, Government files, 1983 Meetings and Correspondence, Rabbi Henry Hoschander to Allan MacEachen, June 5, 1983; Leon Oziel to Allan MacEachen, June 16, 1983; Government files, 1985 Meetings and Correspondence, Judy Feld Carr to Allan MacEachen, November 7, 1983; CJC, DA5/26/10A, Judy Feld Carr to John Roberts, November 9, 1983; EA, 45-ME-13-3, Vol. 14, Telegram of K. Macartney to Beirut, February , 1983.

6 EA, 45-ME-13-3, Vol. 13, Jackson to Ottawa, May 4, 1983.

7 EA, 45-ME-13-3, Vol. 16, Beirut to Ottawa, December 15, 1983.

8 Interview with Judy Feld Carr, August 4, 1995, Toronto; Interview with Rabbi Ibrahim Hamra, October 1, 1994, Toronto.

9 CJC, DA5/26/10A, Judy Feld Carr to J. P. Schioler, July 3, 1983; JFC Papers, Government files, 1984 Meetings and Correspondence, Donald and Judy Carr to M. D. Bell, January 3, 1984.

10 EA File 45-ME-13-3 Vol. 15, House of Commons—Briefing Note re the Jewish Community is increasingly concerned over the fate of 5000 Jews resident in Syria, May 31, 1983; JFC Papers, Government files, 1983 Meetings and Correspondence, J. P. Schioler to Rabbi Erwin Schild, June 7, 1983; J. P. Schioler to Donald and Judy Carr, June 9, 1983; Lloyd Axworthy to Rabbi Henry Hoschander, July 6, 1983; J.P. Schoiler to Leon Oziel, August 12, 1983; M. D. Bell to Judy Feld Carr, November 17, 1983; Government files, 1985 Meetings and Correspondence, J. P. Schoiler to Rabbi Henry Hoschander, August 12, 1983.

11 JFC Papers, Government files, 1983 Meetings and Correspondence, Roland de Corneille to John Roberts, November 24, 1983; CJC, DA 5/26/10B, John Roberts to Judy Feld Carr, January 18, 1984.

12 For a discussion of Canadian immigration policy during this period, see Harold Troper, "Canadian Immigration Policy Since 1945," *International Journal* 68 (1993), 255–81.

13 JFC Papers, Government files, 1984 Meetings and Correspondence, Judy Feld Carr to John Roberts, January 23, 1984; CJC, DA5/26/10B, John Roberts to Judy Feld Carr, February 22, 1984.

14 CJC, DA 5/26/10A, John Roberts to Judy Feld Carr, February 29, 1984.

15 *Canadian Jewish News*, March 8, 1984; JFC Papers, Government files, 1984 Meetings and Correspondence, handwritten notes, "Questions and Statements to Roberts," February 26, 1984.

16 *Canadian Jewish News*, January 5, 1984; *Jewish Press*, January 6, 1984; *Jewish Week*, January 6, 1984; *Jewish Chronicle*, January 6, 1984; *Jewish Week—American Examiner*, January 13, 1984.

17 EA, 45-ME-13-3, Vol. 16, M. D. Bell to Alan Rose, January 5, 1984.

18 EA, 45-ME-13-3, Vol. 16, Telegram, Washington to Ottawa, January 3, 1984.

19 *Wall Street Journal*, February 2, 1984.

20 EA, 45-ME-13-3, Vol. 16, Telegram, Beirut to Ottawa, January 7, 1984; Damascus to Ottawa, March 13, 1984; Washington to Ottawa, January 26, 1984; Washington to Ottawa, March 7, 1984.

21 EA, 45-ME-13-3, Vol. 16, Telegram, Beirut to Ottawa, January 9, 1984; Damascus to Ottawa, March 13, 1984.

22 EA, 45-ME-13-3, Vol. 17, Beirut to Ottawa, June 11, 1984.

23 JFC Papers, Case files, Fortuna Antebi Naftali—Aleppo, handwritten note on telephone call, November 18, 1984; Judy Feld Carr to Alan Rose, November 27, 1984; Alan Rose to Judy Feld Carr, December 14, 1984.

24 EA, 4-ME-13-3, Volume 17, Amman to Ottawa, November 4, 1984; Amman to

Ottawa, November 15, 1984; CJC, DA 5/26/10B, Judy Feld Carr to Alan Rose, November 27, 1984; Alan Rose to Judy Feld Carr, December 14, 1984.

25 *House of Commons Debates*, March 5, 1984, 1763-1764; *Globe and Mail*, March 6, 1984.

26 JFC Papers, Case files, Fortuna Antebi Naftali—Aleppo, Judy Feld Carr to Maurice Antebi, January 29, 1984.

27 JFC Papers, Case files, Fortuna Antebi Naftali—Aleppo, Judy Feld Carr to Albert and Edmond Antebi, January 29, 1984; Judy Feld Carr to Leonard Seidenman, January 29, 1984; handwritten notes on telephone call, Leonard Seidenman to Judy Feld Carr, February 1, 1984; Judy Feld Carr to Leonard Seidenman, March 26, 1984; Judy Feld Carr to Morris Antebi, April 12, 1984; Judy Feld Carr to Edmond Antebi, April 13, 1984.

28 Interview with Judy Feld Carr, April 7, 1996, Toronto; JFC Papers, Case files, Fortuna Antebi Naftali—Aleppo, handwritten notes on telephone call, Judy Feld Carr to Edmond Antebi, March 13, 1984.

29 All those who donated $5 or more received a receipt from the Feld Fund and a thank-you note. For the records of this one-time fundraising effort, see JFC Papers, Case files, Fortuna Antebi Naftali—Aleppo, Naftali family donations; interview with Judy Feld Carr, April 6, 1996; *Beth Tzedec Bulletin*, May 1984.

30 JFC Papers, Case files, Fortuna Antebi Naftali—Aleppo, handwritten note on telephone call, Edmond Antebi to Judy Feld Carr, April 2, 1984; handwritten note on telephone call, Edmond Antebi to Judy Feld Carr, April 3, 1984; Judy Feld Carr to Rabbi Abraham Cooper, April 8, 1984; *Western Jewish News*, June 14, 1984.

31 JFC Papers, Case files, Fortuna Antebi Naftali—Aleppo, handwritten note on telephone call, Edmond Antebi to Judy Feld Carr, June 22, 1984, 1984; handwritten note on telephone call, Edmond Antebi to Judy Feld Carr, October 19, 1984.

32 JFC Papers, Case files, Fortuna Antebi Naftali—Aleppo, Alan Rose to Judy Feld Carr, April 9, 1984.

33 Interview with Judy Feld Carr, March 25, 1994, Toronto.

34 Interview with Batya Barakat, November 21, 1996 (telephone).

35 JFC Papers, Case files, Barakat/Akiva Family—Aleppo, "Batya's Testimony," translated from Arabic, CJC Plenary, May 8, 1986.

36 JFC Papers, Case files, Barakat/Akiva Family—Aleppo, "Batya's Testimony," translated form Arabic, CJC Plenary, May 8, 1986; handwritten note of telephone conversation, Judy Feld Carr to Baruch Barakat, January 12, 1982.

37 *Long Island Jewish World*, August 21, 1981

38 JFC Papers, Case files, Barakat/Akiva Family—Aleppo, handwritten note of telephone conversation Batya Akiva to Judy Feld Carr, n.d.; Judy Feld Carr to Edwin Shapiro, January 5, 1982.

39 JFC Papers, Case files, Barakat/Akiva Family—Aleppo, Dr. Joseph Ranshoff to Dr. Hirsch Sacks, January 12, 1983; Leonard Seidenman to Judy Feld Carr, March 8, 1983.

40 JFC Papers, Case files, Barakat/Akiva Family—Aleppo, Leonard Seidenman to

Judy Feld Carr, February 14, 1983; Leonard Seidenman to Judy Feld Carr, March 8, 1983.

41 JFC Papers, Case files, Barakat/Akiva Family—Aleppo, Judy Feld Carr to Mike Akiva, March 22, 1984.

42 JFC Papers, Case files, Barakat/Akiva Family—Aleppo, Mrs Badrih Akiva [Batya Barakat] to Haver Perez DeCuellar, June 14, 1983; To whom it may concern, November 16, 1983.

43 JFC Papers, Case files, Barakat/Akiva Family—Aleppo, Judy Feld Carr to Batya Barakat, May 25, 1984; hand-written note of telephone call, Batya Barakat to Judy Feld Carr, May 27, 1984; handwritten note of telephone call, Batya Barakat to Judy Feld Carr, June 15, 1984; handwritten note of telephone call, Batya Barakat to Judy Feld Carr, June 21, 1984; handwritten note of telephone call, Batya Barakat, June 25, 1984; hand written note of telephone call, Batya Barakat to Judy Feld Carr, July 2, 1984; Judy Feld Carr to Yitzhak Shelef, October 1983.

44 JFC Papers, Case files, Barakat/Akiva Family—Aleppo, "Batya's Testimony," translated form Arabic, CJC Plenary, May 8, 1986; Interview with Batya Barakat, November 21, 1996 (telephone).

45 Interview with Judy Feld Carr, April 11, 1996, Toronto.

46 Interview with Judy Feld Carr, April 11, 1996, Toronto.

47 JFC Papers, Case files, Suad Tzion Lalo and Ava Lalo (originally Qamishli now Aleppo), Judy Feld Carr to Batya Barakat, February 26, 1985.

48 Interview with Judy Feld Carr, April 11, 1996, Toronto.

49 JFC Papers, Case files, Suad Tzion Lalo and Ava Lalo (originally Qamishli now Aleppo), handwritten note "Call Shelef," n.d.; handwritten note, February 26, 1985; handwritten note, April 14, 1984; Martin Shaw to Judy Feld Carr, June 4, 1985.

50 JFC Papers, Case files, Suad Tzion Lalo and Ava Lalo (originally Qamishli now Aleppo), Judy Feld Carr to Martin Shaw, June 10, 1985.

51 JFC Papers, Case files, Suad Tzion Lalo and Ava Lalo (originally Qamishli now Aleppo), Judy Feld Carr to Rabbi Farhi, June 5, 1985.

CHAPTER EIGHT:
So They Can Marry

1 JFC Papers, Government files, 1985 Meetings and Correspondence, Judy Feld Carr to Milton Harris, February 7, 1985.

2 JFC Papers, Government files, 1985 Meetings and Correspondence, M. D. Bell to Sheila Dropkin, April 9, 1985; Meeting with External Affairs and Immigration, February 7, 1985.

3 JFC Papers, Government files, 1985 Meetings and Correspondence, Meeting With External Affairs and Immigration, February 7, 1985; JFC Papers, Case files, Syrian Jewish Women 1985–89, Judy Feld Carr to Lawrence David Lederman, February 14, 1985; handwritten note, February 10, 1985; handwritten note, February 12, 1985; see lists—Unmarried Women in Damascus, February 11, 1985, Girls to help leave Damascus, February 1985, Women to leave Syria, June

1986; Judy Feld Carr to Milton Harris, February 7, 1985.

4 EA, 45-ME-13-3, Vol. 18, Dispatch, Cairo to Ottawa, March 20, 1985.

5 JFC Papers, Case files, Syrian Jewish Women 1985–89, handwritten note on conversation with Herb Abrams, March 20, 1985.

6 JFC Papers, Case files, Syrian Jewish Women 1985–89, telex received by Phil Granovsky, April 15, 1985; telex for Phil Granovsky to send to Jerusalem, April 16, 1985; report from Philip Granovsky of telephone call he received this afternoon from Yehuda Dominitz, April 17, 1985.

7 JFC Papers, Case files, Syrian Jewish Women 1985–89, Ralph Fisher—Ottawa, April 17, 1985; handwritten notes on telephone conversation Yitzhak Shelef to Judy Feld Carr, April 19,1985; Judy Feld Carr to Yitzhak Shelef, n.d.; Telex to Yehuda Dominitz, April 22, 1985.

8 JFC Papers, Government files, 1985 Meetings and Correspondence, handwritten note of telephone conversation with Bob Elliot, June 20, 1985.

9 JFC Papers, Government files, 1985 Meetings and Correspondence, handwritten notes for Meeting to Take Place on April 30, 1985, n.d.; Meeting in Ottawa with External Affairs and Immigration Department, re Jewish Girls in Damascus, Syria, April 30, 1985; Case files, Syrian Jewish Women 1985–89, handwritten notes, April 30, 1985.

10 CJC, DA5, box 26, file 10B, Network Canada, press release n.d.; Network Canada, telegram text, n.d.; Jay Raisen to Milton Harris, April 26, 1985.

11 JFC Papers, Case files, Syrian Jewish Women 1985–89, handwritten notes, Dinner with Yeshuahu Anug and David Ariel, July 5, 1985; handwritten notes, meeting with Yehuda Dominitz, July 31, 1985; handwritten notes, Moshe Cohen, July 31, 1985; Moshe Cohen to Yitzhak Ben Aron, August 4, 1985 (Hebrew with handwritten English Translation attached); Moshe Cohen to Judy Feld Carr, August 12, 1985.

12 JFC Papers, Government files, 1985 Meetings and Correspondence, handwritten note of telephone call from Mr. Elliot, September 16, 1985.

13 JFC Papers, Case files, Syrian Jewish Women 1985–89, Robert Elliott to Judy Feld Carr, December 3,1985.

14 JFC Papers, Case files, Syrian Jewish Women 1985–89, Robert Elliott to Judy Feld Carr, December 3,1985.

15 JFC Papers, Case files, Syrian Jewish Women 1985–89, Judy Feld Carr to Robert Elliott, December 9, 1985.

16 JFC Papers, Case files, Syrian Jewish Women 1985–89, Judy Feld Carr to Robert Elliott, December 9, 1985; Joe Clark to Robert Kaplan, October 10, 1986.

17 JFC Papers, Case files, Syrian Jewish Women 1985–89, Judy Feld Carr to Percy Sherwood, October 23, 1986; *Canadian Jewish Bulletin*, March 1986; *Canadian Jewish News*, March 13, 1986; *Jewish Western Bulletin*, March 1986.

18 JFC Papers, Government files, 1986 Meetings and Correspondence, handwritten note of telephone call from Percy Sherwood, March 21, 1986.

19 JFC Papers, Government files, 1986 Meetings and Correspondence, handwritten note, Minutes of Lunch Meeting, April 4, 1986.

20 JFC Papers, Case files, Syrian Jewish Women 1985–89, Judy Feld Carr to Percy

Sherwood, May 16, 1986; Judy Feld Carr to Percy Sherwood, May 30, 1986; Judy Feld Carr to Percy Sherwood, June 10, 1986; interview with Judy Feld Carr, May 21, 1996.

21 JFC Papers, Government files, 1986 Meetings and Correspondence, handwritten note, conversation with Sherwood, June 4, 1986.

22 JFC Papers, Government files, 1986 Meetings and Correspondence, Percy Sherwood to Judy Feld Carr, September 8, 1986.

23 JFC Papers. Government files, 1986 Meetings and Correspondence, Arrangements for the Contact of the Fifteen Jewish Women in Damascus, September 15, 1986; meeting in Ottawa, September 30, 1986; handwritten minutes of meeting, September 30, 1986; Judy Feld Carr to Dorothy Reitman, October 1, 1986; Judy Feld Carr to Percy Sherwood, October 1, 1986.

24 JFC Papers, Government files, 1986 Meetings and Correspondence, handwritten note, Call from Percy Sherwood, October 7, 1986; handwritten notes, telephone call from "immigration," October 10, 1986; handwritten notes, telephone call from "immigration," October 28, 1986.

25 George E. Gruen Papers [AJC Papers], IRD-IM 1990, Syria-Jews, Memorandum, George Gruen to IRD Files re Jews arrested in Syria, October 14, 1986.

26 *Globe and Mail*, November 27, 1986.

27 JFC Papers, Government files, 1986 Meetings and Correspondence, handwritten note, Message of Support, n.d.

28 JFC Papers, Government files, 1986 Meetings and Correspondence, handwritten note, For the 15 women, October 15, 1986; note on telephone call to Percy Sherwood, October 25, 1986; handwritten minutes, Meeting, Ottawa—External Affairs, November 6, 1986; handwritten note, telephone call   December 3, 1986; Government files, 1987 Meetings and Correspondence, Meeting with Colleen Cupples, Bob Peotsche, Herb Abrams, Toronto, March 17, 1987.

29 Judy Feld Papers, Government files, 1987 Meetings and Correspondence, meeting with Colleen Cupples, Bob Peotsche, Herb Abrams, Toronto, March 17, 1986; interview with Judy Feld Carr, May 21, 1996, Toronto.

30 JFC Papers. Government files, 1986 Meetings and Correspondence, handwritten note, telephone call December 18, 1986.

31 JFC Papers. Government files, 1987 Meetings and Correspondence, handwritten note, telephone call from Percy Sherwood, March 9, 1987; meeting with Colleen Cupples, Bob Peotsche, Herb Abrams, Toronto, March 17, 1987.

32 Judy Feld Papers, Government files, 1987 Meetings and Correspondence, meeting with Colleen Cupples, Bob Peotsche, Herb Abrams, Toronto, March 17, 1987; D. M. Bell to Jackie Boxer, March 16, 1987; Julia Resnick Gasner to Joe Clark, November 2, 1987; Case Files, Syrian Jewish Women 1986–89, Alan Feld to Brian Mulroney, June 16, 1987; Brian Mulroney to Alan Feld, September 3, 1987.

CHAPTER NINE:
Prisoners of Damascus

1 JFC Papers, Case files, Darwish/Sabato Imprisonment, handwritten note, telephone call, October 7, 1990; telephone call to Benny Avileah, October 18, 1990.

2 JFC Papers, Case files, Darwish/Sabato Imprisonment, telephone call to Benny Avileah, October 31, 1990.

3 JFC Papers, Government files, 1990 Meetings and Correspondence, Judy Feld Carr to Joe Clark, November 9, 1990; Judy Feld Carr to Percy Sherwood, November 9, 1990; Eric B. Wang to Judy Feld Carr, December 3, 1990; Judy Feld Carr to Eric B. Wang, December 17, 1990.

4 *Ayidiot Ha Achronot*, November 10, 1994 (English translation).

5 JFC Papers, Government files, 1991 Meetings and Correspondence, Eric B. Wang to Judy Feld Carr, February 26, 1991; Bulletin (Amnesty International), "Syrian Jews Arrested Trying to Flee Country," September 1991.

6 JFC Papers, Case files, Darwish/Sabato Imprisonment, handwritten note, telephone call Sammy Guindi to Judy Feld Carr, n.d.; Telephone call to Judy Feld Carr, October 21, 1991.

7 Interview with Judy Feld Carr, August 22, 1996.

8 JFC Papers, Case files, Darwish/Sabato Imprisonment, telephone call from Sammy Guindi, n.d.; Rabbi Farhi to Judy Feld Carr, August 15, 1991; interview with Judy Feld Carr, August 22, 1996.

9 JFC Papers, Case files, Darwish/Sabato Imprisonment, Henri Farhi to Judy Feld Carr, August 15, 1991; Henri Farhi to Judy Feld Carr, November 26, 1991.

10 *Canadian Jewish News*, December 5, 1991; JFC Papers, Case files, Darwish/ Sabato Imprisonment; telegram of Henri Farhi to Judy Feld, November 29, 1991; handwritten note, telephone call Camilia Guindi to Judy Feld Carr, November 29, 1991.

11 Interview with Elie Swed, January 27, 1997, Tel Aviv.

12 Interview with Elie Swed, January 27, 1997, Tel Aviv; JFC Papers, Case files, Swed Arrival in New York, April 9, 1994, meeting with Swed family, Elie, Selim and Sara, and their children and sister Olga Swed in Brooklyn apartment, May 23, 1994.

13 Interview with Elie Swed, January 27, 1997, Tel Aviv.

14 Interview with Elie Swed, January 27, 1997, Tel Aviv; interview with Judy Feld Carr, August 26, 1996, Toronto.

15 Interview with Sara Swed, January 26, 1997, Bat Yam, Israel.

16 Interview with Sara Swed, January 26, 1997, Bat Yam, Israel.

17 JFC Papers, Case files, Swed Arrival in New York, April 9, 1994, meeting with Swed family, Elie, Selim and Sara, and their children and sister Olga Swed in Brooklyn apartment, May 23, 1994; interview with Elie Swed, January 27, 1997, Tel Aviv.

18 Interview with Selim Swed, January 26, 1997, Tel Aviv; interview with Elie Swed, January 27, 1997, Tel Aviv.

[19] Interview with Elie Swed, January 27, 1997, Tel Aviv; interview with Selim Swed, January 26, 1997, Tel Aviv.

[20] JFC Papers, Correspondence files, Amnesty International/United Nations Advocacy for Swed Brothers 1992, Judy Feld Carr to Michael Schelew, April 18, 1989; Correspondence files, Sara Swed—Damascus November 1989—December 1990, Judy Feld Carr to Leah Hazan, September 1988.

[21] George Gruen Papers, Country—Syria—Jews 89, Anti-Defamation League, News, June 1989; Roger Pinto to George Gruen, March 23, 1989; Abraham J. Bayer to Stephen Shalom, November 21, 1989; draft letter Stephan J. Solarz and Benjamin A. Gilman to Colleague, n.d.; draft letter to George Bush, n.d.; Lord Plumb to Hafez al-Assad, March 10, 1989; International Herald Tribune, June 22, 1989; Jerusalem Post International Edition, November 19, 1989.

[22] JFC Papers, Case file, Syrian Jewish Women 1985–89, Joe Clark to Barbara McDougall, April 17, 1989; Correspondence files, Amnesty International/United Nations Advocacy for Swed Brothers 1992, notes on Meeting with Richard Adams, November 30, 1988; notes on telephone conversation with Richard Adams, February 21, 1989; Judy Feld Carr to Michael Schelew, April 18, 1989;

[23] JFC Papers, Correspondence files, Amnesty International/United Nations Advocacy for Swed Brothers 1992, Judy Feld Carr to Michael Schelew, April 18, 1989; Amnesty International, Urgent Action—Update, December 1, 1988; Judy Feld Carr, notes on telephone call from Michael Schelew, n.d.; Michael Schelew to Judy Feld Carr, June 8, 1989; Report on the Enforced or Involuntary Disappearance of a Person, June 29, 1989; Judy Feld Carr note on telephone call from Michael Schelew, June 22, 1989; Judy Feld Carr to Michael Schelew, June 23, 1989; Michael Schelew to Judy Feld, July 6, 1989; Mirta S. de Teitelbaum to Judy Feld, August 1, 1989; Georg Mautner-Markhof to Judy Feld, September 22, 1989; Correspondence files. Sara Swed, Damascus Nov. 89–Dec. 90, Judy Feld Carr to Leah Hazan, July 7, 1989; Canadian Jewish News, May 5, 1988; United States Department of State, Country Reports on Human Rights Practices for 1988 (Washington: Department of State, 1989), 1514; CJC, DA5/26/10B, Roger Pinto and Yossi Gilbert Youna to Sir, August 11, 1988; Alan Rose to Roger Pinto, August 22, 1988.

[24] JFC Papers, Correspondence files, Amnesty International/United Nations Advocacy for Swed Brothers 1992, Georg Mautner-Markhof to Judy Feld, November 1, 1989.

[25] Jerusalem Post, November 1, 1989.

[26] Interview with Jack Lalo, November 17, 1996, Brooklyn.

[27] Interview with Esther Lalo, November 17, 1996, Brooklyn.

[28] Interview with Esther Lalo, November 17, 1996, Brooklyn; interview with Judy Feld Carr, August 26, 1996, Toronto.

[29] Interview with Elie Swed, January 27, 1997, Tel Aviv; interview with Sara Swed, January 26, 1997, Bat Yam, Israel; interview with Selim Swed, January 26, 1997, Bat Yam, Israel; interview with Jack Lalo, November 17, 1996, Brooklyn; interview with Esther Lalo, November 17, 1996, Brooklyn.

30 Interview with Sara Swed, January 26, 1997, Bat Yam, Israel; JFC Papers, Correspondence files, Sara Swed—Damascus Nov. 89–Dec. 90, Sara Swed to Judy Feld, October 10, 1989; Judy Feld Carr note on telephone call from Batya Barakat, October 10, 1989.

31 JFC Papers, Correspondence files, Sara Swed—Damascus Nov. 89–Dec. 90, Leah Hazan to Judy Feld Carr, September 23, 1988; Judy Feld Carr notes on telephone call from Moshe Benzioni, July 11, 1988.

32 JFC Papers, Correspondence files, Sara Swed—Damascus, Nov. 89–Dec. 90, Judy Feld Carr to Solomon Sasson, April 3, 1989.

33 JFC Papers, Correspondence files, Sara Swed—Damascus, Nov. 89–Dec. 90, Judy Feld to Sara Swed, March 29, 1989

34 JFC Papers, Correspondence files, Sara Swed—Damascus, Nov. 89–Dec. 90, Sara Mousa Katri (Swed) to Judy Feld, April 11, 1989.

35 JFC Papers, Correspondence files, Sara Swed—Damascus, Nov. 89–Dec. 90, Judy Feld to Sara Swed, April 25, 1989.

36 JFC Papers, Correspondence files, Sara Swed—Damascus, Nov. 89–Dec. 90, Sara Swed to Judy Feld, May 8, 1989.

37 George Gruen Papers, IRD-IM 1990, Syrian Jews, Stephen J. Solarz *et al* to George Bush, January 23, 1990.

38 JFC Papers, Correspondence files, Sara Swed—Damascus, Nov. 89–Dec. 90, Judy Feld Carr to Leah Hazan, August 8, 1989; Judy Feld Carr to Leah Hazan, April 3, 1990; Judy Feld Carr to Leah Hazan, May 13, 1990; Correspondence files, Amnesty International/United Nations Advocacy for Swed Brothers 1992, Amnesty International, Urgent Action sheet, January 31, 1990; Memorandum Stephen Shalom to Kenneth Stein, re Syrian Jewry, March 5, 1990; Judy Feld Carr notes on telephone call from Abe Bayer, March 27, 1990; Percy Sherwood to Judy Feld Carr, May 31, 1990; Howard M. Metzenbaum and Robert Dole to Hafaz al-Assad, May 23, 1990; Joe Clark to Judy Feld Carr, June 12, 1990.

39 JFC Papers, Correspondence files, Sara Swed—Damascus, Nov. 89–Dec. 90, Albert Ayal to Judy Feld Carr, March 28, 1990; Judy Feld Carr to Albert Ayal, March 28, 1990; Judy Feld Carr to Janice Bergman, May 17, 1990; Judy Feld Carr to Percy Sherwood, April 3, 1990; Sara Swed to Judy Feld, April 25, 1990.

40 JFC Papers, Correspondence files, Sara Swed—Damascus, Nov. 89–Dec. 90, Sara Swed to Judy Feld Carr, May 3, 1990.

41 JFC Papers, Correspondence files, Sara Swed—Damascus, Nov. 89–Dec. 90, Judy Feld Carr to Leah Hazan, May 13, 1990; Correspondence files, Amnesty International/United Nations Advocacy for Swed Brothers 1992, Albert Ayal to Judy Feld Carr, April 13, 1990; Stephen J. Solarz to Ezra S. Ashkenazi, September 17, 1990.

42 JFC Papers, Correspondence files, Sara Swed—Damascus, Nov. 89–Dec. 90, Judy Feld Carr notes on telephone call to Benny Avileah, September 26, 1989; Judy Feld Carr notes, January 2, 1990; Judy Feld Carr notes, January 4, 1990.

43 JFC Papers, Court file, Swed Brothers, Damascus, 1990, Transcript of trial (translation), May 21, 1991; Correspondence files, Amnesty International/United Nations Advocacy for Swed Brothers, 1992, Amnesty International, Urgent

Action Update, May 31, 1991.

44 JFC Papers, Case files, Advocacy for Swed Family to Nov. 91; Sara Swed to Judy Feld, May 22, 1991.

45 JFC Papers, Correspondence files, Sara Swed—Damascus Jan. 1991–92. Sara Swed to Judy Feld, May 25, 1991; Sara Swed to Judy Feld, May 26, 1991; Judy Feld Carr to Leah Hazan, May 25, 1991; *Canadian Jewish News,* June 13, 1991; *Globe and Mail,* June 17, 1991; Correspondence files, Amnesty International/ United Nations Advocacy for Swed Brothers 1992. Judy Feld Carr to Benny Avileah, May 25, 1991.

46 JFC Papers, Correspondence files, Amnesty International/United Nations Advocacy for Swed Brothers 1992, Les Scheininger to Judy Feld Carr, June 14, 1991; Judy Feld Carr to Barbara McDougall, June 18, 1991; Barbara McDougall, June 18, 1991; Doug to David Dreier and Rabbi Abraham Cooper, July 26, 1991; Judy Feld Carr to David Dreier, July 31, 1991; Correspondence files, Sara Swed— Damascus, Jan. 1991–92, Judy Feld Carr to Leah Hazan, August 8, 1991; *Canadian Jewish News,* February 6, 1992.

47 JFC Papers, Correspondence files, Sara Swed—Damascus Jan. 1991–92 Judy Feld to Sara Swed, September 6, 1991.

48 JFC Papers, Correspondence files, Amnesty International/United Nations Advocacy for Swed Brothers 1992, Judy Feld Carr notes on discussion with Rabbi Ibrahim Hamra, March 21, 1992; Judy Feld Carr notes on discussion with Rabbi Ibrahim Hamra and Denis Grégoire de Blois, March 23, 1992; Judy Feld Carr to Barbara McDougall, March 30, 1992; fax, Judy Feld Carr to Ian Sadinsky, April 1, 1992; Correspondence files, Sara Swed—Damascus Jan. 1991–92, Judy Feld Carr to Leah Hazan, March 24, 1992.

49 JFC Papers, Correspondence files, Sara Swed—Damascus Jan. 1991–2, fax, Albert Ayal to Judy Feld Carr, April 18, 1992; Swed Release, Sunday, April 19, 1992, Judy Feld Carr note on telephone call from Grégoire de Blois, April 19, 1992; Judy Feld Carr note on telephone call from Mr. Continay, April 19, 1992; Judy Feld Carr note on telephone call from Rabbi Ibrahim Hamra, April 19, 1992; fax Judy Feld Carr to Grégoire de Blois, April 19, 1992; press release, National Task Force on Syrian Jews, April 19, 1992; fax, Judy Feld Carr to Oren David, April 19, 1992; *Jerusalem Post,* April 21, 1992; *Ottawa Citizen,* April 22, 1992; *Canadian Jewish News,* April 23, 1992.

50 JFC Papers, Correspondence files, Sara Swed—Damascus Jan. 1991–92, Leah Hazan to Judy Feld Carr, May 8, 1992; Sara Swed to Judy Feld Carr, April 28, 1992; Elie Swed to Judy Feld Carr, April 24, 1992 Swed Release, Sunday, April 19, 1992. Solomon Sasson, April 20, 1992; Barbara McDougall to Judy Feld Carr, April 29, 1992.

CHAPTER TEN:
Opening the Gates

1 Interview with Judy Feld Carr, August 26, 1996; April, 14, 1997, Toronto.

2 A useful outline of the peace process as it related to the issue of Syrian Jews and

the roles of the United States, Israel, and Syria, see Lawrence Joffe, *Keesing's Guide to the Middle-East Peace Process* (London: Catermill International, 1996), 70–80, 114–17.

3 Interview with Yehuda Dominitz, January 29, 1997, Jerusalem; *Jerusalem Post,* September 21, 1991.

4 *Jerusalem Report,* December 26, 1991, 8–9.

5 JTA, April 28, 1992; *New York Times,* May 1, 1992; *New York Times,* April 28, 1992.

6 George E. Gruen, "Jews in the Middle East and North Africa," *American Jewish Year Book,* 1994 (New York: American Jewish Committee and Jewish Publication Society of America, 1994), 454; *Jerusalem Post,* May 5, 1992.

7 JFC Papers, Correspondence files, JDC 1990–1992, fax of Judy Feld Carr to Gideon Taylor, June 21, 1992; interview with Judy Feld Carr, July 30, 1997, Toronto; *Jerusalem Post International Edition,* June 6, 1992; *Canadian Jewish News,* June 18, 1992; *Guardian Weekly,* June 28, 1992; *Jerusalem Report,* July 16, 1992, 27–29.

8 JFC Papers, Case files, Judy Feld Carr to John B. Craig, October 24, 1988; handwritten note on telephone conversation, October 25, 1988; Judy Feld Carr to Batya [Barakat], March 16, 1990.

9 JFC Papers, Case files, Judy Feld Carr to Batya [Barakat], May 19, 1989. Judy Feld Carr to N. Hasbani, May 8, 1990; N. Hasbani and Judy Feld Carr, n.d.; Judy Feld Carr to N. Hasbani, June 26, 1990.

10 JFC Papers, Case files, Edward Gluck to whom it may concern, April 27, 1990; Robert Matalon to whom it may concern, June 13, 1990.

11 JFC Papers, Case files, handwritten note on telephone conversation Moussa Sarwa to Judy Feld Carr, September 10, 1990.

12 JFC Papers, Case files handwritten note on telephone conversation, Batya Barakat to Judy Feld Carr, August 8, 1991.

13 JFC Papers, Case Files, handwritten note on telephone conversation, Batya Barakat to Judy Feld Carr, February 18, 1992; handwritten note on telephone conversation, Batya Barakat to Judy Feld Carr, February 25, 1992; fax, Judy Feld Carr to Seymour Reich, March 1, 1992; draft letter, Seymour Reich to Waled Al Moualen, n.d.

14 JFC Papers, Case files, note to file, March 3, 1992; fax, Judy Feld Carr to Seymour Reich, March 3, 1992; note to file, May 6, 1992.

15 JFC Papers, Case files, Judy Feld Carr to Batya Barakat, May 7, 1992; Judy Feld Carr to Batya Barakat, May 24, 1991.

16 JFC Papers, Case files, handwritten note on telephone conversation, January 27, 1992; Danielle Hanien to Judy Feld Carr, February 17, 1992.

17 JFC Papers, Case files, handwritten note on telephone conversation, March 4, 1992.

18 JFC Papers, Case files, Judy Feld Carr to Jeanette Kaltan, February 18, 1992.

19 JFC Papers, Case Files, Letter to Mrs. Judy, March 4, 1992 (translation).

20 JFC Papers, Case files, Letter from Mrs. Judy, March 15, 1992.

21 JFC Papers, Case files, Letter from Mrs. Judy, April 29, 1992.

22 JFC Papers, Case files, handwritten note on telephone conversation, May 12, 1992.

23 JFC Papers, Correspondence files, JDC 1990–1992, fax of Judy Feld Carr to Gideon Taylor, June 21, 1992; *Globe and Mail,* September 29, 1992.

24 JFC Papers, Correspondence files, JDC 1990–1992, fax of Judy Feld Carr to Gideon Taylor, June 21, 1992.

25 JFC Papers, Correspondence files, December 1993, Abraham J. Bayer to Judith Feld Carr, December 7, 1993.

26 Interview with Maurice Nseiri, January 27, 1997, Tel Aviv; *Toronto Star,* April 25, 1993.

27 Interview with Judy Feld Carr, May 15, 1997, Toronto.

28 George E. Gruen, "Jews in the Middle East and North Africa," 438–64.

29 JFC Papers. Government files. Handwritten note of telephone conversation, Grégoire de Blois to Judy Feld Carr, March 2, 1993; JTA, February 22, 1993; JTA, February 26, 1993; JTA, March 11, 1993.

30 JFC Papers, Correspondence files, December 1993, Edward Kennedy *et al.* to Bill Clinton, May 19, 1993.

31 JFC Papers, Correspondence files, December 1993, Eliot L. Engel to Warren Christopher, December 1, 1993; Permanent Mission of Canada to the United Nations, press release no. 07, December 3, 1993, 2; Government files, 1993 Meetings and Correspondence, Canadian Jewish Congress Communique, "National Task Force Pleased with Canadian Representations for Syrian Jewry," May 21, 1993, Toronto.

32 Montreal *Gazette,* December 6, 1993; *New York Times,* December 6, 1993; *Wall Street Journal,* December 6, 1993; *Washington Post,* December 6, 1993; *Wall Street Journal,* December 10, 1993; JFC Papers, Correspondence files, December 1993, Abraham J. Bayer to Judith Feld Carr, December 7, 1993.

33 *Canadian Jewish News,* January 6, 1994.

34 JTA, December 10, 1993; JTA, January 4, 1994; JFC Papers, Correspondence files, December 1993, Judy Feld Carr to Abraham Bayer, December 13, 1993; Rabbi Farhi to Judy Feld Carr, December 24, 1993; fax, Judy Feld Carr to Bluma Zuckerbrot, December 29, 1993; Fax, Judy Feld Carr to Denis Grégoire de Blois, December 29, 1993.

35 *Los Angeles Times,* January 4, 1994.

36 JFC Papers, Correspondence files, December 1993, fax, Seymour D. Reich to Judith Feld Carr *et al,* January 7, 1994; Judy Feld Carr handwritten note on conference call, January 7, 1994; fax, Seymour D. Reich to Judith Feld Carr *et al,* January 10, 1994; Judy Feld Carr handwritten note on conference call, January 10, 1994; JTA, January 6, 1994.

37 JFC Papers, Correspondence files, December 1993, Judy Feld Carr to George Cohon, January 1, 1994.

38 JFC Papers, Correspondence files, December 1993, handwritten note on telephone conversation, Judy Feld Carr to George Cohon, January 4, 1994.

39 JFC Papers, Correspondence files, December 1993, handwritten note on tele-

phone conversation, George Cohon to Judy Feld Carr, January 15, 1994; handwritten note on telephone conversation, Marc Weiner to Judy Feld Carr, January 15, 1994; interview with Judy Feld Carr, Toronto, April 14, 1997.

40 JFC Papers, Correspondence files, December 1993; fax, Judy Feld Carr to Reva Price, January 27, 1994; handwritten note on telephone conversation, Judy Feld Carr to Ibrahim Hamra, January 28, 1994; handwritten notes on conference call, February 7, 1994; JTA, January 28, 1994; Montreal *Gazette*, January 29, 1994.

41 JFC Papers, Government files, 1994 Meetings and Correspondence, fax, Judy Feld Carr to Denis Grégoire de Blois, April 18, 1994; Judy Feld Carr to Friends, April 19, 1994; interview with Selim Swed, January 27, 1997, Tel Aviv.

42 *Globe and Mail*, June 13, 1994.

43 JFC Papers, Correspondence files, Letter to Judy Feld Carr, June 25, 1990; Letter to Judy Feld Carr, July 9, 1990; interview with Judy Feld Carr, July 30, 1997.

44 JFC Papers, Correspondence files, Smuggled Books, Israel Shatzman to Judy Feld Carr, July 16, 1993; Rafael Weiser to Judy Feld Carr, May 5, 1994; fax, Judy Feld Carr to Rafael Weiser, June 12, 1994..

45 Interview with Judy Feld Carr, July 30, 1997, Toronto.

46 Interview with Judy Feld Carr, July 30, 1997, Toronto; JFC Papers, Correspondence files, Smuggled Books from Aleppo, Beth Tzedec Sabbath flyer, May 14, 1994; *Canadian Jewish News*, June 9, 1994; handwritten note Torah from Aleppo, n.d.; *Canadian Jewish News*, October 13, 1994.

47 JTA, August 10, 1995; JFC Papers, Correspondence files, Damascus Keter, clipping from *Washington Jewish News*, faxed August 10, 1995.

48 There is at least one other "Damascus Keter" housed in the collection of the World Jewish Bible Center in Jerusalem. It is on permanent exhibit as part of *The Bible in Manuscript and Printed Books* exhibition in the Jewish National Library in Jerusalem.

49 JFC Papers, Correspondence files, Damascus Keter, Judy Feld Carr, handwritten note, July 1993.

50 Interview with Judy Feld Carr, April 14, 1997, Toronto.

51 Interview with Ibrahim Hamra, January 26, 1997, Holon, Israel; interview with Judy Feld Carr, April 14, 1997, Toronto.

52 Much of the following narrative is drawn from several interviews given in confidence. Those confidences will not be violated and, therefore, names of key players are deliberately withheld.

53 JFC Papers, Correspondence files, Damascus Keter, Judy Feld Carr, handwritten note, Exit of the Keter, n.d.

54 JFC Papers, Correspondence files, Damascus Keter, Codex from Damascus, Syria, November 1993: English translations of contacts (originals in Judeo-Arabic and Hebrew—Rashi script).

55 Interview with Judy Feld Carr, April 14, 1997, Toronto; JFC Papers, Correspondence files, Smuggled Books, Judy Feld Carr to Israel Shatzman, November 2, 1993; Rafael Weiser to Judy Feld Carr, December 19, 1993; Shlomo to Judy, December 12, 1993; Rafael Weiser to Judy Feld Carr, June 16, 1993.

EPILOGUE:
Survival and Renewal

[1] *Jerusalem Post International Edition,* January 6, 1996; interview with Alan Feld, February 1, 1997, Tel Aviv; interview with Judy Feld Carr, December 29, 1997, Toronto.

[2] Marianne Sanua, "The Jews of Syria: Their Final Exodus," *Congress Monthly* 62/2 (March/April 1995),12–14.

[3] There were also Westerners who were sometimes able to visit with the Syrian Jewish community, but more often than not they were accompanied by a Muhabarat agent who controlled what was seen, who was talked with, and whose presence prevented unguarded conversation. For an interesting case in point, see Tudor Parfitt, *The Thirteenth Gate: Travels Among the Lost Tribes of Israel* (Bethesda: Adler and Adler, 1987), 5–35.

[4] Interview with Yehuda Dominitz, January 29, 1997, Jerusalem.

A NOTE ON SOURCES

Research for this book is based almost exclusively on primary historical materials. Efforts were made to locate and examine relevant documentary materials, much of it in private hands. For security reasons, some materials, including materials held by Judy Feld Carr, must remain confidential for the time being. I believe their absence in no way detracts from the veracity of the final work. Interviews were also sought with those who had direct knowledge of events discussed. This was not always possible. While nearly all those I contacted granted me an interview and spoke openly and on the record, several individuals either refused an interview or spoke on condition of complete confidentiality. In the preparation of this book I respected all these wishes and, in some cases where it was necessary to protect anonymity, names have been changed in the text. Even with these constraints, the research materials collected paint a remarkable picture of activism on behalf of Syrian Jewry.

MANUSCRIPT MATERIALS

Judy Feld Carr Papers, Toronto
  Case files
  Clipping files
  Correspondence files
  Court file
  Government files
  Subject files

Ronald Feld Papers, Toronto

Department of Foreign Affairs and
  International Trade, Ottawa
  Social Affairs—Human Rights—
    Middle East
  Social Affairs—Human Rights—
    Middle East—Minorities and Race
    Relations
George E. Gruen Papers, New York
  AJC files

Canadian Jewish Congress National
  Archives
  Staff and Departmental files
  Chronological boxes

INTERVIEWS

David Ariel   January 30, 1997, Jerusalem
Benny Avileah   January 30, 1997, Jerusalem
Batya Barakat   November 21, 1996, telephone
Donald Carr   April 7, 1996, Toronto
                       November 3, 1997, Toronto
Judy Feld Carr   August 17, 1993, Toronto
                       August 24, 1993, Toronto
                       September 2, 1993, Toronto

	September 9, 1993, Toronto
	September 21, 1993, Toronto
	October 15, 1993, Toronto
	October 21, 1993, Toronto
	October 28, 1993, Toronto
	November 11, 1993, Toronto
	November 23, 1993, Toronto
	December 14, 1993, Toronto
	July 31, 1995, Toronto
	August 4, 1995, Toronto
	August 7, 1995, Toronto
	August 21, 1995, Toronto
	March 25, 1996, Toronto
	April 7, 1996, Toronto
	April 11, 1996, Toronto
	May 21, 1996, Toronto
	August 21, 1996, Toronto
	August 22, 1996, Toronto
	August 26, 1996, Toronto
	April 14, 1997, Toronto
	May 15, 1997, Toronto
	July 30, 1997, Toronto
Hanna Cohen	July 17, 1995, Toronto
Shula Cohen	January 29, 1997, Jerusalem
Helen Cooper	December 16, 1997, Toronto
Denis Grégoire de Blois	July 12, 1995, Ottawa
Yehuda Dominitz	January 29, 1997, Jerusalem
Rabbi Henri Farhi	November 15, 1996, New York
Alan Feld	February 1, 1997, Tel Aviv
Murad Guindi	August 3, 1996, Toronto
George Gruen	March 16, 1995, New York
Rabbi Ibrahim Hamra	October 1, 1994, Toronto
	January 26, 1997, Hulon
Olga (Dahab) Koski	January 28, 1997, Yaffa
Shlomo Koski	January 28, 1997, Yaffa
Philip Katz	May 29, 1995, Montreal
Jehudi Kinar	October 2, 1996, Toronto
Albert Laham	January 26, 1997, Bat Yam
Laura Laham	January 26, 1997, Bat Yam

Esther Lalo	November 17, 1996, New York
Jack Lalo	November 17, 1996, New York
Moshe Ma'oz	November 3, 1997, Toronto
Maurice Nseiri	January 27, 1997, Tel Aviv
Moshe Nahum	January 28, 1997, Rishon L'Tzion
Shelly Nahum	January 28, 1997, Rishon L'Tzion
Carole Roberson	November 5, 1997, Toronto
Alan Rose	May 31, 1995, Montreal
Rabbi Jacques Sasson	January 26, 1997, Tel Aviv
Lulu Sasson	November 16, 1996, New York
Moshe Sasson	January 29, 1997, Jerusalem
Salamon Sasson	November 16, 1996, New York
David Satok	December 20, 1994, Toronto
	April 21, 1995, Toronto
Rabbi Mitchell Serels	March 13, 1995, New York
Imir Shammosh	August 3, 1996, Toronto
Janice Stein	December 29, 1996, Toronto
Elie Swed	January 27, 1997, Tel Aviv
Salim Swed	January 26, 1997, Bat Yam
Sarah Swed	January 26, 1997, Bar Yam
David Sultan	January 20, 1997, Toronto
David Zifkin	July 19, 1995, telephone

INDEX